The Ultimate Sydney Trav

All You Need to Know Before You Go with Recommendations on Must-See Attractions, Things to Do, Hidden Gems, Where to Stay, Places to Eat, and Ways to Save

Sebastian Felix

Disclaimer Notice

The information provided in this book is intended for general informational purposes only and reflects the author's research and personal experiences. While every effort has been made to ensure the accuracy and reliability of the content, the author and publisher make no guarantees or warranties regarding the completeness, timeliness, or applicability of the information contained herein. Readers are encouraged to seek professional advice and conduct their research before making decisions based on the contents of this book. The author and publisher shall not be held liable for any errors, omissions, or actions taken based on the information presented.

Contents

Chapter 1: Introduction 7

Welcome to Sydney 7

Overview of Sydney 8

History of Sydney 9

How to Use This Guide 9

Why Visit? Top Reasons to Visit Sydney, New South Wales 11

Chapter 2: Know Before You Go 15

Best Time to Visit 15

Getting to Sydney 22

Visa and Entry Requirements 24

Budgeting and Costs 27

Chapter 3: Accommodation 33

Types of Accommodations in Sydney 33

Chapter 4: Attractions and Landmarks 37

20 Must-See Sights and Attractions in Sydney, New South Wales 37

Chapter 5: Getting Around Sydney 59

Public Transportation 59

Taxis and Rideshares 68

Biking and Walking 74

Car Rentals and Driving Tips 80

Tips on Using Sydney's Public Transportation System 86

Chapter 6: Hidden Gems and Off-the-Beaten-Path 89

Lesser-known Attractions and Unique Experiences in Sydney 89

Chapter 7: Where to Stay in Sydney 95

Guide to Sydney Neighborhoods and Districts 95

Best Places to Stay Based on Interests 117

Recommended Areas and Hotels 133

Chapter 8: Cultural Experiences 143

Art Galleries and Museums in Sydney 143

Theaters and Performing Arts 157

Local Festivals and Events 161

Aboriginal Culture and Tours 165

Architectural and Historical Walking Tours 168

Chapter 9: Cuisine and Dining Choices 173

Overview of Local Cuisine 173

Must-Try Dishes 176

Seafood Restaurants 182

Best Cafés and Breakfast Spots 187

Fine Dining and Michelin-starred Restaurants 193

Food Trucks and Food Halls 200

Vegan and Vegetarian Restaurants 203

Cooking Classes and Food Tours 208

Chapter 10: Shopping in Sydney 211

Shopping Districts and Malls 211

Local Markets and Artisanal Shops 214

Boutique Stores and Designer Labels 217

Aboriginal Art and Souvenirs 219

Chapter 11: Nightlife and Entertainment 223

Bars and Rooftop Lounges 223

Nightclubs and Live Music Venues 227

Theater and Performing Arts 229

Sydney Harbor Dinner Cruises 233

Best Craft Beer and Wine Bars 236

Casino and Entertainment Complexes 239

Chapter 12: Outdoor Activities and Recreation 243

Top-Rated Beaches in Sydney 243

Harbor Cruises and Sailing 251

Whale Watching Tours 253

Surfing and Water Sports 255

Botanical Gardens and Parks 257

Chapter 13: Sydney with Families 263

Family-Friendly Attractions 263

Kids-friendly Beaches and Parks 267

Chapter 14: Sydney Itinerary 271

5 Days in Sydney: The Perfect Sydney Itinerary 271

Day 1: Explore Sydney's Iconic Landmarks 271

Day 2: Bondi Beach and Coastal Walks 275

Day 3: Discover Sydney's Culture and History 279

Day 4: Day Trip to the Blue Mountains 283

Day 5: Sydney's Hidden Gems and Final Farewell 288

Top-Rated Guided Tours 293

Chapter 15: Practical Information 299

Money and Currency 299

Language and Communication 301

Safety Tips 303

Health and Medical Services 305

Electricity and Adapters 308

Time Zone and Climate 310

Tipping Guidelines 311

Internet and Wi-Fi Access 312

Local Customs and Etiquette 314

Emergency Contacts and Numbers 316

Useful Apps and Websites 319

Basic Australian Slang 323

Packing List: What to Bring for Every Season in Sydney 324

Visitor Information Centers 327

Travel Insurance 328

Chapter 16: Day Trips and Excursions 333

10 Amazing Day Trips from Sydney 333

Conclusion 337

Chapter 1: Introduction

Welcome to Sydney

Welcome to Sydney, Australia's dynamic and cosmopolitan harbor city, renowned for its iconic landmarks, stunning beaches, and vibrant cultural scene. Nestled along the shores of the Tasman Sea and surrounded by natural beauty, Sydney offers visitors a blend of urban sophistication and laid-back charm.

Harbor Icon: Sydney's most famous landmark, the Sydney Opera House, symbolizes the city's creative spirit and architectural prowess. Its distinctive sail-like design graces the scenic Sydney Harbor, a bustling waterway dotted with ferries, yachts, and waterfront dining venues.

Coastal Splendor: From the golden sands of Bondi Beach to the secluded coves of the Northern Beaches, Sydney's coastline is a paradise for sun-seekers and surfers alike. Coastal walks, such as the Bondi to Coo gee Coastal Walk, offer panoramic views of the Pacific Ocean and access to picturesque swimming spots.

Cultural Melting Pot: Sydney's multicultural makeup is reflected in its diverse neighborhoods, each offering unique experiences. Explore the historic charm of The Rocks, the trendy cafes of Surry Hills, or the vibrant street art in Newtown, where global flavors and local creativity collide.

Gastronomic Delights: Indulge in Sydney's thriving food scene, which celebrates fresh produce and innovative culinary techniques. From seafood markets at Sydney Fish Market to upscale dining at waterfront restaurants, Sydney offers a feast for every palate.

Outdoor Adventure: Beyond its urban core, Sydney boasts expansive parks, including the Royal Botanic Garden and Centennial Parklands, where outdoor enthusiasts can hike, cycle, or simply relax amidst lush greenery. The Blue Mountains National Park, a short drive from the city, offers bushwalking trails and breathtaking vistas.

Historical and Contemporary Blend: Delve into Sydney's rich history at the convict-built Hyde Park Barracks Museum or explore its modern art scene at the Art Gallery of New South Wales. Festivals like Vivid Sydney illuminate the city with light installations, while Sydney's sporting events, including the Sydney Cricket Ground, showcase Australia's love for sportsmanship.

Overview of Sydney

Sydney is a sprawling metropolis that stretches from the coast inland, encompassing diverse neighborhoods, natural reserves, and cultural hotspots. Understanding Sydney's layout and attractions helps visitors navigate the city's offerings with ease.

Geography: Situated on Australia's southeastern coast, Sydney spans the Sydney Basin, encompassing the Sydney CBD (Central Business District) along with surrounding suburbs and natural features such as Sydney Harbor, Parramatta River, and the Blue Mountains to the west.

Population: With over 5 million residents, Sydney is Australia's largest city and a hub of commerce, culture, and tourism. Its multicultural population contributes to a dynamic social fabric and a vibrant arts scene.

Economy: Sydney's economy thrives on finance, tourism, technology, and creative industries. It hosts major international corporations, financial institutions, and tech startups, contributing to its status as a global city.

Transportation: Sydney offers a comprehensive public transport network, including trains, buses, ferries, light rail, and taxis, making it easy to explore the city and its surroundings. Sydney Airport (SYD) serves as a major gateway for domestic and international travelers.

History of Sydney

Sydney's history is shaped by Indigenous heritage, European colonization, and waves of migration, culminating in a modern city that blends old-world charm with contemporary dynamism.

Indigenous Roots: The Sydney area has been inhabited by Aboriginal peoples, including the Gadigal and Eora clans, for thousands of years. Their cultural heritage remains integral to Sydney's identity and is honored through local initiatives and cultural institutions.

Colonial Settlement: In 1788, Captain Arthur Phillip established the first British settlement at Sydney Cove, marking the beginning of European colonization in Australia. The area served as a penal colony for convicts transported from Britain, shaping early urban development.

19th Century Growth: Throughout the 19th century, Sydney grew rapidly as a trading port and administrative center of New South Wales.

The Gold Rush of the 1850s fueled population growth and economic prosperity, transforming Sydney into a cosmopolitan city.

20th Century Transformation: The 20th century saw Sydney expand further, with landmark events such as the completion of the Sydney Harbor Bridge in 1932 and the hosting of the 2000 Summer Olympics, which showcased Sydney's global stature and multicultural diversity.

Modern Sydney: Today, Sydney continues to evolve as a center of finance, culture, and innovation. Urban renewal projects, such as the Barangaroo and Darling Harbor redevelopment, highlight Sydney's commitment to sustainable growth and enhancing public spaces.

How to Use This Guide

This guide is designed to help you explore Sydney's diverse attractions, plan your itinerary, and make the most of your visit. Whether you're interested in cultural experiences, outdoor adventures, or culinary delights, this guide provides comprehensive information to enhance your Sydney experience.

Planning Your Trip: Essential tips on when to visit, entry requirements, health and safety advice, currency exchange, and packing suggestions to prepare for your journey.

Getting to and Around Sydney: Detailed guidance on arriving in Sydney by air, train, car, or ferry, as well as navigating the city using public transport, taxis, and walking routes.

Where to Stay: Recommendations for accommodations in Sydney's neighborhoods, from luxury hotels and boutique stays to budget-friendly hostels and vacation rentals.

Top Attractions: A curated list of must-see sights, including landmarks, museums, parks, and beaches, with insights into their history, significance, and visiting tips.

Cultural Experiences: Explore Sydney's cultural scene, from Aboriginal heritage and contemporary art galleries to theater performances and annual festivals celebrating diversity.

Dining and Nightlife: Discover Sydney's culinary offerings, from waterfront dining to bustling markets, and nightlife hotspots that showcase the city's vibrant social scene.

Outdoor Activities: Recommendations for outdoor enthusiasts, including coastal walks, beach activities, national parks, and sporting events that highlight Sydney's natural beauty and active lifestyle.

Family-Friendly Activities: Family-friendly attractions and activities, ensure fun and educational experiences for visitors of all ages in Sydney.

Practical Information: Essential resources, including tourist information centers, emergency contacts, local laws, internet connectivity, and postal services to facilitate a seamless stay in Sydney.

Maps and Navigation: Useful maps to navigate Sydney's neighborhoods, public transport routes, and day trip destinations, ensuring you maximize your time in the city.

Final Tips and Recommendations: Insider advice on making the most of your visit, including budget-saving tips, safety precautions, and hidden gems that showcase Sydney's unique character.

Appendices: Additional resources, such as a glossary of Australian terms, conversion charts, emergency phrases, suggested reading, and an index for quick reference.

With this guide, you'll embark on a memorable journey through Sydney's past and present, discovering its iconic landmarks, cultural diversity, and natural wonders along the way.

Why Visit? Top Reasons to Visit Sydney, New South Wales

Sydney, Australia, is a captivating city that blends natural beauty, rich history, and modern vibrancy. Here are the top 10 compelling reasons to visit Sydney:

1. Iconic Landmarks: Sydney Opera House and Harbour Bridge

Sydney's skyline is world-renowned, thanks to its two most iconic structures—the Sydney Opera House and the Sydney Harbour Bridge. The Opera House, with its unique sail-like design, is a UNESCO World Heritage site and a hub for cultural performances, while the Harbour Bridge offers thrilling walks and climbs with breathtaking views of the harbour. Whether you're catching a show or walking the bridge, these landmarks are must-see attractions that define Sydney.

2. Pristine Beaches

Sydney is synonymous with stunning beaches. Bondi Beach is one of the most famous in the world, known for its golden sands, vibrant surf culture, and crystal-clear waters.

For a more relaxed atmosphere, Manly Beach and Coogee Beach are fantastic options, offering family-friendly environments and perfect spots for swimming, surfing, or enjoying the coastal walk. Sydney's beach culture is irresistible for anyone who loves the ocean.

3. Natural Wonders and Outdoor Adventures

Sydney offers a stunning mix of urban and natural landscapes. The Royal Botanic Garden is an oasis of greenery set against the backdrop of the harbour, while Blue Mountains National Park is just a short trip from the city, offering dramatic cliffs, waterfalls, and hiking trails. Outdoor enthusiasts can also kayak in Sydney Harbour, take scenic coastal walks, or explore Ku-ring-gai Chase National Park, known for its Aboriginal rock art and diverse wildlife.

4. World-Class Dining Scene

Sydney is a culinary hotspot with a dining scene that offers something for every palate. From fine dining establishments with waterfront views to trendy cafes and multicultural food markets, the city has it all. Areas like Surry Hills, Chinatown, and Circular Quay offer endless options, ranging from fresh seafood to modern Australian fusion cuisine. Don't miss Sydney's seafood specialty: the famous Sydney rock oysters.

5. Vibrant Arts and Culture

Sydney is a thriving cultural hub, home to a wide array of museums, galleries, and festivals. The Art Gallery of New South Wales, the Museum of Contemporary Art, and the Australian Museum are just a few of the venues that showcase both indigenous and international art. The city's dynamic arts scene is also evident during major cultural events such as the Sydney Festival and Vivid Sydney, an annual festival of light, music, and ideas.

6. A Multicultural Metropolis

Sydney is one of the most multicultural cities in the world, and its diversity is reflected in everything from its food to its festivals. Wander through Chinatown, explore the vibrant neighborhoods of Newtown and Surry Hills, or enjoy the bustling markets in Paddy's Market or Haymarket. The city celebrates its diversity through food, art, and community events, offering a rich tapestry of cultural experiences for visitors.

7. Perfect Climate

With its temperate climate, Sydney is a year-round destination. Summers (December to February) are ideal for beach lovers, while the cooler months (June to August) offer pleasant weather for sightseeing and outdoor activities. The mild winters are perfect for exploring the city's parks, taking part in cultural events, or enjoying a harbour cruise without the summer crowds.

8. Adventures on Sydney Harbour

Sydney Harbour is a playground for water-based activities. Whether you're sailing on a luxury yacht, taking a ferry ride to Taronga Zoo, or kayaking past secluded beaches, the harbour offers stunning views and endless adventures. You can also enjoy a Sydney Harbour Cruise to witness the iconic skyline from the water at sunset or explore hidden coves for a more tranquil experience.

9. Proximity to Wildlife Experiences

Australia is famed for its unique wildlife, and Sydney offers a great gateway to experience it. Taronga Zoo provides a chance to get up close with kangaroos, koalas, and other native animals, all with spectacular views of the city. If you want a more immersive experience, head to Featherdale Wildlife Park or embark on a whale-watching tour during the migration season (May to November). Sydney's proximity to nature and wildlife is a treat for animal lovers.

10. Shopping and Fashion

Sydney is a shopper's paradise, from luxury boutiques to quirky markets. The Queen Victoria Building (QVB) offers an elegant shopping experience with high-end retailers in a stunning 19th-century building. For those looking for more eclectic finds, the markets of The Rocks and Paddington are great for picking up local art, fashion, and souvenirs. Whether you're after cutting-edge Australian design or unique vintage finds, Sydney's shopping scene will keep you entertained.

11. Vibrant Nightlife

Sydney comes alive after dark with a nightlife scene that caters to all tastes. The Rocks, with its historic pubs and modern bars, offers a blend of old-world charm and contemporary vibes. Kings Cross is known for its lively clubs and entertainment venues, while Darlinghurst and Oxford Street are the epicenters of Sydney's LGBTQ+ scene, hosting some of the city's most vibrant parties and events. For a more relaxed evening, numerous rooftop bars and jazz clubs provide stunning views and live music.

12. Family-Friendly Attractions

Sydney offers a plethora of activities for families. The Taranga Zoo, located on the shores of Sydney Harbor, is home to a wide variety of animals and offers interactive exhibits and educational programs. The SEA LIFE Sydney Aquarium and the Wild Life Sydney Zoo provide fascinating insights into marine and terrestrial wildlife. Luna Park, with its historic amusement rides and carnival atmosphere, is a favorite among children and adults alike.

13. Sustainable and Eco-Friendly Travel

Sydney is committed to sustainability and offers numerous eco-friendly travel options. Many hotels and businesses have adopted green practices, and the city's extensive public transport system reduces the need for car travel. Visitors can enjoy eco-tours, such as guided walks through national parks and wildlife sanctuaries that emphasize conservation and responsible tourism. The city also promotes cycling, with dedicated bike lanes and bike-sharing programs making it easy to explore Sydney sustainably.

Chapter 2: Know Before You Go

Best Time to Visit

Sydney, known for its stunning beaches, iconic landmarks, and vibrant culture, offers something for every traveler all year round. However, the best time to visit Sydney largely depends on your personal preferences regarding weather, activities, and events. Here's a detailed guide on what to expect during each season:

Spring (September to November)

Weather:

Temperatures: 11°C to 25°C (51°F to 77°F)

Spring in Sydney is mild and pleasant, with blooming flowers and longer days.

Highlights:

Outdoor Activities: Ideal for beach outings, hiking, and exploring parks and gardens.

Events: Sydney hosts the Sydney Fringe Festival in September, Sculpture by the Sea in October-November, and Good Food Month in October.

Crowds: Moderate tourist crowds, making it easier to find accommodation and navigate popular attractions.

Why Visit:

- Perfect weather for outdoor activities.
- Opportunity to experience vibrant local festivals and food events.
- Moderate tourist presence, offering a more relaxed experience compared to the peak summer months.

Summer (December to February)

Weather:

Temperatures: 18°C to 26°C (64°F to 79°F), occasionally higher.

Sydney's summer is warm to hot, with plenty of sunshine.

Highlights:

Beaches: Best time for swimming, surfing, and sunbathing at Bondi, Manly, and Coo gee beaches.

Events: Major events like New Year's Eve fireworks over Sydney Harbor, Sydney Festival in January, and Australia Day celebrations on January 26.

Outdoor Activities: Perfect for outdoor festivals, concerts, and sports events.

Why Visit:

- Peak beach season with vibrant beach culture.
- Experience Sydney's world-famous New Year's Eve fireworks.
- A plethora of outdoor activities and festivals.
- However, be prepared for large crowds and higher prices for accommodation and flights.

Autumn (March to May)

Weather:

Temperatures: 14°C to 22°C (57°F to 72°F)

Autumn is mild and comfortable, with less humidity than summer.

Highlights:

Nature: Great time to explore national parks, the Blue Mountains, and coastal walks as the foliage starts to change color.

Events: Sydney hosts the Mardi Gras Parade in March, the Royal Easter Show in April, and the Vivid Sydney Light Festival in May and June.

Crowds: Fewer tourists compared to summer, making it easier to enjoy attractions.

Why Visit:

- Mild weather is ideal for outdoor exploration and hiking.
- Unique events like Vivid Sydney, which transforms the city with spectacular light displays.

- Lower accommodation and flight prices compared to the peak summer season.

Winter (June to August)

Weather:

Temperatures: 8°C to 17°C (46°F to 63°F)

Winter in Sydney is mild compared to many other places but can be cooler and wetter.

Highlights:

Indoor Activities: Perfect time for exploring museums, art galleries, and indoor attractions.

Events: Vivid Sydney continues into June, the Sydney Film Festival in June, and the Bondi Winter Magic Festival.

Whale Watching: June to August is prime time for spotting migrating whales along the coast.

Why Visit:

- Enjoy cultural and indoor activities away from the summer heat.
- Unique winter events and festivals.
- Fewer tourists, offering a more tranquil experience and lower accommodation prices.

General Tips

Avoiding Peak Tourist Season: If you prefer to avoid large crowds and higher prices, consider visiting in the shoulder seasons (spring and autumn).

Weather Considerations: Sydney's weather is generally mild, but it's always good to check forecasts and pack accordingly. Summer can be quite hot, so bring sun protection, and winter can be chilly in the evenings, so a jacket is advisable.

Events and Festivals: Sydney's event calendar is packed year-round. Planning your visit around specific events can enhance your experience, but be sure to book accommodations well in advance during these times.

Beach Lovers: If beach activities are a priority, late spring to early autumn is the best period. Water temperatures are warmest from December to March.

Best Time to Visit Sydney Based on Interests and Preferences

General Sightseeing and Outdoor Activities:

Best Time: Spring (September to November) and Autumn (March to May)

Why: During these seasons, Sydney experiences mild temperatures and pleasant weather. Spring brings blooming flowers and green landscapes, while autumn offers clear skies and vibrant foliage. Both periods are ideal for exploring Sydney's outdoor attractions like parks, beaches, and coastal walks without the extremes of summer heat or winter cold.

Beach and Water Activities:

Best Time: Summer (December to February)

Why: Sydney's beaches, including iconic spots like Bondi Beach and Manly Beach, are most enjoyable in summer. Expect warm temperatures perfect for swimming, surfing, and sunbathing. The city comes alive with beach festivals and outdoor events during this time. However, be prepared for larger crowds and higher accommodation prices, especially around Christmas and New Year.

Cultural Events and Festivals:

Best Time: Throughout the Year, with Peaks in Summer and Autumn

Why: Sydney hosts numerous cultural events and festivals year-round. The Sydney Festival in January showcases music, dance, theater, and visual arts. Chinese New Year celebrations in late January or early February feature parades, markets, and performances. Autumn sees events like the Sydney Writers' Festival and Vivid Sydney, a spectacular light festival transforming the cityscape.

Wildlife Viewing and Nature Tours:

Best Time: Winter (June to August)

Why: Winter in Sydney offers cooler temperatures, making it comfortable for outdoor activities like bushwalking and wildlife tours. It's an excellent time to visit wildlife sanctuaries, such as Taranga Zoo or the nearby Blue Mountains, where you can spot native animals like kangaroos and koalas. The Blue Mountains also look stunning in winter with misty landscapes and clear views.

Food and Wine Experiences:

Best Time: Throughout the Year, with a Special Focus on Spring and Autumn

Why: Sydney's culinary scene thrives year-round, but spring and autumn are particularly pleasant for dining outdoors. Restaurants and cafes often showcase seasonal menus with fresh produce. Wine lovers should visit Hunter Valley, a short drive from Sydney, known for its vineyards and wine tastings. Many wineries host events during the harvest seasons in autumn.

Surfing and Water Sports:

Best Time: Spring and Autumn

Why: While summer offers warmer water temperatures, spring and autumn provide a good balance of weather and manageable crowds. Surfing enthusiasts can catch good waves along Sydney's coastline, especially in less crowded spots during these seasons. Manly Beach and Cronulla are popular surfing destinations accessible from central Sydney.

Hiking and Outdoor Adventures:

Best Time: Spring and Autumn

Why: Mild temperatures and clear skies in spring and autumn make hiking and outdoor adventures enjoyable. Explore national parks like Royal National Park or Ku-ring-gai Chase National Park, which offer a range of hiking trails and scenic lookouts. Avoid hiking during summer due to high temperatures and bushfire risks.

Month-by-month Guide to Visiting Sydney

January:

January is the peak of summer in Sydney, with temperatures often reaching highs of around 26-29°C (79-84°F). It's a great time for beachgoers and outdoor enthusiasts, with Bondi and other beaches bustling with activity. However, it's also the peak tourist season, so expect crowds at major attractions and higher accommodation prices. The city hosts various events and festivals, including the Sydney Festival, which showcases arts and cultural performances.

February:

February continues to be warm and sunny, making it ideal for beach activities and outdoor events. The weather remains consistently pleasant, with temperatures ranging from 22-27°C (72-81°F). The Chinese New Year celebrations add a vibrant touch to the city, with dragon boat races, lantern festivals, and street parades in Chinatown and other areas.

March:

March marks the transition from summer to autumn in Sydney. The weather is still warm and enjoyable, with temperatures ranging from 20-25°C (68-77°F). It's a good time to explore outdoor attractions like the Royal Botanic Garden or take a cruise on Sydney Harbor. The Sydney Gay and Lesbian Mardi Gras Parade, a major cultural event, typically occurs in early March, drawing visitors from around the world.

April:

April brings mild autumn weather to Sydney, with temperatures cooling to 17-22°C (63-72°F). The city is less crowded than during the summer months, making it a pleasant time to visit popular attractions like the Sydney Opera House and the Sydney Harbor Bridge. The annual Royal Easter Show, showcasing agriculture, entertainment, and food, is a highlight for families and visitors interested in local culture.

May:

May continues with mild autumn temperatures, ranging from 14-19°C (57-66°F). It's an ideal time for exploring Sydney's outdoor spaces, such as coastal walks and national parks, as well as enjoying the changing foliage in parks like Centennial Park. The Vivid Sydney festival, usually held towards the end of May, features spectacular light installations, music, and ideas talks across the city.

June:

June marks the beginning of winter in Sydney, with temperatures ranging from 11-17°C (52-63°F). While it's cooler, it's still a great time to explore indoor attractions like museums, galleries, and cozy cafes. The Sydney Film Festival and the Sydney Writers' Festival are major cultural events during this month, offering enriching experiences for visitors interested in film and literature.

July:

July is typically the coldest month in Sydney, with temperatures averaging 9-16°C (48-61°F). It's a quieter period for tourism, making it a good time to visit popular attractions without the summer crowds. Winter festivals, such as the Bastille Festival and Bondi Winter Magic, offer opportunities to experience local food, art, and entertainment in a festive atmosphere.

August:

August continues with cool winter weather in Sydney, with temperatures ranging from 9-17°C (48-63°F). It's a good time for whale watching, as humpback whales migrate along the coast. The city hosts events like the Sydney Science Festival and the City2Surf, a popular running event that attracts participants from around the world.

September:

September brings the arrival of spring in Sydney, with temperatures warming to 13-21°C (55-70°F). The city bursts with color as flowers bloom in parks and gardens, such as the Royal Botanic Garden and Blue Mountains Botanic Garden. It's a great time for outdoor activities like hiking, cycling, and picnicking. The Sydney Fringe Festival and the Sydney International Boat Show are major events during this month.

October:

October continues with pleasant spring weather, with temperatures ranging from 15-23°C (59-73°F). It's an ideal time to explore Sydney's coastal walks, such as the Bondi to Coo gee walk, and enjoy outdoor dining at waterfront restaurants. The NRL Grand Final and the Sculpture by the Sea exhibition at Bondi Beach are highlights for sports fans and art enthusiasts alike.

November:

November sees warmer spring temperatures in Sydney, averaging 18-25°C (64-77°F). It's a popular time for beachgoers and outdoor enthusiasts, with daylight saving starting towards the end of the month, extending evening activities. The Sydney International Tennis tournament and the Sydney to Hobart Yacht Race preparations add excitement to the city's cultural and sporting calendar.

December:

December marks the beginning of summer in Sydney, with temperatures rising to 21-26°C (70-79°F). It's a festive time of year, with Christmas decorations adorning the city and holiday events taking place. Bondi Beach and other coastal areas are popular for Christmas Day picnics and beach gatherings. New Year's Eve in Sydney, featuring the iconic fireworks display over Sydney Harbor, is a world-renowned celebration to welcome the new year.

Getting to Sydney

Sydney, Australia's largest and most iconic city, is a bustling metropolis known for its stunning harbor, vibrant culture, and diverse attractions. Whether you're traveling from within Australia or from abroad, here's a comprehensive guide to getting to Sydney.

By Air

1. Major Airports:

Sydney Kingsford Smith Airport (SYD): The primary international and domestic gateway to Sydney, located just 8 km south of the city center. It consists of three terminals: T1 (International), T2 (Domestic), and T3 (Domestic - primarily Qantas flights).

2. International Flights:

Direct Flights: Sydney is well-connected globally with direct flights from major cities in Asia, North America, Europe, the Middle East, and Oceania. Airlines such as Qantas, Emirates, Singapore Airlines, and American Airlines provide direct services.

Transit Options: If a direct flight isn't available, common transit hubs include Dubai, Singapore, Hong Kong, and Los Angeles.

3. Domestic Flights:

Connections within Australia: Major Australian cities like Melbourne, Brisbane, Perth, Adelaide, and Canberra offer frequent domestic flights to Sydney. Airlines such as Qantas, Virgin Australia, and Jetstar operate numerous daily flights.

4. Airport Transfers:

Train: The Airport Link train connects Sydney Airport to the city center and other major suburbs. It runs every 10 minutes, with a travel time of about 13 minutes to Central Station.

Taxi and Rideshares: Taxi and rideshare services like Uber are readily available at designated pickup zones outside each terminal. The trip to the city center typically takes 20-30 minutes, depending on traffic.

Shuttle Services: Various shuttle companies offer door-to-door services to hotels and other locations in Sydney. These can be pre-booked or arranged upon arrival.

Bus: Public buses also service the airport, providing a cost-effective transfer option.

By Sea

1. Cruise Ships:

International Cruises: Sydney is a popular stop for international cruises, with ships docking at the Overseas Passenger Terminal in Circular Quay, right in the heart of the city, or at White Bay Cruise Terminal, which is a short distance from the city center.

Domestic Cruises: Domestic cruise lines also offer routes that include Sydney as a key destination.

2. Ferry Services:

Regional Ferries: Ferries from nearby regions such as Newcastle or the Central Coast can be an enjoyable and scenic way to arrive in Sydney, docking at various points along the harbor.

By Land

1. Train:

Interstate Trains: Sydney's Central Station is the main hub for interstate train services. The Indian Pacific connects Sydney with Perth, via Adelaide, offering a unique and scenic cross-country journey. NSW Train Link services connect Sydney to Melbourne, Brisbane, and other regional destinations.

Regional Trains: NSW Train Link provides regional rail services to and from cities like Newcastle, the Blue Mountains, and the South Coast.

2. Bus/Coach:

Interstate Coaches: Several companies, including Greyhound Australia and Firefly Express, operate long-distance bus services connecting Sydney with other major cities such as Melbourne, Brisbane, and Canberra. These services often run overnight, providing a cost-effective travel option.

Regional Coaches: NSW Train Link and private companies offer extensive coach networks to regional towns and cities within New South Wales.

3. Car:

Major Highways: Sydney is accessible via several major highways. The Hume Highway (M31) connects Sydney with Melbourne, while the Pacific Highway (M1) links Sydney to Brisbane. The Princes Highway (A1) serves those coming from the south coast, including Canberra and Wollongong.

Driving Tips: Driving in Sydney's CBD can be challenging due to traffic and limited parking. However, the city's motorway network and well-signposted routes make driving to and from Sydney relatively straightforward.

Visa and Entry Requirements

When planning a trip to Sydney, Australia, it's essential to understand the visa and entry requirements to ensure a smooth and hassle-free arrival. Here's a comprehensive guide to help you navigate the process:

Visa Requirements

Visitor Visas

visitor (subclass 651): Available to passport holders from the European Union and a few other European countries. This visa is free and allows stays of up to 3 months for tourism or business purposes.

Electronic Travel Authority (ETA) (subclass 601): Available to passport holders from a wide range of countries including the United States, Canada, Japan, South Korea, Singapore, and Hong Kong. The ETA allows stays of up to 3 months and carries a small service fee.

Visitor Visa (subclass 600): This visa is for those who do not qualify for the visitor or ETA. It allows stays from 3 to 12 months for tourism or business purposes and requires a visa application charge.

Working Holiday Visas

Working Holiday Visa (subclass 417): Available to passport holders from eligible countries aged 18-30 (or 35 for some countries). This visa allows you to work and travel in Australia for up to 12 months.

Work and Holiday Visa (subclass 462): Similar to the subclass 417 but for passport holders from other eligible countries. This visa also permits working and traveling for up to 12 months.

Student Visas

Student Visa (subclass 500): Required for international students wishing to study full-time in Australia. The visa allows you to stay for the duration of your study program, usually up to 5 years and includes permission to work part-time.

Business and Skilled Migration Visas

Temporary Skill Shortage Visa (subclass 482): Allows skilled workers to work in Australia for up to 4 years. This visa requires sponsorship by an approved business.

Employer Nomination Scheme (subclass 186): A permanent visa for skilled workers who are nominated by an employer.

Skilled Independent Visa (subclass 189): A points-based visa for skilled workers who are not sponsored by an employer, a state or territory, or a family member.

Entry Requirements

Passport Validity

Ensure your passport is valid for at least six months beyond your intended stay in Australia. While Australia does not have an official rule requiring six months of validity, airlines, and transit countries may have such a requirement.

Health Requirements

Health Insurance: It is highly recommended to have health insurance for the duration of your stay. International visitors are not covered by Australia's national health scheme (Medicare) unless a reciprocal agreement is in place.

Health Examinations: Depending on your length of stay and the activities you intend to engage in, you may need to undergo health examinations or provide a medical certificate.

Character Requirements

You must be of good character to visit or live in Australia. This includes providing police certificates and other documents if required.

You may be asked to provide a police clearance certificate from each country you have lived in for 12 months or more over the last 10 years after you turned 16.

Proof of Funds

You may need to demonstrate that you have sufficient funds to support yourself during your stay. This can include bank statements, pay slips, or an employment contract.

Declaration of Travel History

You will need to declare your travel history and provide details about any other visas you have applied for or been granted in the past.

Application Process

Determine Your Visa Type

Visit the Australian Government Department of Home Affairs website to determine the correct visa type for your visit.

Gather Required Documents

Prepare all necessary documents, including your passport, proof of funds, health insurance, and any other supporting documentation required for your specific visa type.

Submit Your Application

Apply online through the Immi Account portal on the Department of Home Affairs website. Some visas can be processed electronically, while others may require a visit to an Australian visa office.

Pay the Visa Fee

Pay the applicable visa application fee. Fees vary depending on the visa type and processing times.

Wait for Processing

Visa processing times can vary. Check the estimated processing times on the Department of Home Affairs website and ensure you apply well in advance of your travel dates.

Receive Your Visa Grant Notification

If your application is approved, you will receive a visa grant notification with your visa details. Print this document and keep it with your travel documents.

Arrival in Sydney

Immigration and Customs

Upon arrival in Sydney, you will go through immigration and customs. Present your passport, visa grant notification, and any required documents to the border officers.

Declaration Form

Complete the incoming passenger card provided during your flight. Declare any items that may be restricted or subject to duties.

Biosecurity Checks

Be aware of Australia's strict biosecurity laws. Declare all food, plant material, and animal products to avoid fines or penalties.

Budgeting and Costs

Sydney is known for its stunning landscapes, vibrant culture, and iconic landmarks like the Sydney Opera House and Harbour Bridge. However, it's also one of the more expensive cities in the world, making budgeting crucial for any traveler. Whether you're a backpacker or looking for a mid-range or luxury experience, understanding the costs associated with visiting Sydney can help you make the most of your trip. Here's a breakdown of what you can expect in terms of expenses across different categories.

1. Accommodation Costs

Sydney offers a wide range of accommodation options, from budget hostels to luxury hotels, and the costs will vary significantly depending on your preferences.

Budget Accommodations:

Hostels and Budget Hotels: Prices range from AUD 30-$60 per night for dormitory-style rooms and around AUD 70-$120 for private budget hotel rooms. These can be found in central areas like Kings Cross, Surry Hills, and Bondi Beach.

Airbnb: Private rooms or budget apartments on Airbnb can cost around AUD 70-$150 per night, offering a local experience while saving money.

Mid-Range Accommodations:

For mid-range hotels, expect to pay between AUD 150-$300 per night. These hotels are often located in central areas like the CBD (Central Business District) or Darling Harbour, offering good access to main attractions.

Luxury Accommodations:

If you're looking to splurge, luxury hotels in iconic locations like Circular Quay or The Rocks can cost upwards of AUD 400-$800 per night, especially during peak tourist seasons.

Tips:

- Book in advance, especially during peak periods (December to February) when prices soar.
- Consider staying slightly outside the city center in areas like Redfern or Newtown, where you can find cheaper options while still having good transport links.

2. Food and Dining Costs

Sydney has a diverse and vibrant food scene, but dining out can be pricey depending on where and how you eat.

Budget Meals:

If you're looking to save on food, budget eateries, takeaways, and fast-food options range from AUD 10-$20 per meal. Asian food courts, especially in places like Chinatown and Haymarket, offer delicious meals for under AUD 15.

Grocery Stores: If you plan to cook your meals, budget about AUD 60-$100 per week on groceries from supermarkets like Coles, Woolworths, or Aldi.

Mid-Range Dining:

A meal at a mid-range restaurant will typically cost AUD 25-$40 per person without drinks. Popular casual dining spots around Darlinghurst, Surry Hills, and Newtown offer a great range of cuisines.

Fine Dining:

Sydney is home to several Michelin-starred restaurants and fine dining establishments where meals can easily cost upwards of AUD 100-$200 per person. Some top spots include Quay, Bennelong, and Aria, which offer iconic harbour views but at a premium.

Tips:

- Look out for lunch specials and happy hour deals at many restaurants, especially in tourist areas.
- Try Sydney's diverse and affordable ethnic cuisine—Vietnamese, Thai, and Lebanese food, for example, offers good value for money.

3. Transportation Costs

Sydney has an extensive public transportation system, including buses, trains, ferries, and light rail, all accessible with an Opal Card (Sydney's travel card system).

Public Transport:

For budget-conscious travelers, public transport is affordable. Fares vary by distance, with prices ranging from AUD 3.20-$6.30 per ride for adults on buses and trains. Ferries, especially for trips to popular spots like Manly, can cost up to AUD 8.20 per trip.

Opal Card Caps: Public transport is capped at AUD 16.80 per day and AUD 50 per week, making it easier to budget for extended stays. On Sundays, the fare is capped at AUD 2.80 for unlimited travel.

Taxis and Rideshares:

Taxis are more expensive, with an average ride costing AUD 15-$30 for short trips. Uber and other rideshare services are generally cheaper, with base fares starting around AUD 7-$10.

Bike Rentals and Walking:

Sydney's central area is very walkable, and many tourist attractions are close together. Bike rentals are also available, with options like Lime bikes costing around AUD 10 per hour.

Tips:

- Use public transport wherever possible, especially for ferries, which offer scenic views for a fraction of the cost of harbor tours.
- Plan your trips to coincide with the daily cap for Opal Card travel to maximize value.

4. Sightseeing and Activities Costs

Many of Sydney's top attractions are free or affordable, making it easier to stick to a budget while still enjoying everything the city has to offer.

Free Attractions:

Sydney has plenty of free activities such as walking across the Harbour Bridge, visiting the Royal Botanic Gardens, exploring The Rocks historical area, and relaxing on famous beaches like Bondi and Manly.

Art lovers can visit the Art Gallery of NSW and the Museum of Contemporary Art, both of which offer free entry.

Paid Attractions:

Sydney Opera House Tour: Guided tours start at AUD 43 for adults, but you can walk around and admire the exterior for free.

Sydney Tower Eye: Costs around AUD 25-$40 depending on the type of experience (observation deck or combined experiences).

Taronga Zoo: Entry costs AUD 50 for adults but offers a whole day's worth of entertainment and iconic views of the city.

Day Tours and Experiences:

Wine tours, Blue Mountains excursions, or whale-watching tours can range from AUD 100-$200 per person. Look for deals online or group discounts to save on day trips.

Tips:

- Take advantage of free walking tours (e.g., I'm Free Walking Tours) to explore the city on foot without spending much.
- Plan and book online for discounts on major attractions.

5. Entertainment and Nightlife Costs

Sydney's nightlife is diverse, with everything from bars and clubs to theatres and outdoor cinemas.

Budget Entertainment:

Enjoy free live music at bars like The Argyle or Soda Factory, or visit the open-air cinema at Bondi during the summer (tickets from AUD 20).

Entry to many bars is free, but expect to pay around AUD 8-$12 for a beer and AUD 14-$18 for cocktails.

Theatre and Events:

Sydney has a thriving arts scene, with theatre tickets ranging from AUD 50 to AUD 150 depending on the show and seating. You can find cheaper options for local performances or events at smaller venues.

Tips:

- Happy hours at bars can significantly reduce costs, with drinks often half-price.
- Look out for free festivals or outdoor events, especially during the summer months.

6. Overall Budgeting Tips for Sydney Travelers

Daily Budget:

Backpackers: AUD 80-$120 per day (staying in hostels, using public transport, eating at budget eateries, and visiting free attractions).

Mid-Range Travelers: AUD 150-$250 per day (staying in mid-range hotels or Airbnb, dining at casual restaurants, and visiting paid attractions).

Luxury Travelers: AUD 400+ per day (staying in luxury hotels, dining at fine restaurants, and enjoying guided tours and experiences).

Use Public Transport: Sydney's public transport is efficient and affordable, making it the best way to explore the city on a budget.

Free Activities: Take advantage of the many free activities Sydney offers, from coastal walks to museums.

Book in Advance: For both accommodation and activities, booking ahead can save money, especially during peak seasons.

Chapter 3: Accommodation

Types of Accommodations in Sydney

Sydney, a vibrant metropolis known for its iconic landmarks, stunning beaches, and diverse culture, offers a wide range of accommodation options to suit every budget and preference.

Luxury Hotels

Sydney boasts an array of luxury hotels offering unparalleled comfort and high-end amenities. Key properties include The Langham, with its elegant rooms and opulent spa, and the Park Hyatt, known for its stunning views of the Sydney Opera House. These hotels typically feature fine dining options, 24-hour concierge service, and full-service spas. Located in central areas like The Rocks and Circular Quay, they offer easy access to major attractions. Expect to pay between AUD 400 to AUD 1,000 per night, depending on the season and room type.

Boutique Hotels

Boutique hotels in Sydney offer a personalized experience with unique design elements and intimate settings. Properties such as the QT Sydney blend contemporary decor with quirky details, providing a stylish retreat in the heart of the city. They often include features like on-site restaurants, personalized service, and a distinct aesthetic. Located in vibrant neighborhoods like Surry Hills and Darlinghurst, these hotels generally range from AUD 200 to AUD 400 per night.

Serviced Apartments

Serviced apartments cater to longer stays with amenities similar to those of a hotel but with added space and kitchen facilities. The Adina Apartment Hotel in Sydney's central business district offers comfortable apartments with fully equipped kitchens and laundry facilities. These apartments are often located near business hubs or transport links, making them ideal for both business and leisure travelers. Prices range from AUD 150 to AUD 300 per night.

Budget Hotels and Hostels

For budget-conscious travelers, Sydney provides numerous budget hotels and hostels that offer affordable accommodation without compromising on comfort.

Places like the Wake Up! Sydney Central Hostel offers dormitory-style rooms and private options with basic amenities and social activities. Located in areas like Surry Hills and near Central Station, these options typically cost between AUD 30 to AUD 150 per night.

Holiday Parks and Camping

For a more adventurous stay, holiday parks and camping sites offer a unique way to experience Sydney. The BIG4 Sydney Lakeside Holiday Park provides cabin accommodations and camping sites close to nature reserves and beaches. These parks usually feature communal facilities like BBQ areas and swimming pools. They are often located in suburban areas or near the coast, with prices ranging from AUD 80 to AUD 200 per night for cabins and less for campsites.

Short-Term Rentals

Short-term rentals, including options like Airbnb and Vacation Rentals by Owner (VRBO), offer a range of choices from cozy apartments to entire homes. These rentals provide flexibility and a local living experience. Examples include chic city apartments in Darling Harbor and spacious homes in Bondi Beach. Features typically include fully equipped kitchens, living areas, and sometimes unique amenities like pools or terraces. Located throughout Sydney, these rentals vary widely in price, generally ranging from AUD 100 to AUD 500 per night depending on size, location, and amenities.

Luxury Apartments

Luxury apartments in Sydney offer high-end living with premium facilities and prime locations. Examples include the Bondi Beach Apartments and The Woolloomooloo Wharf Apartments. These properties feature modern interiors, stunning views, and amenities such as private pools, gyms, and concierge services. They are often located in sought-after areas such as Bondi Beach and the CBD. Prices for these upscale accommodations range from AUD 300 to AUD 800 per night.

Guesthouses and B&Bs

Guesthouses and bed-and-breakfasts in Sydney provide a cozy and often more personal alternative to larger hotels. Properties like the Woolloomooloo Bay Bed and Breakfast offer comfortable rooms with homey touches, often including breakfast and personalized recommendations from hosts.

Located in quieter, residential areas or close to popular suburbs, these options generally cost between AUD 100 to AUD 250 per night.

Eco-Friendly Accommodations

Sydney is home to eco-friendly accommodations that prioritize sustainability. Hotels such as the Ovolo Woolloomooloo feature green practices, including energy-efficient systems and waste reduction programs. These accommodations often include environmentally conscious amenities and are situated in both central and suburban locations. Prices range from AUD 200 to AUD 400 per night, reflecting their commitment to sustainability and quality.

Serviced Residences

Serviced residences combine the convenience of hotel services with the comfort of home. The Fraser Suites Sydney, for example, offers spacious apartments with kitchen facilities, housekeeping services, and access to fitness centers and pools. Positioned in central areas, these residences cater to both short and long-term stays and typically cost between AUD 250 to AUD 500 per night.

Historical Hotels

Sydney also features historical hotels that offer a blend of classic charm and modern comfort. The Old Clare Hotel in Chippendale, for instance, is a beautifully restored building with a rich history, combining original architectural elements with contemporary design. Guests can enjoy stylish rooms, a rooftop bar, and a sophisticated dining experience. Located in vibrant areas like Chippendale and The Rocks, these hotels provide a unique experience with prices ranging from AUD 200 to AUD 400 per night.

Waterfront Hotels

For those who want to enjoy stunning water views, Sydney's waterfront hotels offer picturesque settings and luxurious amenities. The Pier One Sydney Harbor, for example, is located on the water's edge with direct access to the Sydney Harbor Bridge and Circular Quay. Features include elegant rooms with harbor views, an outdoor terrace, and fine dining options. Positioned in prime waterfront locations, these hotels generally cost between AUD 300 to AUD 600 per night, depending on the view and season.

Booking Tips

1. Book Early: Sydney is a popular destination, and accommodations, especially the best ones, fill up quickly. Book several months in advance, especially for travel during peak seasons (summer, major holidays, and festivals).

2. Use Reliable Booking Platforms: Trusted sites like Booking.com, Expedia, and Airbnb provide user reviews, price comparisons, and flexible booking options. Additionally, checking the hotel's official website can sometimes yield exclusive deals or packages.

3. Consider Location: Choose accommodation based on your planned activities. Staying in central locations like the CBD, Darling Harbor, or The Rocks offers easy access to major attractions. For a beach experience, consider Bondi or Manly.

4. Read Reviews: Reviews on platforms like TripAdvisor and Google can provide insights into the experience of past guests. Look for comments on cleanliness, service, location, and value for money.

5. Check Amenities: Ensure the accommodation meets your needs: free Wi-Fi, breakfast options, parking, swimming pool, gym, or child-friendly services. Some hotels also offer complimentary airport transfers or shuttles to popular tourist spots.

6. Flexibility with Dates: If possible, be flexible with your travel dates. Mid-week stays can sometimes be cheaper than weekends. Using the "flexible dates" feature on booking sites can help identify the most affordable times to stay.

7. Look for Package Deals: Some hotels offer packages that include breakfast, dinner, or tickets to local attractions. These can be cost-effective and convenient.

8. Join Loyalty Programs: If you frequently travel, joining hotel loyalty programs (like Marriott Bonvoy, Hilton Honors, or Accor Live Limitless) can earn your points, discounts, and exclusive perks.

9. Check Cancellation Policies: Ensure you understand the cancellation policy before booking. Some rates are non-refundable but offer significant discounts, while others allow for free cancellation up to a certain date.

10. Consider Off-Peak Travel: Traveling during off-peak seasons can result in lower accommodation rates and less crowded attractions. Sydney's shoulder seasons (spring and autumn) often provide pleasant weather and better deals.

Chapter 4: Attractions and Landmarks

20 Must-See Sights and Attractions in Sydney, New South Wales

Sydney is a city teeming with iconic landmarks, cultural sites, beautiful beaches, and natural wonders. Whether you're a first-time visitor or a seasoned traveler, these 20 must-see attractions capture the essence of Sydney and provide unforgettable experiences.

1. Sydney Opera House

The Sydney Opera House is one of the world's most iconic buildings and a symbol of Australia's rich cultural heritage. Designed by Danish architect Jørn Utzon, this UNESCO World Heritage Site is renowned for its distinctive sail-like shells, which house multiple performance venues. Opened in 1973, the Opera House hosts over 1,500 performances annually, including opera, ballet, theatre, and concerts. Its stunning location on Bennelong Point offers panoramic views of Sydney Harbor, making it a perfect spot for photography and sightseeing. The venue also offers guided tours, providing insights into its architectural marvels and backstage areas.

- **Opening Hours:** Daily from 9:00 AM to 5:00 PM for tours; performance times vary.

- **Address:** Bennelong Point, Sydney NSW 2000, Australia

How to Get There:

- By Train: Circular Quay Station is a 5-minute walk.
- By Bus: Numerous routes stop at Circular Quay.
- By Ferry: Circular Quay Wharf is a short stroll away.

Admission Fee:

- Tours: Adult $42, Concession AUD 32, Child AUD 22, Family packages available.
- Performances: Prices vary by show.

Insider Tip: Arrive early for tours or performances to explore the Opera House's surroundings, including the Royal Botanic Garden and the Sydney Harbor Bridge, for fantastic photo opportunities. Booking tickets in advance for popular shows is highly recommended to avoid disappointment.

2. Sydney Harbor Bridge

The Sydney Harbor Bridge, an iconic symbol of Sydney, Australia, is renowned for its striking architecture and historical significance. Spanning 1,149 meters (3,770 feet) across Sydney Harbor, the bridge connects the Central Business District (CBD) with the North Shore.

Completed in 1932, it boasts a steel arch design, making it the largest steel arch bridge in the world. The bridge's main span measures 503 meters (1,650 feet) and rises 134 meters (440 feet) above the water, offering panoramic views of the city, the harbor, and the Sydney Opera House. Visitors can experience the bridge up close through the Bridge Climb, a thrilling ascent to the summit, which provides breathtaking vistas of the harbor and beyond. The bridge also accommodates vehicles, trains, cyclists, and pedestrians, highlighting its multifunctional role in Sydney's transport network. Its engineering marvel and scenic backdrop make it a central feature of Sydney's skyline and a must-visit landmark for tourists and locals alike.

Opening Hours

- Bridge Climb: Daily from early morning to late evening (varies by season and tour type)
- Pylon Lookout Museum: 10:00 AM - 5:00 PM daily

Address: Sydney Harbor Bridge, Sydney, NSW 2000, Australia

How to Get There

- Train: Alight at Milsons Point Station (North Shore) or Circular Quay Station (CBD).
- Bus: Numerous bus service routes that stop near both ends of the bridge.
- Ferry: Ferries to Circular Quay provide a scenic route to the bridge.

Admission Fee

- Bridge Climb: Prices vary (approximately AUD 200-400 depending on the climb type and time).
- Pylon Lookout Museum: Around AUD 19 for adults, AUD 12.50 for children.

Insider Tip: For a free experience, walk across the pedestrian path for spectacular views, particularly during sunset when the city is bathed in a golden glow.

3. Darling Harbor

Darling Harbor is a vibrant waterfront precinct in Sydney, renowned for its diverse attractions and lively atmosphere. It offers a blend of entertainment, dining, and cultural experiences. Key highlights include the SEA LIFE Sydney Aquarium, where you can explore underwater wonders; the WILD LIFE Sydney Zoo, home to native Australian animals; and the Australian National Maritime Museum, showcasing maritime heritage. Darling Harbor also features the ICC Sydney, which hosts various events, and the Darling Quarter, perfect for family-friendly activities. The area comes alive at night with illuminated fountains and a bustling dining scene along the waterfront.

- **Opening Hours:** Varies by attraction; generally, 9 AM to 10 PM.
- **Address:** Darling Harbor, Sydney, NSW 2000, Australia

How to Get There:

- By Train: Alight at Town Hall Station and walk.
- By Light Rail: Alight at Convention, Exhibition, or Pyrmont Bay stops.
- By Ferry: Ferries stop at Darling Harbor Wharf.

Insider Tip: Visit during the evening to enjoy the Harbor's vibrant nightlife and catch the spectacular fireworks display every Saturday at 9 PM.

4. The Rocks

The Rocks is a historic precinct in Sydney, renowned for its cobblestone streets, heritage buildings, and vibrant atmosphere. Nestled between the Sydney Harbor Bridge and Circular Quay, The Rocks offers a unique blend of history and modernity. Wander through narrow laneways filled with boutique shops, art galleries, and cafes. Visit the Museum of Contemporary Art or explore the area's colonial past at the Rocks Discovery Museum. On weekends, the Rocks Markets come alive with local artisans, food stalls, and live entertainment. The Rocks also boasts some of Sydney's oldest pubs, where you can enjoy a drink while soaking in the historic ambiance.

Opening Hours

- General Area: Open 24/7
- Rocks Discovery Museum: Daily, 10:00 AM – 5:00 PM
- Rocks Markets: Saturday and Sunday, 10:00 AM – 5:00 PM

Address: The Rocks, Sydney, NSW 2000, Australia

How to Get There

- By Train: Take a train to Circular Quay Station. The Rocks is a short walk from the station.
- By Bus: Numerous bus routes stop at Circular Quay.
- By Ferry: Alight at Circular Quay Ferry Terminal and walk to The Rocks.

Insider Tip: Visit on a weekend to experience the vibrant Rocks Markets and explore the hidden laneways for unique photo opportunities and boutique shopping. Don't miss the sunset views from the Observatory Hill Park, offering a stunning panorama of Sydney Harbor.

5. Taranga Zoo

Taranga Zoo is a premier wildlife sanctuary located on the picturesque shores of Sydney Harbor, offering breathtaking views of the city skyline. Home to over 4,000 animals from 350 species, the zoo provides an immersive experience with diverse wildlife, from native Australian species like kangaroos and koalas to exotic animals like elephants and giraffes. The zoo is dedicated to conservation and education, offering interactive exhibits and informative talks. Highlights include the Lemur Forest Adventure, the Sumatran Tiger Trek, and the iconic Free Flight Bird Show. Visitors can also enjoy the Sky Safari cable car, which provides a unique aerial view of the zoo and harbor.

- **Opening Hours:** Daily from 9:30 AM to 5:00 PM
- **Address:** Bradley's Head Road, Mossman NSW 2088, Australia

How to Get There:

- By Ferry: Take the ferry from Circular Quay to Taranga Zoo Wharf, followed by a short shuttle bus ride or a walk to the entrance.
- By Bus: Bus routes 238 and 244 run directly to the zoo.
- By Car: Parking is available on-site for a fee.

Admission Fee:

- Adults: AUD 49
- Children (4-15 years): AUD 29
- Concessions and family passes are available.

Insider Tip: Arrive early to catch the morning feeding sessions and avoid the crowds. Don't miss the Sky Safari for a spectacular aerial view of the zoo and Sydney Harbor.

6. Sydney Tower Eye

Rising 309 meters above the heart of Sydney, the Sydney Tower Eye offers unparalleled panoramic views of the city and its iconic landmarks. From its observation deck, visitors can marvel at sweeping vistas that stretch from the

Sydney Harbor Bridge to the Blue Mountains. The experience includes interactive touchscreens detailing key points of interest visible from the tower, enhancing the visit with educational insights into Sydney's history and geography. For those seeking an adrenaline rush, the Skywalk—an outdoor glass-floored platform at 268 meters—provides a thrilling opportunity to walk above the city.

- **Opening Hours:** Daily from 9:00 AM to 9:00 PM (last entry at 8:00 PM)
- **Address:** Sydney Tower Eye, 100 Market St, Sydney NSW 2000, Australia
- **How to Get There:** The Sydney Tower Eye is centrally located in the CBD. It's a short walk from Town Hall Station and easily accessible by bus or taxi.
- **Insider Tip:** To avoid crowds, visit early in the morning or during weekdays. Sunset offers particularly stunning views as the city lights up. Consider combining your visit with a meal at the tower's 360 Bar and Dining for a memorable dining experience with equally spectacular views.

7. Queen Victoria Building

The Queen Victoria Building (QVB) stands as a testament to Sydney's Victorian-era architecture and is a premier shopping destination steeped in history. Built in the late 19th century and meticulously restored, the QVB features Romanesque Revival architecture, complete with stained glass windows, intricate tile work, and a grand central dome. Its elegant corridors are lined with high-end boutiques, jewelers, cafes, and restaurants, making it a delightful place to shop and explore. The building also houses the Great Australian Clock, a mechanical marvel featuring dioramas of historical scenes.

Opening Hours:

- Monday to Saturday: 9:00 AM - 6:00 PM
- Sunday: 11:00 AM - 5:00 PM

Address: 455 George St, Sydney NSW 2000, Australia

How to Get There: The QVB is centrally located in Sydney's CBD, within walking distance from Town Hall Station and Wynyard Station. Buses also stop nearby on George Street.

Insider Tip: Visit during the Christmas season to witness the stunning decorations and the famous Swarovski crystal Christmas tree in the central dome, a sight that attracts visitors from around the world.

8. Circular Quay

Circular Quay is a quintessential Sydney landmark, serving as both a transport hub and a gateway to the city's iconic harbor. Located at the northern end of Sydney's central business district (CBD), Circular Quay offers stunning views of the Sydney Opera House, Sydney Harbor Bridge, and the sparkling waters of Port Jackson. It's a bustling precinct where ferries depart for various harbor destinations, including Manly, Taranga Zoo, and Watsons Bay. The area is dotted with outdoor cafes, restaurants, and street performers, making it a vibrant spot for both locals and tourists to relax and soak in the Sydney atmosphere.

- **Opening Hours: Circular** Quay is accessible 24/7 for pedestrian access. However, individual shops, restaurants, and attractions have varied operating hours.
- **Address:** Circular Quay, Sydney NSW 2000, Australia.

How to Get There:

- By Train: Alight at Circular Quay Station, a major transport hub on the City Circle Line.
- By Ferry: Numerous ferries operate from Circular Quay Wharf, connecting various harbor destinations.
- By Bus: Several bus routes stop near Circular Quay, making it accessible from different parts of Sydney.

Insider Tip: For stunning views of the Sydney Opera House and Harbor Bridge, take a leisurely walk along the waterfront promenade towards the Opera House. Sunset and evening times offer particularly picturesque views, with the city skyline illuminated against the harbor backdrop.

9. Sydney Observatory

Sydney Observatory is a historic site atop Observatory Hill with a rich heritage dating back to 1858. Located near the Rocks district, it offers panoramic views of Sydney Harbor and interactive exhibits on astronomy and space science. Visitors can explore telescopes, a planetarium, and historical displays, learning about celestial navigation and the observatory's pivotal role in Australia's scientific history. Guided tours and night sky viewing sessions provide insights into stars, planets, and astronomical phenomena.

- **Opening Hours:** Open daily except Mondays. Hours vary; check the official website for details.
- **Address:** 1003 Upper Fort St, Millers Point NSW 2000, Australia
- **How to Get There:** Take a scenic walk from Circular Quay or catch a bus to Observatory Hill. Limited parking is available nearby.
- **Admission Fee:** General admission: AUD 10. Concessions and family tickets are available. Night tours may have different pricing.
- **Insider Tip:** Visit during evening sessions to observe celestial objects through telescopes. Check the observatory's website for special events like meteor showers or planet alignments for a unique stargazing experience.

10. Sydney Fish Market

Sydney Fish Market is a bustling hub for seafood enthusiasts, offering an authentic taste of Australia's maritime culture. As one of the largest fish markets globally, it showcases an impressive array of fresh seafood—from Sydney rock oysters and prawns to a variety of fish and crustaceans. Visitors can explore the market's diverse stalls, where vendors offer everything from raw catches to gourmet seafood meals.

The market's vibrant atmosphere, filled with the sights and sounds of auctioneers and chefs, provides an immersive experience of Sydney's seafood industry. Beyond shopping, visitors can enjoy waterfront dining at seafood restaurants overlooking the harbor or participate in cooking classes to learn the art of preparing fresh seafood dishes.

Opening Hours:

- Open daily from 7:00 AM to 4:00 PM
- Closed on Christmas Day

Address: Bank St & Pyrmont Bridge Rd, Sydney NSW 2009, Australia

How to Get There:

- By Public Transport: Take the light rail to Pyrmont Bay Station or catch buses to nearby stops.
- By Car: Limited parking available; consider using public transport or rideshare.

Insider Tip: Arrive early (around 7:00 AM) for the freshest selection and to experience the morning fish auction, where local seafood is sold to restaurants and the public. Combine your visit with a seafood lunch at one of the market's acclaimed eateries for a complete Sydney culinary experience.

11. Barangaroo Reserve

Barangaroo Reserve, situated on the western edge of Sydney's CBD, is a striking urban park that seamlessly blends natural beauty with Aboriginal heritage. Named after a powerful Cammeray gal woman, Barangaroo offers visitors lush green spaces, native plantings, and stunning views of Sydney Harbor. The park's design incorporates sustainable principles and features cultural artifacts and interpretative signage that highlight its Indigenous history. Visitors can stroll along scenic walking paths, relax in shaded picnic areas, and admire the sandstone foreshore. Barangaroo Reserve also hosts cultural events and performances, celebrating its rich Aboriginal heritage.

- **Opening Hours:** Open daily from 9:00 AM to 5:00 PM (subject to change for special events).
- **Address:** Hickson Road, Barangaroo NSW 2000, Australia.

- **How to Get There:** Barangaroo Reserve is easily accessible by walking from Circular Quay (approx. 15 minutes), by ferry to Barangaroo Wharf, or by bus to nearby stops on George Street.
- **Insider Tip:** Visit at sunset for breathtaking views of Sydney Harbor Bridge and the city skyline. The park's layout and design create unique perspectives that are especially magical during the golden hour.

12. Kings Cross

Kings Cross, once notorious for its nightlife and colorful history, has transformed into a vibrant cultural hub in Sydney. Located east of the CBD, this area now blends its edgy past with trendy cafes, eclectic bars, and boutique shops. The iconic Coca-Cola billboard marks its entrance, while nearby streets like Darlinghurst Road offer a mix of dining options, from casual eateries to fine dining. At night, Kings Cross comes alive with its lively bars and clubs, catering to a diverse crowd seeking entertainment.

- **Opening Hours:** Generally, bars and clubs in Kings Cross operate until late, with specific hours varying by venue.
- **Address:** Kings Cross, Sydney, New South Wales, Australia.

- **How to Get There:** Kings Cross is easily accessible by train (Kings Cross Station), bus, or a short walk from nearby neighborhoods like Potts Point or Darlinghurst.
- **Insider Tip:** During the day, explore the area's history with a walk around the Kings Cross Heritage Trail. For a memorable experience, visit on a Sunday when the Kings Cross Market is in full swing, offering local produce, crafts, and live music. Keep in mind that while Kings Cross has cleaned up its image, it's still wise to exercise typical urban caution, especially late at night.

13. The Strand Arcade

The Strand Arcade is a cherished gem in Sydney's CBD, renowned for its Victorian architecture and upscale shopping experience. Built-in 1891, this historic shopping arcade exudes elegance with its ornate iron-lace balconies, glass roof, and mosaic-tiled floors. It houses a curated selection of boutiques, offering fashion, jewelry, beauty products, and gourmet treats. Whether browsing for designer labels or enjoying a leisurely coffee, The Strand Arcade provides a blend of heritage charm and modern luxury.

Opening Hours:

- Monday to Wednesday: 9:00 AM - 6:00 PM
- Thursday: 9:00 AM - 8:00 PM

- Friday: 9:00 AM - 6:00 PM
- Saturday: 9:00 AM - 5:00 PM
- Sunday: 10:00 AM - 4:00 PM

Address: 412-414 George St, Sydney NSW 2000, Australia

How to Get There:

- By Train: Alight at Town Hall Station (3-minute walk).
- By Bus: Various bus routes stop near Town Hall or George St.

Insider Tip: Visit during weekdays to avoid crowds and enjoy a relaxed shopping experience. Don't miss the beautiful window displays during festive seasons.

14. Manly Beach

Manly Beach is a quintessential Sydney destination renowned for its stunning coastal scenery, vibrant surf culture, and laid-back atmosphere. Situated on Sydney's Northern Beaches, manly offers a picturesque escape from the city bustle, accessible via a scenic 30-minute ferry ride from Circular Quay. The beach itself features golden sands and clear waters, perfect for swimming, surfing, and sunbathing.

Surrounding the beach, visitors can explore a variety of shops, cafes, and restaurants, adding to the lively seaside ambiance. The Manly Corso, a pedestrian mall, is a hub of activity, offering everything from casual eateries to boutique shopping. Outdoor enthusiasts can enjoy the scenic Manly to Spit Bridge coastal walk, which offers breathtaking views of Sydney Harbor and native bushland.

- **Opening Hours:** Manly Beach is accessible 24/7, but lifeguard patrols operate from 8:30 AM to 5:00 PM during the swimming season.
- **Address:** Manly Beach, North Steyn, Manly NSW 2095, Australia.
- **How to Get There:** From Circular Quay, take the iconic Manly Ferry, which departs regularly and offers spectacular harbor views. Alternatively, you can take a bus from the city center directly to Manly.
- **Insider Tip:** Visit early in the morning or late afternoon to avoid the crowds and experience the serene beauty of the beach. Don't miss out on trying the famous fish and chips from one of the local eateries along the Corso.

15. Royal Botanic Garden

The Royal Botanic Garden in Sydney is a lush, tranquil oasis situated on the edge of Sydney Harbor, offering visitors an escape from the bustling city. Established in 1816, it is one of the oldest scientific institutions in Australia and features an extensive collection of plants from Australia and around the world.

The garden spans 74 acres, with themed sections such as the Rose Garden, Palm Grove, and the Cadi Jam Ora: First Encounters Garden, which highlights the significance of native plants to the Aboriginal people. Visitors can enjoy guided tours, seasonal events, and educational programs. The garden also offers spectacular views of the Sydney Opera House and Harbor Bridge, making it a prime spot for photography and leisurely walks.

- **Opening Hours:** Daily, 7:00 AM to 8:00 PM (hours may vary seasonally)
- **Address:** Mrs. Macquarie's Road, Sydney NSW 2000, Australia
- **How to Get There:** Easily accessible by public transport. Take a train to Martin Place or Circular Quay, then walk. Buses and ferries to Circular Quay are also convenient options.
- **Insider Tip:** Visit early in the morning for a peaceful experience and to catch the stunning sunrise over the harbor. Don't miss the Calyx, an innovative horticultural space with changing exhibitions.

16. Art Gallery of New South Wales

The Art Gallery of New South Wales (AGNSW) is a premier cultural institution located in the heart of Sydney. Established in 1871, it offers a rich and diverse collection of Australian, European, and Asian art. Visitors can explore extensive collections of contemporary and traditional artworks, including significant pieces by Indigenous Australian artists.

The gallery's stunning neoclassical architecture is complemented by modern extensions, providing a harmonious blend of old and new. Special exhibitions, educational programs, and art workshops regularly enhance the gallery experience. The AGNSW also features a delightful cafe and a well-stocked gallery shop, making it a perfect destination for art enthusiasts and casual visitors alike.

Opening Hours:

- Monday to Sunday: 10:00 AM - 5:00 PM
- Wednesdays: Open until 10:00 PM for Art After Hours

Address: Art Gallery Road, The Domain, Sydney NSW 2000, Australia

How to Get There:

- By Train: Alight at St James or Martin Place stations, then a short walk through The Domain.
- By Bus: Numerous buses stop nearby on Elizabeth Street.
- By Car: Paid parking is available at the gallery and nearby Domain Car Park.

Insider Tip: Visit on Wednesday evenings for "Art After Hours" – enjoy extended opening hours, free talks, films, and live music. Plus, the gallery is less crowded during these times, allowing for a more relaxed experience.

17. Watsons Bay

Watsons Bay is a charming seaside suburb in Sydney, known for its stunning views, historic sites, and delicious seafood.

As one of the oldest fishing villages in Australia, it offers a unique blend of natural beauty and historical significance. Visitors can explore the picturesque South Head Heritage Trail, which leads to the Hornby Lighthouse and offers panoramic views of the Sydney Harbor and the Pacific Ocean. The area is also famous for Doyles on the Beach, one of Sydney's iconic seafood restaurants, where you can enjoy fresh fish and chips by the water. With its tranquil beaches, scenic walks, and rich history, Watsons Bay is a perfect escape from the hustle and bustle of the city.

- **Opening Hours:** Watsons Bay is open to the public 24/7, but specific attractions like Doyles on the Beach and the Hornby Lighthouse have varied opening hours.
- **Address:** Watsons Bay, NSW 2030, Australia

How to Get There:

- By Ferry: Take a ferry from Circular Quay to Watsons Bay, which offers a scenic 20-minute ride.
- By Bus: Buses 324 and 325 from the city center directly to Watsons Bay.
- By Car: Drive via New South Head Road, but parking can be limited.

Insider Tip: Visit during weekdays to avoid the weekend crowds and enjoy a picnic at Robertson Park for the best views of the sunset over Sydney Harbor.

18. Chinese Garden of Friendship

The Chinese Garden of Friendship, located in Darling Harbor, is a tranquil oasis amidst the bustling city of Sydney. Designed in collaboration with Sydney's sister city, Guangzhou, this traditional Chinese garden embodies the harmony between man and nature. Opened in 1988, the garden features elements of water, plants, stone, and architecture, reflecting the Taoist principles of Yin-Yang and Wu-Xing. Visitors can explore serene landscapes, including waterfalls, koi ponds, pavilions, and weeping willows. The garden's intricate design includes paths leading to hidden nooks, perfect for quiet contemplation. Highlights include the Dragon Wall, symbolizing the bond between Guangzhou and Sydney, and the Teahouse, where visitors can enjoy traditional Chinese tea and snacks.

- **Opening Hours:** Daily from 10:00 AM to 5:00 PM, except on Good Friday and Christmas Day.
- **Address:** Pier Street, Darling Harbor, Sydney, NSW 2000
- **How to Get There:** Easily accessible by public transport. Take the train to Town Hall Station, then a short walk to Darling Harbor. Alternatively, catch a bus to the Haymarket area or the light rail to the Paddy's Market stop.
- **Admission Fee:** Adults $8, Concession $4, Family (2 adults and 2 children) $20. Children under 12 enter free with a paying adult.
- **Insider Tip:** Visit on a weekday morning for a quieter experience and the best photo opportunities without the crowds. Don't miss the guided tours, which offer deeper insights into the garden's design and cultural significance.

19. Luna Park

Luna Park, an iconic amusement park located on the northern shore of Sydney Harbor, is a must-see attraction offering a blend of nostalgic charm and modern thrills. Opened in 1935, the park's entrance is marked by the famous smiling face, welcoming visitors into a world of fun and excitement. The park features a mix of classic and contemporary rides, including the Ferris wheel, which offers stunning views of the Sydney Opera House and Harbor Bridge, and the adrenaline-pumping Wild Mouse roller coaster. In addition to rides, Luna Park hosts various events, live performances, and carnival games, making it a perfect destination for families, friends, and couples.

- **Opening Hours** Luna Park's opening hours vary throughout the year. Generally, it is open from 11:00 AM to 10:00 PM on weekends, public holidays, and school holidays. Check the official website for specific dates and times.
- **Address** 1 Olympic Drive, Milsons Point NSW 2061, Australia

How to Get There

- By Train: Take the T1 North Shore Line to Milsons Point Station, which is a short walk from the park.
- By Ferry: Ferries to Milsons Point Wharf depart from Circular Quay and Darling Harbor, with a short walk to the park from the wharf.
- By Bus: Numerous bus routes service Milsons Point and North Sydney, with stops near the park.

Admission Fee: Luna Park offers various ticket options, including unlimited ride passes and single-ride tickets. Prices vary, so check the website for current rates and special offers.

Insider Tip: Visit during the evening to enjoy the park's dazzling lights and catch stunning sunset views over Sydney Harbor from the Ferris wheel.

20. Chinatown

Sydney's Chinatown, located in Haymarket, is a bustling and vibrant precinct that offers a rich cultural experience. Known for its colorful streets, delicious Asian cuisine, and lively atmosphere, Chinatown is a must-visit for food enthusiasts and cultural explorers alike. Dixon Street, the main pedestrian thoroughfare, is lined with a plethora of restaurants, cafes, and shops, offering everything from authentic Chinese dishes to trendy Asian fusion cuisine.

Chinatown is also home to the Friday Night Markets, where you can enjoy a variety of street food, unique crafts, and live performances. During the Lunar New Year, Chinatown becomes even more vibrant with festivities, parades, and traditional lion dances, making it an exciting time to visit.

Opening Hours:

- Most shops and restaurants: 10:00 AM - 10:00 PM daily
- Friday Night Markets: 4:00 PM - 11:00 PM every Friday

Address: Dixon Street, Haymarket, NSW 2000, Sydney, Australia

How to Get There:

- By Train: Take the train to Central Station, then walk 10 minutes via Eddy Avenue and George Street.
- By Light Rail: Alight at Paddy's Markets stop on the L1 Dulwich Hill Line.
- By Bus: Numerous bus routes stop near Chinatown. Check local schedules for the best route.

Insider Tip: Visit on a Friday evening to experience the bustling Night Markets, where you can sample a wide array of street food and enjoy the lively ambiance. Don't miss the custard-filled "Dragon Beard Candy" for a unique treat!

Chapter 5: Getting Around Sydney

Public Transportation

Navigating Sydney can be both an exciting and straightforward experience, thanks to its well-developed transportation network. Whether you prefer public transport, taxis, rideshares, biking, walking, or renting a car, Sydney offers various options to suit your travel needs.

Public Transportation

A. Trains

Sydney's train network, operated by Sydney Trains, is one of the most efficient and extensive ways to get around the city and its surrounding suburbs. The network is well-connected, covering key areas of Sydney and providing easy access to major attractions, business districts, and residential areas.

Overview of Sydney's Train Network

The Sydney Trains network comprises several lines, each identified by a specific color and letter. The lines serve various parts of the city and suburbs, with Central Station serving as the primary hub where most lines converge. The train services are reliable, frequent, and cover a wide area, making them an excellent choice for both tourists and locals.

Key Train Lines

T1 North Shore & Western Line

- Route: Berowra to Emu Plains/Richmond via Sydney CBD
- Key Stops: North Sydney, Chatswood, Parramatta, Blacktown, Penrith

T2 Inner West & Leppington Line

- Route: Leppington to City Circle via Granville and Inner West
- Key Stops: Ashfield, Strathfield, Granville, Liverpool

T3 Bankstown Line

- Route: Liverpool/Lidcombe to City Circle via Bankstown
- Key Stops: Bankstown, Campsie, Sydenham

T4 Eastern Suburbs & Illawarra Line

- Route: Bondi Junction to Cronulla/Waterfall
- Key Stops: Kings Cross, Central, Hurstville, Sutherland

T5 Cumberland Line

- Route: Scofield's to Leppington via Parramatta
- Key Stops: Blacktown, Parramatta, Cabramatta

T6 Carlingford Line

- Route: Clyde to Carlingford (Note: This line is currently being converted to light rail and is expected to reopen as part of the Parramatta Light Rail project)

T7 Olympic Park Line

- Route: Lidcombe to Olympic Park
- Key Stops: Olympic Park

T8 Airport & South Line

- Route: Macarthur to City Circle via Sydney Airport
- Key Stops: Revesby, Wolli Creek, Domestic Airport, International Airport

T9 Northern Line

- Route: Hornsby to Gordon via Strathfield
- Key Stops: Eastwood, Epping, Rhodes, North Sydney

Using the Opal Card

The Opal card is a smartcard used for fare payments across Sydney's public transport network, including trains. It offers convenience and cost savings, especially for frequent travelers.

- **Purchasing an Opal Card:** You can buy an Opal card at train stations, convenience stores, and online.
- **Topping Up:** Top up your Opal card at stations, convenience stores, or online. Auto top-up options are also available.
- **Using the Opal Card:** Tap on at the start and tap off at the end of your journey. The fare is automatically calculated based on the distance traveled.

Timetables and Schedules

Sydney Trains operates on a regular schedule, with increased frequency during peak hours (morning and evening commutes). Timetables are available at stations and online. For real-time information, use transport apps such as Trip View, Opal Travel, or Google Maps.

Accessibility

Sydney Trains is committed to providing accessible services for all passengers. Most stations are equipped with lifts, ramps, and accessible toilets. Assistance is available for passengers with disabilities, and accessible seating is provided on trains.

Safety and Etiquette

Safety: Sydney Trains places a high priority on passenger safety. Stations are monitored by CCTV, and security personnel are present at major stations.

Etiquette: Allow passengers to alight before boarding, keep noise levels down, and offer your seat to those in need.

B. Buses

Sydney’s bus network is extensive and efficient, covering areas that are not accessible by trains or ferries. Buses are an integral part of the city's public transportation system, providing locals and tourists with convenient options for traveling within the city and its suburbs.

Overview

Sydney Buses, operated by Transport for NSW, offers comprehensive coverage across the city, connecting major landmarks, suburbs, and business districts. The network is designed to complement the train and ferry systems, ensuring that passengers can reach almost any destination within the Sydney metropolitan area.

Key Features

1. Extensive Network:

Sydney's bus network includes over 600 routes, ranging from high-frequency routes within the CBD to suburban and regional services.

Major interchanges such as Circular Quay, Wynyard, Town Hall, and Central Station provide seamless transfers between buses, trains, and ferries.

2. Opal Card System:

The Opal card is a reusable smartcard that makes traveling on buses, trains, ferries, and light rail easy and efficient.

Passengers can top up their Opal cards at numerous locations, including stations, convenience stores, and online.

3. Real-Time Information:

Apps like Trip View, Transport for NSW, and Google Maps provide real-time updates on bus arrivals, routes, and schedules.

Electronic displays at major bus stops and interchanges offer real-time departure information.

4. Accessibility:

Most buses in Sydney are equipped with low floors and ramps, making them accessible for passengers with mobility impairments, prams, and wheelchairs.

Priority seating is available for elderly passengers, pregnant women, and people with disabilities.

Popular Bus Routes

1. CBD and Surrounding Areas:

Route 333: The Bondi Link, running from Circular Quay to Bondi Beach via Bondi Junction. It's an express service with limited stops, making it a quick option for beachgoers.

Route 555: The free CBD shuttle, operating between Circular Quay and Central Station, provides a convenient way to explore the downtown area.

2. Inner West and Eastern Suburbs:

Route 370: Connecting Coo gee Beach to Leichhardt, passing through Newtown and the University of Sydney.

Route 400: An orbital route connecting Bondi Junction, Sydney Airport, and Burwood, providing a crucial link for travelers.

3. Northern Beaches and North Shore:

Route 100: The B-Line, a high-frequency service running from the CBD to the Northern Beaches, including stops at Wynyard, Spit Junction, and Mona Vale.

Route 144: From Manly to Chatswood, serving key locations such as Warringal Mall and St Leonard's.

Practical Tips for Bus Travel

1. Opal Card Usage:

Tap on the card reader when boarding the bus and tap off when disembarking to ensure the correct fare is charged.

Daily, weekly, and Sunday travel caps apply, making it cost-effective for regular travelers.

2. Planning Your Journey:

Use transport apps to plan your journey and receive real-time updates on bus arrivals and service changes.

Check bus stop signs for route numbers, timetables, and maps.

3. During Peak Hours:

Buses can be crowded during peak commuting times (7-9 AM and 4-6 PM). If possible, travel outside these hours for a more comfortable experience.

Priority bus lanes in the CBD and other key areas help buses avoid traffic congestion, ensuring a faster journey.

4. Night Services:

Nightrider buses operate during the early morning hours when trains are not running, providing essential transport links across the city and suburbs.

Routes like N10 (Town Hall to Sutherland) and N30 (Town Hall to Macquarie Park) are part of the Nightrider network.

C. Ferries

Sydney's ferries are not only a practical mode of transportation but also a quintessential part of the city's charm, offering breathtaking views of the harbor and its iconic landmarks. Operated by Sydney Ferries, the network connects various points around the harbor, making it an essential and enjoyable way to get around.

Overview of Sydney Ferries

Sydney Ferries operates from the main terminal at Circular Quay, which is the hub for several routes spanning the harbor. The service runs seven days a week, providing both commuters and tourists with reliable and scenic transport options.

Key Ferry Routes

1. Circular Quay to Manly

Duration: Approximately 30 minutes

Highlights: This is one of the most popular routes, offering stunning views of the Sydney Opera House, Harbor Bridge, and the entrance to Sydney Harbor. Manly Beach is a major attraction at the end of the route.

Frequency: Regular services, especially during peak hours.

2. Circular Quay to Taranga Zoo

Duration: Approximately 12 minutes

Highlights: Quick access to Taranga Zoo, with spectacular views of the harbor and city skyline.

Frequency: Frequent services throughout the day.

3. Circular Quay to Watsons Bay

Duration: Approximately 25 minutes

Highlights: Scenic route passing by Garden Island and Shark Island, ending at the picturesque Watsons Bay, known for its seafood restaurants and coastal walks.

Frequency: Regular services, with increased frequency during weekends.

4. Circular Quay to Parramatta

Duration: Approximately 1 hour and 30 minutes

Highlights: This long route offers a unique perspective of Sydney, traveling up the Parramatta River and showcasing a mix of urban and natural landscapes.

Frequency: Less frequent compared to other routes, advisable to check schedules.

5. Circular Quay to Darling Harbor

Duration: Approximately 15 minutes

Highlights: Connects two major tourist hubs, passing under the Harbor Bridge and by Barangaroo Reserve.

Frequency: Regular services, with more options during peak tourist seasons.

6. Circular Quay to Cockatoo Island

Duration: Approximately 20 minutes

Highlights: Direct access to Cockatoo Island, a UNESCO World Heritage site with a rich history and unique events.

Frequency: Regular services, with additional services during events.

Using the Ferry System

Opal Card

The Opal card is the primary payment method for Sydney Ferries. It's a reusable smartcard that can be topped up online, at stations, or various retail outlets.

Tapping On and Off: Always remember to tap on and off at Opal card readers located at ferry wharves to ensure you're charged the correct fare.

Tickets

Single-ride tickets can also be purchased at terminals for those who do not have an Opal card. However, using an Opal card is generally more cost-effective.

Accessibility

Most ferries and wharves are accessible to passengers with disabilities, including those using wheelchairs or with limited mobility. Accessible facilities include ramps, designated spaces, and accessible restrooms.

Tips for Ferry Travel

1. Plan Ahead: Check the latest schedules on the Transport for NSW website or use apps like Trip View for real-time updates. Consider weather conditions, as services may be affected by severe weather.

2. Best Times for Scenic Views: For the best experience and photography opportunities, plan your trips during sunrise or sunset when the harbor is particularly picturesque.

3. Combine Routes: Create your harbor tour by combining different ferry routes. For instance, start with a trip to Manly, then head back and switch to the Darling Harbor service.

4. Peak Times: Avoid peak commute times if you prefer a less crowded experience. Peak hours are typically 7:00-9:00 AM and 4:30-6:30 PM on weekdays.

5. Special Cruises: Look out for special ferry cruises or evening services that might offer themed tours, such as harbor lights cruises or cultural heritage tours.

D. Light Rail

The light rail system in Sydney is an efficient and scenic way to navigate the city, offering a modern and convenient alternative to buses and trains. The network has expanded in recent years, providing comprehensive coverage of key areas within Sydney.

The Sydney Light Rail network consists of three main lines: L1, L2, and L3. These lines connect the Central Business District (CBD) with various suburbs and key destinations.

L1 Dulwich Hill Line: This line runs from Central Station through the inner western suburbs to Dulwich Hill.

L2 Randwick Line: This line connects Circular Quay with Randwick, passing through key locations such as Surry Hills, Moore Park, and the University of New South Wales.

L3 Kingsford Line: Similar to the L2, but branches off to Kingsford, covering areas like Kensington and UNSW.

Routes and Key Stops

1. L1 Dulwich Hill Line:

- Central Station: Major transport hub connecting trains, buses, and light rail.
- Paddy's Markets: Located near Chinatown, ideal for shopping and dining.
- The Star: Casino and entertainment complex.
- Fish Market: Famous for fresh seafood.
- Glebe: Trendy neighborhood with cafes and boutiques.
- Lilyfield: Residential suburb with parklands.
- Dulwich Hill: Final stop, a quiet residential area.

2. L2 Randwick Line:

- Circular Quay: Hub for ferries, trains, and buses, with views of the Opera House and Harbor Bridge.
- QVB: Historic Queen Victoria Building, a shopping destination.
- Surry Hills: Known for its vibrant dining scene.
- Moore Park: Home to the Sydney Cricket Ground and Entertainment Quarter.
- Randwick: Final stop, near the Randwick Racecourse and Prince of Wales Hospital.

3. L3 Kingsford Line:

- Follows L2 route up to Kensington Junction, then:
- UNSW: University of New South Wales, a major educational institution.
- Kingsford: Final stop, a bustling suburb with diverse dining options.

Using the Light Rail

1. Opal Card: To travel on the light rail, you'll need an Opal card. This smart card can be topped up online, at stations, or in convenience stores. Tap on at the start and tap off at the end of your journey to ensure the correct fare is charged.

2. Accessibility: All light rail vehicles and stations are wheelchair accessible. Stations have ramps or lifts, and designated spaces are available on the trams.

3. Frequency and Timings: Light rail services run frequently, especially during peak hours. Check the Transport for NSW website or transport apps for real-time schedules.

4. Tickets and Fares: Besides the Opal card, single-trip tickets can be purchased at light rail stations. Daily, weekly, and monthly travel passes are also available for unlimited travel on public transport.

Advantages of Light Rail

- Scenic Routes: Enjoy picturesque views of the city and harbor.
- Convenience: Frequent services and multiple connections with other public transport.
- Eco-Friendly: Light rail is a sustainable mode of transport, reducing traffic congestion and pollution.
- Accessibility: Easy access for passengers with disabilities.

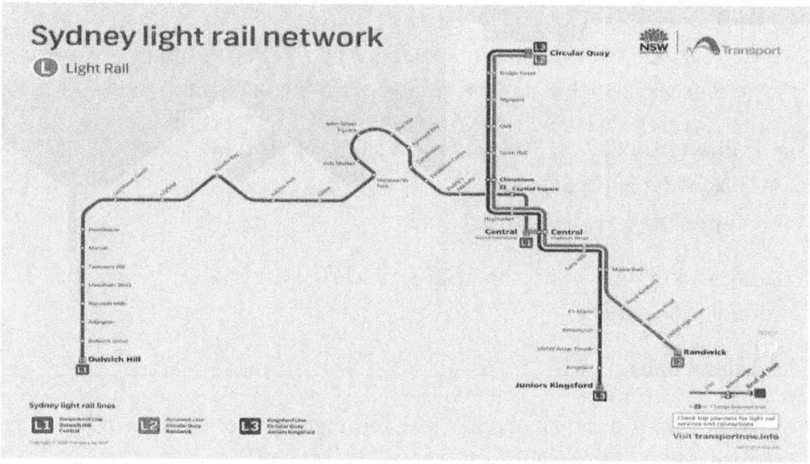

Map of the Sydney Light Rail Network

Taxis and Rideshares

A. Taxis

Taxis are a convenient and reliable mode of transportation in Sydney, especially for those who prefer a direct and private travel option. With a well-regulated taxi industry, you can easily hail a cab on the street, book one via phone, or use a taxi app. Here's everything you need to know about using taxis in Sydney:

Major Taxi Companies

Sydney has several reputable taxi companies that offer a range of services from standard rides to luxury options. Here are some of the key players:

1. 13cabs

13cabs is one of the largest taxi networks in Sydney, known for its extensive fleet and reliable service.

- **Phone:** 13 2227 (13cabs)
- **Website:** 13cabs
- **App:** Available on both iOS and Android platforms

Services: Standard taxis, Silver Service (premium cars), wheelchair-accessible vehicles, and parcel delivery.

2. Silver Service

Silver Service is a premium taxi service offering a more luxurious travel experience with high-end vehicles and professional drivers.

- **Phone:** 13 2227 (13cabs, request Silver Service)
- **Website:** Silver Service
- **App:** Integrated with the 13cabs app

Services: Premium taxis with luxury vehicles, professional drivers, and a focus on comfort and service.

3. Legion Cabs

Legion Cabs is another popular taxi company in Sydney, known for its reliable service and customer satisfaction.

- **Phone:** (02) 131 451
- **Website:** Legion Cabs
- **App:** Available on both iOS and Android platforms

Services: Standard taxis, maxi taxis for groups, and wheelchair-accessible vehicles.

4. Premier Cabs

Premier Cabs offers a range of taxi services across Sydney, focusing on promptness and reliability.

- **Phone:** (02) 1300 773 743
- **Website:** Premier Cabs
- **App:** Available on both iOS and Android platforms

Services: Standard taxis, maxi taxis, and parcel delivery.

Booking a Taxi

1. Hailing a Taxi: You can hail a taxi on the street, especially in busy areas such as the CBD, near tourist attractions, and around shopping districts. Available taxis display a lit "TAXI" sign on the roof.

2. Taxi Ranks: Taxi ranks are designated areas where you can find taxis waiting for passengers. These are typically located at major transport hubs (such as Central Station and Circular Quay), shopping centers, and near popular nightlife spots.

3. Phone Booking: You can book a taxi by calling any of the major taxi companies. This method ensures that a taxi is dispatched to your location, especially useful during peak times or bad weather.

4. Mobile Apps: Most taxi companies have mobile apps that allow you to book a taxi easily. These apps provide real-time tracking, fare estimates, and cashless payment options. The apps for 13cabs, Silver Service, Legion Cabs, and Premier Cabs are available on both iOS and Android platforms.

Fare Structure

1. Metered Fares

Taxis in Sydney charge fares based on a metered system, which includes:

- **Base Fare:** The initial charge when you start your trip.
- **Distance Rate:** A per-kilometer charge.
- **Time Rate:** A charge based on the time spent in traffic, applicable during slow-moving traffic or when the taxi is stationary.

2. Additional Charges

- **Airport Surcharge:** A surcharge applies for trips starting from Sydney Airport.
- **Tolls:** Any tolls incurred during the trip are added to the fare.
- **Late-night surcharge:** An additional charge may apply for trips during late-night hours (usually between 10 PM and 5 AM).
- **Booking Fee:** A small fee for phone or app bookings.

Payment Options

- **Cash:** Most drivers accept cash, but it's advisable to carry small denominations.
- **Credit/Debit Cards:** Major cards like Visa, MasterCard, and American Express are widely accepted. There may be a small processing fee.
- **Mobile Payments:** Services like Apple Pay and Google Pay are accepted by many taxis.

Tips for Using Taxis

Safety: Always ensure the taxi has a valid taxi number plate and driver identification. If in doubt, use recognized taxi companies.

Receipts: Ask for a receipt at the end of your trip. This is useful for expense claims or in case you leave something in the taxi.

Customer Service: If you experience any issues, most taxi companies have customer service departments to handle complaints or lost property inquiries.

B. Rideshares

Ridesharing services have become an integral part of getting around Sydney, offering convenience, flexibility, and often cost-effective transportation options. Several prominent ridesharing companies operate in the city, making it easy for both locals and tourists to find a ride quickly and efficiently. Here's a detailed look at how to use rideshares in Sydney:

Major Rideshare Services

1. Uber

Uber is the most widely used ridesharing service in Sydney. It offers a range of ride options to suit different needs and budgets.

- **UberX:** The standard and most popular option, providing a balance between cost and comfort.
- **Uber Comfort:** For riders looking for newer cars with extra legroom.
- **UberX:** Ideal for groups, offering larger vehicles that can accommodate up to six passengers.
- **Uber Black:** A premium service with high-end vehicles and professional drivers.
- **Uber Assist:** For passengers needing extra assistance, including those with disabilities.

2. Ola

Ola, an Indian rideshare company, operates in Sydney and is known for competitive pricing and frequent discounts.

- **Ola Prime Sedan:** A comfortable option similar to UberX.
- **Ola Prime SUV:** Suitable for larger groups or those needing extra space.
- **Ola Rentals:** Allows booking a car on an hourly basis with the option to make multiple stops.

3. Didi

Didi, a Chinese rideshare giant, is another popular option in Sydney, known for affordable fares and promotions.

- **Didi Express:** The standard service, offering a similar experience to UberX and Ola Prime Sedan.
- **Didi Max:** Larger vehicles for groups or extra luggage.
- **Didi Lux:** A premium service with luxury vehicles.

How to Use Rideshares

1. Download the App: First, download the rideshare app of your choice from the App Store or Google Play Store. Uber, Ola, and Didi each have their own apps.

2. Set Up Your Account: Register for an account by providing your phone number, email address, and payment information. Most apps accept credit cards, debit cards, and PayPal. Some also support cash payments.

3. Booking a Ride:

Enter Your Destination: Open the app and enter your destination in the "Where to?" field.

Choose Your Ride Option: Select the type of ride you want based on your needs and budget. The app will display estimated fares for each option.

Request a Ride: Confirm your pickup location and request a ride. The app will show the estimated time of arrival for your driver.

4. During the Ride

Track Your Driver: The app allows you to track your driver's location in real-time and provides an estimated arrival time.

Driver Details: You'll see your driver's name, photo, vehicle details, and license plate number, ensuring you get into the correct car.

Safety Features: Most apps include safety features like the ability to share your trip status with friends or family and an emergency assistance button.

5. Payment and Rating

Payment: At the end of the ride, payment is automatically processed through the app. If you choose to pay in cash, hand the fare to the driver directly.

Rating: You can rate your driver and provide feedback. High ratings are crucial for drivers to maintain their standing with the rideshare company.

Benefits of Using Rideshares

1. Convenience: Rideshares are available 24/7, making them a reliable option regardless of the time of day or night. The apps allow you to book a ride from virtually anywhere, eliminating the need to hail a taxi on the street.

2. Cost-Effective: Rideshares can be more affordable than traditional taxis, especially with the frequent promotions and discounts offered by companies like Ola and Didi. The apps also provide transparent pricing with fare estimates before you book.

3. Safety: Rideshare apps prioritize passenger safety with features like driver background checks, GPS tracking, and the ability to share your ride details with trusted contacts. In-app support and emergency assistance options further enhance safety.

4. Flexibility: With a variety of vehicle options, rideshares can accommodate different needs, from solo travelers to large groups. Services like Uber Assist cater to passengers requiring special assistance.

5. User-Friendly: The rideshare apps are designed to be intuitive and easy to use. Features like real-time tracking, driver ratings, and cashless payments simplify the entire process, making it accessible even for those unfamiliar with the city.

Tips for Using Rideshares in Sydney

1. Surge Pricing: Be aware of surge pricing, which increases fares during high-demand periods, such as peak commuting hours, major events, or bad weather. If possible, wait for the surge to end or use an alternative transportation method.

2. Airport Rides: When traveling to or from Sydney Airport, rideshare pickups and drop-offs are designated at specific areas. Follow the signs or app instructions to find the correct location.

3. Shared Rides: Some services offer shared ride options, like Uber Pool, which can reduce costs by sharing the ride with other passengers heading in the same direction.

4. Promo Codes: Keep an eye out for promo codes and discounts, especially if you're a new user. These can significantly reduce the cost of your rides.

5. Etiquette: Maintain good etiquette by being ready at the pickup location, respecting the driver and their vehicle, and following any specific guidelines set by the rideshare service.

Biking and Walking

A. Biking

Sydney is an increasingly bike-friendly city, with dedicated bike lanes, shared paths, and scenic routes that make cycling a fantastic way to explore. Whether you're a seasoned cyclist or a casual rider, Sydney offers numerous opportunities to enjoy the city on two wheels.

Benefits of Biking in Sydney

Health and Fitness: Biking is a great way to stay active while sightseeing.

Environmentally Friendly: Reduce your carbon footprint by choosing a green mode of transport.

Cost-Effective: Biking can save you money on transportation costs.

Flexibility: Biking allows you to explore areas that might be difficult to reach by car or public transport.

Popular Biking Routes

1. Sydney Harbor Bridge to Manly Scenic Ride

- **Distance:** Approximately 20 kilometers (12.4 miles)
- **Highlights:** Cross the iconic Sydney Harbor Bridge, explore North Sydney, and enjoy the coastal scenery leading to Manly.

2. Centennial Park

- **Distance:** Various loops, up to 7 kilometers (4.3 miles)
- **Highlights:** Flat terrain, beautiful parklands, and dedicated cycle lanes make this ideal for families and casual riders.

3. Bondi to Coo gee Coastal Ride

- **Distance:** Approximately 6 kilometers (3.7 miles)
- **Highlights:** Stunning coastal views, beaches, and parks. This route combines sections of the famous Bondi to Coo gee Walk with cycle-friendly paths.

4. Bay Run

- **Distance:** 7 kilometers (4.3 miles)
- **Highlights:** A scenic loop around Iron Cove, perfect for a leisurely ride with water views and green spaces.

5. Cooks River Cycleway

- **Distance:** 23 kilometers (14.3 miles)
- **Highlights:** Following the Cooks River from Botany Bay to Strathfield, this route passes parks, wetlands, and residential areas.

Bike Rental Shops

1. Sydney Bike Tours

- **Location:** 30 Harrington Street, The Rocks, Sydney
- **Contact:** +61 2 9241 2277
- **Services:** Offers a variety of bikes for rent, including city bikes, mountain bikes, and e-bikes. Guided tours are also available.

2. Lime

- **Contact:** Through the Lime app (available on iOS and Android)
- **Services:** Dockless electric bike rentals are available throughout the city. Locate and unlock bikes via the app.

3. Bonza Bike Tours

- **Location:** 30 Harrington Street, The Rocks, Sydney
- **Contact:** +61 2 9247 8800
- **Services:** Offers bike rentals, including hybrid bikes, mountain bikes, and electric bikes. Guided tours and custom cycling experiences are also offered.

4. Manly Bike Tours

- **Location:** Shop 6, 54 West Esplanade, Manly, Sydney
- **Contact:** +61 2 8005 7368
- **Services:** Provides bike rentals for exploring Manly and surrounding areas. Options include city bikes, mountain bikes, and electric bikes. Maps and self-guided tour suggestions are available.

5. Sydney Cycleways

- **Location:** Various locations (check website for details)
- **Contact:** Through the Sydney Cycleways website
- **Services:** Offers information on bike paths, safety tips, and bike rental locations. They also provide resources for planning your bike journey around Sydney.

Biking Safety Tips

Wear a Helmet: It's mandatory by law in Australia to wear a helmet while cycling.

Follow Road Rules: Cyclists must adhere to the same road rules as drivers, including obeying traffic signals and signs.

Use Bike Lanes: Where available, use designated bike lanes for safer travel.

Be Visible: Wear bright clothing and use lights and reflectors, especially when riding at dawn, dusk, or night.

Signal Intentions: Use hand signals to indicate turns and stops to other road users.

Stay Alert: Be aware of your surroundings, watch for pedestrians, and avoid distractions.

B. Walking

Walking is one of the best ways to explore Sydney, allowing you to experience the city's vibrant neighborhoods, iconic landmarks, and stunning natural beauty up close. Whether you're wandering through the bustling city center or strolling along the picturesque coastlines, Sydney is a walker's paradise. Here's everything you need to know about walking in Sydney:

Best Walking Areas and Routes

1. Central Business District (CBD)

Sydney's CBD is a compact area that's easy to navigate on foot. Key attractions such as the Sydney Opera House, Circular Quay, The Rocks, and Darling Harbor are all within walking distance. The CBD's grid layout makes it simple to explore, and there are plenty of cafes, shops, and parks to enjoy along the way.

- **Must-See Spots:** Martin Place, Pitt Street Mall, Queen Victoria Building, Hyde Park.

2. The Rocks

The Rocks is Sydney's historic district, filled with cobblestone streets, heritage buildings, and charming markets. Walking through The Rocks offers a glimpse into Sydney's colonial past, with numerous museums, galleries, and historic pubs to explore.

- **Highlights:** The Rocks Discovery Museum, Susannah Place Museum, Dawes Point Park, weekend markets.

3. Circular Quay to Opera House

A walk from Circular Quay to the Sydney Opera House is a quintessential Sydney experience. This short stroll offers stunning views of the Harbor Bridge, ferries coming and going, and the iconic sails of the Opera House.

- **Points of Interest:** Museum of Contemporary Art, First Fleet Park, Opera Bar.

4. Royal Botanic Garden

Adjacent to the Opera House, the Royal Botanic Garden is an expansive and beautifully landscaped park perfect for a leisurely walk. The garden features themed sections, scenic viewpoints, and plenty of spots to relax.

- **Highlights:** Mrs. Macquarie's Chair, the Calyx, the Rose Garden, and panoramic views from the Fleet Steps.

5. Bondi to Coo gee Coastal Walk

This iconic coastal walk stretches for about 6 kilometers along Sydney's eastern coastline, offering breathtaking ocean views, secluded beaches, and dramatic cliffs. It's a must-do for nature lovers and photography enthusiasts.

- **Route:** Bondi Beach, Tamayama Beach, Bronte Beach, Clovelly Beach, Coo gee Beach.
- **Facilities:** Lookout points, restrooms, cafes, and swimming spots along the way.

6. Harbor Bridge Walk

Walking across the Sydney Harbor Bridge provides spectacular views of the harbor, the Opera House, and the city skyline. The pedestrian pathway on the eastern side of the bridge is accessible and safe.

- **Starting Points:** The Rocks (south side) or Milsons Point (north side).
- **Extras:** Visit the Pylon Lookout for panoramic views and historical displays.

7. Darling Harbor

Darling Harbor is a lively waterfront precinct with attractions like the SEA LIFE Sydney Aquarium, WILD LIFE Sydney Zoo, and the Australian National Maritime

Museum. Walking here is especially enjoyable in the evening when the area is beautifully lit.

- **Attractions:** Cockle Bay Wharf, King Street Wharf, Pyrmont Bridge, Tumbling Park.

8. Barangaroo Reserve

This newly developed area offers scenic walks along the western edge of the CBD. The reserve features landscaped gardens, walking paths, and cultural installations, making it a perfect spot for a relaxing stroll.

- **Highlights:** Tumbling Walk, Nawi Cove, Barangaroo Headland Park.

Tips for Walking in Sydney

1. Wear Comfortable Shoes: Sydney's diverse terrains, from paved city streets to coastal pathways, require comfortable footwear. Good walking shoes will enhance your experience and prevent fatigue.

2. Stay Hydrated: Carry a water bottle, especially during warmer months, as Sydney's sun can be intense. There are numerous water refill stations throughout the city and parks.

3. Use Sun Protection: Always apply sunscreen, wear a hat, and use sunglasses to protect yourself from the sun. Sydney's UV index can be high, even on cloudy days.

4. Safety First: Sydney is generally safe for walking, but it's always wise to stay aware of your surroundings, particularly at night. Stick to well-lit areas and avoid secluded spots after dark.

5. Maps and Apps: Use maps and navigation apps like Google Maps or City mapper to plan your walking routes. The NSW Transport app also provides useful information on pedestrian pathways and attractions.

6. Discover Hidden Gems: While walking, be open to exploring side streets and lesser-known areas. Sydney is full of hidden gems, from small cafes and boutiques to street art and pocket parks.

7. Join a Walking Tour: Consider joining a guided walking tour to learn more about Sydney's history, culture, and local stories. Tours are available for various interests, including historical walks, food tours, and art walks.

Walking Tours and Guided Experiences

1. Free Walking Tours: Companies like I'm Free Walking Tours offer complimentary tours of Sydney, covering major attractions and historical sites. These tours operate on a tip-based system and are a great way to get acquainted with the city.

2. The Rocks Walking Tours: Explore the oldest part of Sydney with a guided tour through The Rocks. Learn about the area's convict history, heritage buildings, and intriguing stories from knowledgeable guides.

3. Ghost Tours: For a spooky adventure, join a ghost tour in The Rocks or around Sydney's historic sites. These tours delve into the city's haunted history and paranormal legends.

4. Food and Drink Tours: Experience Sydney's culinary scene with guided food and drink tours. Explore local markets, taste Australian wines, and discover hidden eateries and bars.

5. Aboriginal Cultural Tours: Join an Aboriginal cultural tour to learn about the indigenous heritage of Sydney. Guides share stories, traditional knowledge, and the significance of landmarks from an Aboriginal perspective.

Car Rentals and Driving Tips

A. Car Rentals

Renting a car in Sydney can offer you the freedom and flexibility to explore the city and its surroundings at your own pace. Whether you're planning day trips to nearby attractions like the Blue Mountains or Hunter Valley, or simply want the convenience of your vehicle for city travel, here's everything you need to know about car rentals in Sydney.

Major Car Rental Companies

1. Avis

- **Website:** www.avis.com.au
- **Phone:** +61 2 9353 9000

- **Locations:** Multiple locations including Sydney Airport, Central Business District (CBD), and key suburbs.
- **Features:** Wide range of vehicles from economy to luxury, GPS rental, child seats, and roadside assistance.

2. Hertz

- **Website**: www.hertz.com.au
- **Phone:** +61 2 8303 2090
- **Locations:** Available at Sydney Airport, CBD, and several suburban locations.
- **Features:** Comprehensive vehicle selection, flexible rental options, and additional services like Never Lost® GPS and Hertz Gold Plus Rewards.

3. Budget

- **Website:** www.budget.com.au
- **Phone:** +61 2 9353 9000
- **Locations:** Offices at Sydney Airport, downtown Sydney, and various suburban branches.
- **Features:** Competitive rates, diverse fleet including SUVs and luxury cars, and optional extras like GPS and child safety seats.

4. Europcar

- **Website:** www.europcar.com.au
- **Phone:** +61 2 8303 2290
- **Locations:** Sydney Airport, city center, and major suburban areas.
- **Features:** Wide range of vehicles, including eco-friendly options, flexible rental terms, and additional driver options.

5. Thrifty

- **Website:** www.thrifty.com.au
- **Phone:** +61 2 8303 2400
- **Locations:** Available at Sydney Airport, CBD, and other strategic locations around Sydney.
- **Features:** Affordable rates, extensive fleet including commercial vehicles, and additional services such as GPS and baby seats.

6. Enterprise

- **Website:** www.enterprise.com.au
- **Phone:** +61 2 8303 2700
- **Locations:** Sydney Airport, downtown, and various suburbs.

Booking and Requirements

1. Booking a Rental Car

Online Reservations: Most car rental companies offer online booking through their websites. This is often the most convenient and ensures you get the vehicle type you prefer.

Phone Reservations: You can also call the rental company to make a reservation or inquire about availability and rates.

In-Person Reservations: If you prefer, you can visit a rental office directly, though availability may be limited without prior booking.

2. Requirements

Driver's License: A valid driver's license is required. International visitors should have their home country license and, in some cases, an International Driving Permit (IDP).

Age Requirements: Most companies require drivers to be at least 21 years old, though some have higher age requirements for certain vehicle categories. Drivers under 25 may incur a young driver surcharge.

Credit Card: A credit card in the driver's name is typically required for the security deposit. Debit cards are accepted by some companies but often come with additional conditions.

Insurance: Basic insurance is usually included, but additional coverage options are available and recommended for added peace of mind.

Additional Considerations

1. Insurance Options

Collision Damage Waiver (CDW): Reduces the renter's liability in case of an accident.

Theft Protection: Covers loss or damage due to theft.

Personal Accident Insurance (PAI): Provides medical coverage for the driver and passengers in case of an accident.

2. Additional Drivers

Most companies allow additional drivers for an extra fee. The additional driver must meet the same age and license requirements as the primary driver.

3. Optional Extras

GPS Navigation: Handy for navigating Sydney and its surroundings.

Child Seats: Legally required for children under seven years old.

Wi-Fi Hotspots: Some companies offer portable Wi-Fi devices for rent.

4. Fuel Policy

Full-to-Full: The vehicle should be returned with a full tank of fuel, as received.

Pre-Purchase Fuel: Pay for a full tank upfront and return the car with any fuel level.

5. Toll Roads

Sydney has several toll roads. Most rental cars are equipped with an electronic tag (e-TAG) for automatic toll payment. Charges are typically added to your rental bill.

B. Driving Tips

Driving in Sydney can provide a high level of flexibility and convenience, allowing you to explore the city and its surroundings at your own pace. However, navigating a busy metropolis like Sydney comes with its own set of challenges. Here are some detailed driving tips to ensure a smooth and enjoyable experience:

1. Road Rules and Regulations

Drive on the Left: In Australia, vehicles drive on the left side of the road. This can be a significant adjustment for visitors from countries where driving is on the right.

Speed Limits: Speed limits are strictly enforced in Sydney. The general limits are:

- 50 km/h in urban areas.
- 40 km/h in school zones during specified hours.
- 60-70 km/h on major roads.
- 100-110 km/h on highways and motorways.
- Always look for and adhere to posted speed limit signs.

Seat Belts: Seat belts are mandatory for all occupants of the vehicle. Ensure everyone is buckled up before driving.

Mobile Phones: Using a handheld mobile phone while driving is illegal. Use a hands-free system if you need to make calls.

2. Navigating the City

GPS and Maps: Use a reliable GPS navigation system or a smartphone app like Google Maps or Waze for directions. These tools can help you avoid traffic congestion and find the quickest routes.

Traffic Conditions: Sydney experiences heavy traffic, especially during peak hours (7:00-9:30 AM and 4:00-6:30 PM). Plan your trips to avoid these times if possible.

Roundabouts: Roundabouts are common in Sydney. Always give way to vehicles already in the roundabout and indicate your exit.

3. Tolls and Electronic Tolling

Toll Roads: Several major roads and tunnels in Sydney have tolls, including the Sydney Harbor Bridge, Sydney Harbor Tunnel, and various motorways. Tolls are automatically collected electronically.

E-TAG: An electronic tag (e-TAG) is required for toll payments. If you're renting a car, check if it comes with an e-TAG. Otherwise, you can purchase a temporary pass online (Link is the main provider).

Payment Options: If you use a toll road without an e-TAG, you have up to three days to pay the toll online or by phone. Failure to do so can result in hefty fines.

4. Parking

Street Parking: Street parking in Sydney can be challenging, especially in the CBD. Always check the parking signs for restrictions, time limits, and fees.

Parking Meters: Many areas have parking meters that accept coins, credit cards, and sometimes mobile payment apps.

Public Car Parks: Consider using public car parks for longer stays. They are usually more secure and offer various payment options.

Residential Areas: Be mindful of parking restrictions in residential areas to avoid fines. Some areas require a residential parking permit.

5. Fuel Stations and Costs

Fuel Types: Petrol stations offer various types of fuel, including unleaded, premium unleaded, and diesel. Ensure you use the correct type for your vehicle.

Payment: Most fuel stations accept credit cards, but it's a good idea to carry some cash just in case.

Price Variations: Fuel prices can vary significantly between different areas. Apps like Fuel Check can help you find the cheapest fuel prices near you.

6. Safety Tips

Keep Left: Always stay in the left lane unless overtaking. On multi-lane roads, use the right lane for passing only.

Pedestrian Crossings: Be vigilant at pedestrian crossings. Pedestrians have the right of way at designated crossings and intersections.

Animal Crossings: In rural areas and national parks, watch out for wildlife, especially at dawn and dusk.

Breakdowns: In case of a breakdown, pull over safely and use your hazard lights. Contact your rental company or a roadside assistance service.

7. Car Rentals

Requirements: You need a valid driver's license (an international driving permit is recommended if your license is not in English) and a credit card for the deposit.

Insurance: Ensure you have comprehensive insurance coverage. Check what is included in your rental agreement and consider additional coverage for peace of mind.

Rental Companies: Major car rental companies like Avis, Hertz, Budget, and Europcar operate in Sydney. Booking in advance, especially during peak seasons, is advisable.

8. Scenic Drives and Day Trips

Popular Routes: Sydney offers many scenic drives, such as the Grand Pacific Drive to Wollongong and the Blue Mountains via the Great Western Highway.

Day Trips: Renting a car makes it easy to explore surrounding regions like the Hunter Valley, the South Coast, and the Central Coast.

Tips on Using Sydney's Public Transportation System

Sydney's public transportation system is extensive and efficient, comprising trains, buses, ferries, and light rail services. Here's a comprehensive guide to navigating it:

1. Understanding the Opal Card System

Opal Card Overview: The Opal card is a smart card used to pay for travel on Sydney's public transport network. It's essential for seamless travel across trains, buses, ferries, and light rail.

How to Get an Opal Card: You can purchase an Opal card at convenience stores, newsagents, or Opal top-up machines located in train stations. There are also options for online ordering and mobile app management.

Topping Up: The card can be topped up at Opal top-up machines, participating retailers, or via the Opal Travel app. Minimum top-ups are usually around AUD 10.

Daily and Weekly Caps: The Opal card system has daily and weekly travel caps to ensure cost-effectiveness. For instance, the daily cap for adults is AUD 16.20, and the weekly cap is AUD 120.70. This means you won't spend more than these amounts within the specified periods.

2. Train Travel

Ticketing: Once you have your Opal card, simply tap on and off at Opal readers located at train stations. The fare is automatically calculated based on the distance traveled and time of day.

Peak and Off-Peak Hours: Fares vary depending on peak (weekdays, 7-9 AM, and 4-6 PM) and off-peak hours. Traveling during off-peak times is cheaper and can be less crowded.

Important Stations: Key stations include Central Station (a major hub), Circular Quay (near iconic landmarks), and Bondi Junction (gateway to Bondi Beach).

3. Bus Travel

Using Opal Card: Tap your Opal card on the reader when boarding and alighting from the bus. Fares are calculated based on the number of zones traveled.

Routes and Schedules: Buses cover extensive routes, with frequent services throughout the day. Bus stops are well-marked, and schedules are available at bus stops or via the Transport for NSW website and app.

Bus Types: Sydney offers various bus services, including standard buses, express services, and night buses. Check the route number and destination to ensure you're boarding the correct bus.

4. Ferry Travel

Opal Card Use: Tap your Opal card on the reader at the ferry wharf before boarding and when disembarking. Ferries offer scenic views of Sydney Harbor and access to popular spots like Manly and Taranga Zoo.

Popular Routes: The Circular Quay to Manly route is a popular choice for tourists. There are also ferries to Darling Harbor and other waterfront destinations.

Fare Pricing: Ferry fares are based on the distance traveled and are generally more expensive than trains or buses. However, the experience and views often justify the cost.

5. Light Rail

Ticketing: Use your Opal card to tap on and off at light rail stations. The light rail connects key areas such as Central Station to the Inner West and the CBD to the southeastern suburbs.

Routes and Stations: Major stops include Central Station, Haymarket, and the Star Casino. The light rail system is a convenient option for traveling within the city center.

Fare Structure: Light rail fares are based on the distance traveled and time of day, similar to trains and buses.

6. Additional Tips

Travel Apps: Use the Transport for NSW app or Google Maps for real-time schedules, route planning, and service updates. The app also provides information on Opal card balances and top-up options.

Concessions: If you're eligible for concessions (e.g., seniors, students), ensure your Opal card is registered with the appropriate discount. Concession fares are significantly cheaper.

Lost Property: For lost items, contact the Transport for NSW Lost Property Office. They maintain a database of lost items across the public transport network.

Safety and Etiquette: Sydney's public transport is generally safe, but remain vigilant of your belongings. Additionally, observe local etiquette, such as giving up seats for the elderly or disabled and maintaining a respectful noise level.

By familiarizing yourself with the Opal card system and the various modes of public transport, you'll be able to navigate Sydney efficiently and cost-effectively, making your travel experience more enjoyable.

Chapter 6: Hidden Gems and Off-the-Beaten-Path

Lesser-known Attractions and Unique Experiences in Sydney

1. Wendy's Secret Garden

Nestled near Lavender Bay on Sydney's lower north shore, Wendy's Secret Garden is a tranquil, hidden paradise created by Wendy Whiteley, wife of renowned artist Brett Whiteley. This lush, privately maintained public garden is filled with native and exotic plants, winding pathways, and whimsical sculptures, all while offering stunning views of Sydney Harbour. The garden is a peaceful retreat, perfect for a quiet stroll, a picnic, or simply soaking in the natural beauty of this lovingly crafted oasis. It's an unmarked gem that feels like a personal escape from the city's hustle and bustle.

Location: Lavender Bay, Milsons Point

Tips: Best visited during early mornings or late afternoons for peaceful solitude. Bring a picnic to enjoy on the lawns.

2. Paddington Reservoir Gardens

A hidden gem in the trendy suburb of Paddington, this former water reservoir has been transformed into a beautiful sunken garden and urban park. Combining elements of industrial architecture with landscaped greenery, Paddington Reservoir Gardens offers a unique mix of heritage ruins, columns, and arches, reminiscent of ancient Roman baths.

The site is an urban oasis, with plenty of seating, quiet corners, and a stunning design that feels like a secret escape amidst the city. It's an excellent spot for photography, relaxation, or a quiet read.

Location: 251-255 Oxford Street, Paddington

Tips: Visit on weekdays for fewer crowds. Ideal for architecture enthusiasts and photographers.

3. McMahons Point and Blues Point Reserve

Offering some of the best panoramic views of Sydney Harbour, McMahons Point, and Blues Point Reserve are lesser-known locations where you can enjoy a postcard-perfect view of the Harbour Bridge and Opera House without the crowds. Tucked away in a quiet residential area, these points are peaceful places for a leisurely walk, picnic, or watching the sunset over the water. It's one of the best-kept secrets for an alternative viewpoint that's just as impressive as the more tourist-heavy spots.

Location: McMahons Point, North Sydney

Tips: Arrive at sunset for spectacular views. Pack a picnic and enjoy a serene meal with a view.

4. The Coal Loader Centre for Sustainability

This unique site, once a coal-loading platform, has been transformed into a sustainability hub and urban green space. Located in Waverton, the Coal Loader Centre for Sustainability offers visitors interactive exhibits on sustainable living, green roofs, community gardens, and art installations. The highlight is the underground tunnel system, where coal was once transported. Visitors can walk through these tunnels and learn about the site's industrial history. The Centre also hosts workshops, markets, and events focused on environmental awareness and community engagement.

Location: 2 Balls Head Drive, Waverton

Tips: Free entry. Visit the café on-site for a coffee break while enjoying the peaceful green surroundings.

5. Cockatoo Island

A UNESCO World Heritage site, Cockatoo Island is often overlooked despite being a treasure trove of history and industrial heritage. Located in the middle of Sydney Harbour, the island served as a convict prison, shipyard, and industrial site, and now offers fascinating tours of its tunnels, prison cells, and dry docks. The island also hosts art exhibitions, concerts, and even camping experiences where you can spend the night under the stars with a view of Sydney's skyline.

It's a perfect destination for history buffs and those looking for an adventurous day trip away from the crowds.

Location: Sydney Harbour (accessible by ferry)

Tips: Pack water and snacks if you're planning to spend the day. Book in advance for camping or glamping experiences.

6. Chinamans Beach

Hidden just around the corner from the much busier Balmoral Beach, Chinamans Beach is a serene and secluded spot in Mosman. With its crystal-clear waters, white sand, and calm waves, it's perfect for a peaceful swim, a relaxed sunbathing session, or a quiet family outing. Unlike Sydney's famous beaches, Chinamans Beach offers a quieter, more laid-back atmosphere, ideal for those looking to escape the crowds. Its hidden location makes it one of Sydney's best-kept beach secrets.

Location: Mosman, near Balmoral Beach

Tips: No shops or cafes nearby, so bring your food and drinks. Ideal for a quiet, relaxing beach day.

7. The Calyx at the Royal Botanic Garden

Located within Sydney's Royal Botanic Garden, The Calyx is an extraordinary living gallery that features ever-changing exhibitions based on plants and nature. The centerpiece is an enormous vertical garden, one of the largest in the Southern Hemisphere, showcasing thousands of plants in intricate designs. The space hosts art installations, science exhibits, and workshops. Despite its stunning beauty and central location, The Calyx remains relatively undiscovered by tourists, making it a peaceful and inspiring place to explore.

Location: Mrs Macquaries Road, Royal Botanic Garden, Sydney

Tips: Entry is free, though donations are encouraged. Perfect for nature lovers and those interested in botanical art.

8. Maccallum Pool

Located on the western side of Cremorne Point, Maccallum Pool is a unique and picturesque harbour pool with spectacular views of Sydney's skyline and Harbour Bridge. Originally built as a private swimming pool for the residents, it has since been turned into a public facility. With its charming wooden deck and prime location, it's an idyllic spot for a refreshing swim, far from the tourist crowds. The surrounding walking paths also offer scenic views of the harbor.

Location: Cremorne Point, Milson Road

Tips: Visit early to avoid peak times. Bring a towel and some snacks to enjoy a relaxing afternoon by the pool.

9. Secret Gardens of Darling Harbour

Despite being in one of the busiest areas of the city, Darling Harbour's Secret Gardens are a peaceful hideaway unknown to many. These lush, landscaped gardens are tucked away behind modern buildings, providing a sanctuary with beautiful water features, native plants, and winding pathways. It's the perfect place to take a break from the city's buzz, offering a tranquil spot for a walk or a quiet moment of reflection amid the greenery.

Location: Darling Harbour, Sydney

Tips: Ideal for a quiet break while exploring the busy Darling Harbour area. Great for a moment of serenity after visiting nearby attractions.

10. Barangaroo Reserve

Barangaroo Reserve is an urban oasis and a testament to modern landscaping and cultural heritage restoration. Located along the western edge of Sydney Harbour, this hidden gem offers a series of bushwalks and waterfront paths amidst native flora. It's also a place of deep indigenous significance, with interpretive signs explaining the cultural history of the land. The reserve offers breathtaking views of the Harbour Bridge and is a peaceful alternative to the more tourist-heavy areas. It's perfect for nature lovers and those looking to experience a piece of Sydney's indigenous heritage.

Location: Barangaroo, Sydney

Tips: Ideal for walking or cycling. There's a café on-site, so you can enjoy a coffee with a view. Bring a camera to capture the beautiful landscape.

Chapter 7: Where to Stay in Sydney

Guide to Sydney Neighborhoods and Districts

Sydney is a vibrant tapestry of neighborhoods, each offering a unique flavor of the city. Whether you crave iconic landmarks, artsy enclaves, or beachside bliss, Sydney has a place for you. Here's a glimpse into neighborhoods and districts that will leave you wanting to explore more:

The Rocks:

The Rocks, Sydney's oldest neighborhood, is a captivating blend of history, charm, and harborside vibrancy. Stepping into The Rocks is like stepping back in time, with its cobblestone streets lined with charming sandstone buildings, each whispering tales of the city's colonial past. Here's a detailed look at what awaits you in this captivating district:

Characters:

The Storytellers: Engaging tour guides, often dressed in period attire, bring the history of The Rocks to life. They share tales of convicts, sailors, and the early struggles and triumphs of Sydney.

The Artisans: The Rocks boasts a thriving community of artists, potters, jewelers, and leatherworkers. Watch them create unique pieces in their workshops and browse through their galleries to find a one-of-a-kind souvenir.

The Pub Dwellers: Friendly locals and visitors mingle in the numerous historic pubs. Soak up the atmosphere and hear yarns spun by seasoned pub patrons.

The Buskers: Street performers add a touch of liveliness to the area. From talented musicians to captivating magicians, they entertain visitors as they stroll through the streets.

Top Attractions:

The Rocks Historic Precinct: Explore the charming laneways and admire the beautifully restored sandstone buildings. Take a self-guided walking tour or join a guided tour to delve deeper into the neighborhood's rich history.

The Argyle Street Markets: Held every weekend, these vibrant markets are a treasure trove of Australian arts, crafts, souvenirs, and local produce.

The Rocks Discovery Museum: Learn about the fascinating stories of The Rocks through interactive exhibits, archaeological finds, and multimedia presentations.

Cadman's Cottage: Step back in time and explore the oldest surviving house in Sydney, built in 1816. Experience the lifestyle of early Sydney residents.

Sydney Harbor Bridge: Climb the iconic Sydney Harbor Bridge for breathtaking panoramic views of the city and harbor.

Hidden Gems:

The Rocks Millenium Pylon Lookout: Ascend the stairs of this unassuming pylon for stunning views of the Sydney Opera House and the harbor.

Campbell Street: Wander down this quiet street and discover hidden cafes with charming courtyards, perfect for a relaxing break.

Susannah Place Museum: This meticulously restored 1845 terrace house offers a glimpse into the domestic life of a wealthy merchant family in the 19th century.

Kendall Lane: This hidden laneway boasts a delightful collection of street art, adding a touch of urban cool to the historic neighborhood.

The Rocks Sea Road: Hop on a ferry from Circular Quay and enjoy a scenic journey around the harbor, offering a different perspective of The Rocks and the Sydney Opera House.

Experiences:

Ghost Tours: Embark on a spooky evening tour and learn about the resident ghouls and mysteries that haunt The Rocks' historic buildings.

The Rocks Pub Tour: Explore the iconic pubs of The Rocks, sample local beers, and delve into their fascinating histories.

Paddleboarding Tour: Rent a stand-up paddleboard and explore the Sydney Harbor from a unique perspective, paddling under the Sydney Harbor Bridge.

Dining with a View: Indulge in a delicious meal at one of the many waterfront restaurants, soaking up the stunning views of the harbor and the city skyline.

Sunset Cruise: Set sail on a romantic sunset cruise and watch the Sydney Harbor Bridge transform into a stunning spectacle of lights.

Beyond the Tourist Trail:

Volunteer at The Rocks: Immerse yourself in the history and contribute to the preservation of this iconic neighborhood by volunteering at a local historical society.

Take a Painting Class: Unleash your inner artist and learn to capture the charm of The Rocks with a painting class led by a local artist.

Join a Local Book Club: Mingle with Sydneysiders and discuss your favorite reads at a book club held in one of The Rocks' charming pubs.

Attend a Local Festival: Experience the vibrant culture of The Rocks by attending one of the many festivals held throughout the year, such as the Rocks Aroma Festival or the Rocks Christmas Fair.

The Rocks offers something for everyone. Whether you're a history buff, an art enthusiast, a foodie, or simply seeking a charming and vibrant atmosphere, you'll find yourself captivated by this unique corner of Sydney.

Darling Harbor:

Darling Harbor is a dazzling district on Sydney's glittering waterfront, pulsating with family fun, entertainment, and iconic landmarks. It's a one-stop shop for tourists seeking a vibrant mix of attractions, from world-class museums to harbor cruises and delectable dining.

Characters:

Families: Darling Harbor caters beautifully to families with a plethora of child-friendly attractions. SEA LIFE Sydney Aquarium and WILD LIFE Sydney Zoo offer immersive experiences for all ages. Darling Harbor also boasts playgrounds, face painting, and kid-friendly restaurants with dedicated menus.

Culture vultures: Catch a captivating performance at the IMAX Theatre or delve into maritime history at the Australian National Maritime Museum. The precinct also houses the Sydney Lyric Theatre, renowned for its musicals and theatrical productions.

Thrill-seekers: Get your adrenaline pumping with a jet boat ride or a climb to the top of the Sydney Harbor Bridge. For a unique perspective, take a scenic helicopter tour over the harbor and witness the city skyline from above.

Top Attractions:

SEA LIFE Sydney Aquarium: Embark on an underwater adventure encountering an incredible variety of marine life from the vibrant coral reefs to the majestic sharks of the Pacific Ocean.

WILD LIFE Sydney Zoo: Explore diverse Australian ecosystems and get up close with iconic animals like koalas, kangaroos, and even Tasmanian devils.

Sydney Opera House: This architectural marvel is a must-see. Take a guided tour to learn about its history and design, or catch a world-class performance in one of its theaters. (Technically located in The Rocks, but with a strong Darling Harbor presence)

Australian National Maritime Museum: Immerse yourself in Australia's rich maritime history through interactive exhibits and fascinating shipwrecks.

IMAX Theatre: Experience movies on a larger-than-life scale with state-of-the-art technology and immersive sound systems.

Darling Harbor Ferris Wheel: Soar above the harbor on the giant Ferris wheel for breathtaking panoramic views of the city and coastline.

Madame Tussauds Sydney: Meet your favorite celebrities and historical figures in wax form, perfect for a fun and interactive experience.

Hidden Gems:

Cockle Bay Wharf: Venture beyond the main strip to discover Cockle Bay Wharf, a hidden gem offering a more relaxed atmosphere with harborside restaurants and bars. Enjoy live music while savoring fresh seafood overlooking the water.

Chinese Garden of Friendship: Step into a tranquil oasis and experience the beauty of traditional Chinese gardens with serene ponds, intricate pavilions, and manicured gardens.

Pyrmont Bridge Walkway: Enjoy scenic harbor views from a different perspective on the Pyrmont Bridge Walkway. This pedestrian and bicycle path offers a unique way to explore the harbor foreshore.

Star Casino: Try your luck at the tables or enjoy a variety of restaurants and bars at Sydney's premier casino complex.

Experiences:

Harbor Cruise: Set sail on a scenic cruise around Sydney Harbor and witness iconic landmarks like the Sydney Opera House and Harbor Bridge from a unique perspective. Choose from a variety of cruises, including dinner cruises, sunset cruises, and tall ship experiences.

Tall Ship Lunch: Sail aboard a historic tall ship while enjoying a delicious lunch buffet and soaking up the harbor views.

Kayaking Adventure: Explore the harbor from a different angle with a kayaking adventure. Paddle alongside iconic landmarks and enjoy a unique perspective of the city skyline.

Whale Watching Tour: Embark on a thrilling whale-watching tour during migration season (May to November) and witness these magnificent creatures in their natural habitat.

Sydney Festival (January): Immerse yourself in Sydney's vibrant arts scene during the Sydney Festival, a month-long celebration of theater, dance, music, and visual arts. (Darling Harbor often hosts festival events)

Beyond the Tourist Trail:

WILD LIFE Sydney Zoo's Taranga After Dark: Experience the zoo after dark on a special tour and encounter nocturnal animals in their active state.

SEA LIFE Sydney Aquarium's Behind the Scenes Tour: Go beyond the exhibits and delve into the inner workings of the aquarium, learning about animal care and conservation efforts.

Barangaroo Reserve: Escape the hustle and bustle of Darling Harbor with a stroll through Barangaroo Reserve, a tranquil waterfront park with stunning city and harbor views.

Dining Delights:

Darling Harbor offers a diverse range of dining options to cater to all tastes and budgets. From casual cafes and bars to fine dining restaurants with waterfront views, you'll be spoilt for choice.

Accessibility:

Darling Harbor is well-connected by public transport with light rail, train, ferry, and bus services readily available.

Whether you're seeking exhilarating adventures, fascinating wildlife encounters, or a relaxing waterfront stroll, Darling Harbor has something for everyone.

Bondi Beach:

Bondi Beach – the name itself conjures images of golden sands, glistening surfers, and a laid-back beach culture. But Bondi offers more than just a postcard-perfect beach. It's a vibrant neighborhood pulsating with energy, cafes abuzz with conversation, and shops catering to every whim.

Characters:

Surfers: Bondi is a surfer's paradise. Watch experienced surfers carve through the waves at Bondi Beach or South Bondi, or take a lesson and catch your first wave.

Beach Bums: Sunbathers soak up the rays on the expansive beach, families build sandcastles, and joggers pound the pavement along the iconic Bondi to Coo gee Coastal Walk.

Foodies: From trendy cafes serving brunch with a view to casual beachside kiosks offering fish and chips, Bondi caters to all palates.

Celebrities & Trendsetters: Bondi attracts its fair share of celebrities and tastemakers. You might spot them grabbing a coffee, strolling along the beach, or shopping in the boutiques.

Top Attractions:

Bondi Beach: The crown jewel, of course, is the iconic Bondi Beach itself. Swim in the crystal-clear water, perfect your tan, or try your hand at surfing.

Bondi Icebergs: Take a dip in the iconic Bondi Icebergs, an ocean pool carved into the rocks, offering stunning views and a refreshing escape from the waves.

Bondi to Coo gee Coastal Walk: Lace up your walking shoes and embark on this scenic six-kilometer coastal walk, offering breathtaking ocean views, hidden coves, and dramatic cliffs.

Campbell Cove: Tucked away at the southern end of Bondi Beach, Campbell Cove is a secluded haven with a rock pool and a historic boathouse.

Hidden Gems:

Sculptures by the Sea: Held annually between Bondi and Tamayama beaches, this free open-air exhibition showcases contemporary sculptures along the picturesque coastline.

Hendriks Cafe: Tucked away in a laneway, this hole-in-the-wall cafe is a local favorite with delicious coffee and a relaxed atmosphere.

Bondi Farmers Market: Every Saturday, the Bondi Beach Public School comes alive with a vibrant farmers market offering fresh produce, artisan foods, and locally-made crafts.

Gondwana Gallery: This Aboriginal art gallery showcases authentic artworks from Indigenous artists across Australia.

Experiences:

Learn to Surf: Sign up for a surf lesson and experience the thrill of catching a wave at Bondi. Several surf schools offer lessons for all skill levels.

Stand-Up Paddleboarding: Explore the coastline from a different perspective by renting a stand-up paddleboard. Paddle past the surfers and enjoy the serenity of the ocean.

Helicopter Tour: Get a bird's-eye view of Bondi Beach and Sydney's iconic landmarks with a scenic helicopter tour.

Sunset Drinks: As the sun dips below the horizon, grab a drink at a rooftop bar or beachfront restaurant and soak up the magical atmosphere.

Beyond the Beach:

Bondi Beach Markets: Browse through a vibrant mix of stalls selling clothes, jewelry, souvenirs, and local crafts at the Bondi Beach Markets, held every Sunday.

Bondi Pavilion: This historic building houses an art gallery, theatre, and cinema, offering a variety of cultural experiences.

Street Art: Explore the backstreets and laneways around Bondi Beach to discover hidden gems of street art.

Tips:

- Bondi Beach can get crowded, especially during peak season. Arrive early to secure a spot on the beach.
- Public transportation is readily available, with buses running frequently and Bondi Junction train station offering connections to the city center.
- Parking can be challenging, so consider using public transportation or walking if possible.
- Don't forget to pack sunscreen, a hat, and a swimsuit!

Bondi Beach is more than just a beach – it's a vibrant community with something to offer everyone. Whether you're a seasoned surfer, a sun-worshiper, or a curious explorer, Bondi Beach will leave you with memories that will last a lifetime.

Surry Hills and Darlinghurst:

Surry Hills and Darlinghurst, nestled close together in Sydney's inner east, pulsate with a unique energy. Once known for their bohemian flair and alternative lifestyles, these neighborhoods have evolved into vibrant hubs for art, food, and cutting-edge culture.

Characters:

Creative Trailblazers: Surry Hills and Darlinghurst are magnets for artists, musicians, designers, and entrepreneurs. Expect to encounter them sipping lattes in trendy cafes, browsing through independent galleries, or showcasing their talents at pop-up events.

Fashionistas: A curated sense of style permeates the streets. Spot fashion-forward individuals sporting vintage finds, designer labels, or anything in between.

Foodies with a Twist: This is not your average culinary scene. Expect innovative chefs experimenting with global flavors, repurposed industrial spaces housing trendy restaurants, and hidden laneways brimming with unique eateries.

Night Owls: The party doesn't stop after dark. Darlinghurst boasts a lively nightlife scene with LGBTQ+ bars, underground clubs with renowned DJs, and hidden speakeasies. Surry Hills offers a more relaxed vibe with rooftop bars, craft beer pubs, and intimate cocktail lounges.

Top Attractions:

Australian Centre for the Moving Image (ACMI): Delve into the world of film, television, digital culture, and interactive media at this innovative museum.

Art Galleries Galore: Surry Hills and Darlinghurst boast a dense concentration of independent art galleries showcasing everything from established artists to emerging talents. Explore galleries like Anna Schwartz Gallery, GAGPROJECT, and Roslyn Oxley9.

Oxford Street Fashion: Indulge in retail therapy on Oxford Street, Paddington's continuation that bleeds into Darlinghurst. Find a mix of high-end designer stores, vintage clothing shops, and independent boutiques.

Rooftop Revelry: Experience Sydney's skyline from a different perspective. Enjoy a drink and breathtaking views at The Rooftop (hotel), Irene Rooftop, or The Campbell.

Hidden Gems:

Surry Hills laneways: Venture beyond the main streets and discover a hidden world of laneways packed with trendy cafes, quirky bars, and unique street art. Explore Acre Lane, Bourke Street Bakery laneway, and Crown Lane.

Spice Alley: A hidden gem in Chippendale, bordering Darlinghurst, Spice Alley is a haven for Asian street food. Sample authentic flavors from Thailand, Vietnam, Korea, and more.

The Beresford: This heritage-listed building houses a hidden courtyard with a charming cafe and independent design stores.

Golden Age Cinema & Bar: Catch a classic film or cult favorite at this restored cinema, followed by a drink at the on-site bar.

Unforgettable Experiences:

Coffee Connoisseur Tour: Embark on a guided walking tour exploring Surry Hills and Darlinghurst's specialty coffee scene, sampling brews at renowned cafes.

Street Art Scavenger Hunt: Download a map and embark on a self-guided hunt for the vibrant street art that adorns the walls of these neighborhoods.

Vintage Shopping Spree: Hit the racks at vintage clothing stores like Matilda, Archive, and So French So Chic, and unearth unique finds to add to your wardrobe.

Live Music Night: Immerse yourself in Sydney's music scene at live music venues like The Lansdowne, The Metro, or The Oxford Art Factory.

Foodie Delights: Indulge in a progressive dinner, starting with tapas in a hidden laneway bar, followed by a degustation menu at a renowned Surry Hills restaurant, and ending with drinks at a rooftop bar.

Bonus Tip: Be sure to check out the weekly Paddington Markets, overflowing with handmade crafts, vintage treasures, and delicious food from around the world.

Surry Hills and Darlinghurst offer a kaleidoscope of experiences for the curious traveler. So, come prepared to explore hidden gems, encounter creative minds, and savor the unique energy that defines this captivating corner of Sydney.

The Inner West (Newtown, Glebe, Leichhardt):

The Inner West, encompassing Newtown, Glebe, and Leichhardt, pulsates with a unique rhythm that's distinctly Sydney. It's a vibrant tapestry woven with alternative lifestyles, multicultural influences, and a deep appreciation for art, food, and community. Here's your guide to diving into this dynamic district:

Characters:

Newtown: Edgy, artistic, and youthful. Think students, musicians, activists, and a smattering of families, all united by a love for individuality.

Glebe: A village vibe with a strong Greek and Italian influence. Expect families, professionals, and a sprinkle of students, all with a relaxed and easy-going attitude.

Leichhardt: Italian heartland, buzzing with families and a strong sense of community. It's a place where generations come together over steaming plates of pasta and lively conversations.

Top Attractions:

Newtown: Explore the iconic King Street with its vintage clothing stores, quirky record shops, and vibrant live music venues. Catch a performance at the Encore Theatre, a historic venue that's hosted legendary acts. Don't miss the Newtown Festival, a street party celebrating the neighborhood's diversity.

Glebe: Browse the Glebe Markets for unique finds, from handcrafted jewelry to vintage treasures. Delve into the past at the Blackwattle Bay Heritage Walk, or visit the Sydney University campus with its grand sandstone buildings and rich history.

Leichhardt: Take a walking tour through Leichhardt's Italian precinct, Norton Street, savoring delicious pastries, cured meats, and authentic coffee at family-run cafes. Immerse yourself in Italian culture at the Festa Italian, a vibrant celebration of food, music, and dance.

Hidden Gems:

Newtown: Discover the Harold Park Hotel, a historic pub with a rooftop bar offering stunning city views. Unwind at Camperdown Park, a tranquil green space with hidden gardens and a charming rose maze.

Glebe: Seek out Glebe Point Road for its independent bookstores, art galleries, and eclectic mix of cafes and restaurants. Explore the Rozelle Lime Kilns, remnants of Sydney's industrial past offering unique harbor views.

Leichhardt: Step back in time at Leichhardt Library, a heritage-listed building with a beautiful reading room. Catch a flick at the Norton Street Leichhardt Cinemas, an independent cinema showcasing arthouse and foreign films.

Experiences:

Foodie Delights: Embark on a culinary adventure in the Inner West. Newtown offers vegan havens, trendy cafes, and international restaurants. Glebe boasts Greek tavernas, Italian trattorias, and hidden gems serving up global cuisine. Leichhardt is a paradise for Italian food lovers, from casual pizzerias to fine-dining establishments.

Street Art Safari: Unleash your inner explorer with a street art tour of the Inner West. Renowned artists have transformed walls into vibrant canvases, showcasing the creative spirit of the neighborhood.

Live Music Hub: Immerse yourself in Sydney's thriving live music scene. Newtown boasts a plethora of pubs and music venues hosting everything from indie bands to up-and-coming DJs.

Vintage Shopping Spree: Hunt for unique treasures in the Inner West's vintage clothing stores. From classic finds to quirky statement pieces, there's something for every style in Newtown and Glebe.

Beyond the Tourist Trail:

Community Vibe: Mingle with locals at weekend markets like the Glebe Markets or the Carriage works Farmers Market in Eveleigh. These vibrant spaces offer fresh produce, artisan goods, and a chance to experience the heart of the community.

Park Life: Escape the city buzz at the Inner West's many parks. Victoria Park in Glebe is perfect for picnics and sports, while Henson Park in Leichhardt offers walking trails and a dog park.

Alternative Entertainment: Catch a performance at the Sydney Theatre Company's Wharf Theatres in Walsh Bay, or explore the contemporary art scene at the Carriage works Arts Precinct in Eveleigh.

Inner West: A Place to Linger

The Inner West isn't just a collection of sights; it's a feeling. It's about slowing down, savoring delicious food, browsing unique shops, and soaking up the vibrant atmosphere.

Paddington and Woollahra:

Paddington and Woollahra, nestled in Sydney's eastern suburbs, offer a sophisticated escape for the discerning traveler. Beyond the designer boutiques and upscale restaurants lies a charming neighborhood brimming with character, hidden gems, and unique experiences.

Characters:

The Fashionistas: Paddington is a haven for fashion enthusiasts. You'll find them browsing the racks of designer stores on Oxford Street, hunting for vintage treasures, or attending exclusive fashion events.

The Aesthetes: Art lovers and collectors flock to Paddington for its renowned galleries showcasing contemporary Australian and international art. Keep an eye out for impromptu street art installations that add a touch of whimsy to the neighborhood.

The Foodies: From Michelin-starred restaurants to cozy cafes, Paddington and Woollahra cater to every palate. Sample exquisite Italian fare, indulge in modern Australian cuisine, or grab a delicious brunch at a trendy cafe.

The Culture Vultures: History buffs will appreciate the grand Victorian terraces lining the streets. Architecture enthusiasts will be captivated by the iconic Paddington Reservoir Gardens, a hidden oasis featuring restored Victorian water pumps and lush greenery.

Top Attractions:

Oxford Street: This iconic shopping strip is a paradise for fashionistas, with a mix of high-end designer stores, independent boutiques, and vintage shops.

Paddington Markets: Every Saturday, these bustling markets offer a treasure trove of vintage clothing, antiques, handmade crafts, and local produce. Be prepared to bargain and soak up the vibrant atmosphere.

Five Ways: This lively intersection is the heart of Paddington, with a great selection of cafes, restaurants, and bars. People watch from a sidewalk table and enjoy the cosmopolitan vibe.

Queen Street: This hidden gem boasts a charming collection of independent bookstores, art galleries, and specialty shops.

Paddington Reservoir Gardens: Escape the urban bustle and discover this tranquil oasis featuring restored Victorian water pumps, ornamental ponds, and lush greenery.

Hidden Gems:

Trumper Park: Nestled amongst the terraces, this hidden park offers a peaceful escape with stunning views of the city skyline.

Paddington Reservoir: Take a guided tour of this historic reservoir, now transformed into a unique events space.

Saint Mark's Church: Admire the beautiful Gothic Revival architecture of this historic church, a hidden gem on Oxford Street.

Surry Hills Pocket City Farm: Experience urban agriculture firsthand at this community-run farm, offering workshops and fresh, local produce.

Paddington Bear Shop: Delight the little ones (or the young-at-heart) with a visit to this charming shop dedicated to the beloved Paddington Bear.

Unique Experiences:

Foodie Tour: Embark on a culinary adventure through Paddington and Woollahra, sampling gourmet delights at hidden cafes, bakeries, and delis.

High Tea: Indulge in a quintessential English tradition at a luxurious hotel or charming cafe, enjoying delicate pastries and fragrant teas.

Vintage Shopping Spree: Hunt for unique treasures and one-of-a-kind pieces at Paddington's many vintage clothing stores.

Art Gallery Hopping: Immerse yourself in the vibrant art scene by visiting the renowned galleries and hidden studios scattered throughout the neighborhood.

Picnic in the Park: Pack a gourmet spread and head to one of the many parks, like Victoria Park or Paddington Reservoir Gardens, for a relaxing afternoon under the sun.

Beyond the Tourist Trail:

Volunteer at the Paddington Reservoir: Give back to the community by volunteering your time at this unique historical site.

Take a Painting Class: Unleash your inner artist by participating in a painting class led by a local artist.

Attend a Fashion Event: Immerse yourself in the world of high fashion by attending a runway show or designer talk.

Join a Book Club: Connect with fellow bibliophiles by joining a book club at one of Paddington's independent bookstores.

Explore the Backstreets: Wander off the beaten path and discover the hidden laneways and charming streets that add to Paddington's unique character.

Paddington and Woollahra offer more than just glitz and glamour. With its charming streets, diverse offerings, and hidden gems, it's a place to discover Sydney's sophisticated side and create lasting memories.

Manly:

Manly, a relaxed beachside haven just a scenic ferry ride from Sydney's bustling CBD, offers a captivating mix of sun, surf, and a chilled-out atmosphere. Here's a detailed breakdown of Manly's character, top attractions, hidden gems, and experiences to make your visit unforgettable:

Characters:

Surfers & Sun-Seekers: Manly Beach is a magnet for surfers of all levels, with consistent waves and a vibrant surf culture. Families also flock here for the calm swimming areas and pristine sands.

Foodies: Manly boasts a diverse culinary scene. From fresh seafood restaurants overlooking the water to hidden cafes serving up delicious brunches, there's something to tantalize every taste bud.

Nature Lovers: Manly is a gateway to stunning coastal walks and national parks. Hike the scenic Manly Scenic Walkway for breathtaking ocean views or explore the Shelly Beach Aquatic Reserve for its rich marine life.

Bohemian Chic: A relaxed, beachy vibe permeates Manly. Explore the boutiques along the Corso with their locally-made crafts and surf apparel, or discover hidden bars and restaurants tucked away in side streets.

Top Attractions:

Manly Beach: The undisputed star of the show. This iconic stretch of golden sand offers excellent surfing conditions, calm swimming areas, and stunning views of the Pacific Ocean.

Manly Corso: A vibrant pedestrian strip lined with shops, cafes, restaurants, and street performers. Browse for souvenirs, grab a bite to eat, or simply soak up the lively atmosphere.

Manly Scenic Walkway: A must-do for nature lovers. This scenic coastal walk stretches from Shelly Beach to Spit Bridge, offering stunning ocean views, dramatic cliffs, and hidden coves.

Shelly Beach: A protected cove perfect for snorkeling and swimming. Explore the vibrant marine life in the Shelly Beach Aquatic Reserve, a designated underwater sanctuary.

Hidden Gems:

Fair light Beach: Escape the crowds at this secluded beach, a favorite among locals for its relaxed atmosphere and calm waters.

Manly Quarantine Station: Delve into Sydney's history at this beautifully restored quarantine station, offering guided tours and fascinating exhibits.

The Wormhole: This quirky bar hidden down a laneway is a local favorite, with a relaxed atmosphere and eclectic live music.

Manly Freshwater Pool: Take a dip in this historic ocean pool, a unique alternative to the beach that offers stunning views.

Experiences:

Learn to Surf: Embrace the local surfing culture and take a lesson at one of Manly's many surf schools. There are options for all levels, from complete beginners to seasoned surfers looking to hone their skills.

Kayaking Adventure: Explore the stunning coastline from a different perspective by embarking on a kayak tour. Paddle around secluded coves, spot marine life, and enjoy the serenity of the calm waters.

Whaley Watching Cruise: Head offshore on a whale-watching cruise from Manly and witness the majestic humpback whales migrating along the coast (seasonal).

Manly Food & Wine Festival (held annually): Immerse yourself in Manly's vibrant food scene at this annual festival. Sample delicious food from local restaurants, wineries, and breweries, and enjoy live music and entertainment.

Sunset at Manly Wharf: Conclude your day in Manly with a breathtaking sunset. Watch the sky explode with color as the sun dips below the horizon, creating a truly unforgettable experience.

Beyond the Tourist Trail: **Manly Freshwater:** Venture beyond the main beach and explore the charming village of Manly Freshwater. Enjoy a coffee overlooking the picturesque harbor, browse through local art galleries, or visit the Manly Surf School.

North Head National Park: Immerse yourself in nature at North Head National Park. Hike to the summit for panoramic views of the city and coastline, explore the historic military tunnels, or spot whales from the vantage point.

Manly to Spit Bridge Ferry: Take a scenic ferry ride from Manly to Spit Bridge, enjoying breathtaking views of the coastline, secluded coves, and hidden beaches along the way.

Manly offers a perfect escape from the city's hustle and bustle, with its laid-back charm, stunning beaches, and diverse activities.

Chinatown:

Sydney's Chinatown is a vibrant tapestry of sights, smells, and tastes, offering a dynamic experience for every kind of traveler. Here's a deeper dive into this fascinating neighborhood:

Characters:

Shopkeepers and Restaurateurs: The heart of Chinatown beats with the energy of its shopkeepers and restaurateurs. Many families have run businesses here for generations, welcoming visitors with warm smiles and a passion for sharing their heritage.

Local Residents: A close-knit community resides in Chinatown, adding a layer of authenticity to the experience. You might see elderly men playing mahjong in parks, or families enjoying a traditional dim sum lunch.

Foodies and Culture Enthusiasts: Chinatown is a magnet for those seeking an authentic culinary and cultural adventure. Be prepared to rub shoulders with fellow food enthusiasts and travelers eager to experience a slice of Chinese life in Sydney.

Top Attractions:

Paddy's Markets: This bustling market is a treasure trove of bargains, from fresh produce and souvenirs to clothing and electronics. Be ready to haggle and explore the maze-like stalls for unique finds.

Dixon Street: The heart of Chinatown, Dixon Street is lined with restaurants serving everything from Cantonese classics to spicy Sichuan dishes. Be sure to try delicacies like roast duck, dumplings (dim sum), and noodles.

Chinese Garden of Friendship: Escape the city buzz at this tranquil oasis, featuring traditional Chinese landscaping, koi ponds, and pagodas. It's a perfect spot for a peaceful stroll and a break from sightseeing.

Haymarket and Spice Alley: Venture beyond Dixon Street to Haymarket for a more local experience. Explore Spice Alley, a hidden laneway packed with restaurants offering regional Chinese cuisine and Southeast Asian delights.

Hidden Gems:

Tea Houses: Escape the crowds and discover a hidden gem – a traditional tea house. Savor a cup of fragrant tea and indulge in delicate pastries for a truly authentic experience.

Fruit and Vegetable Markets: Find the freshest produce at the lively fruit and vegetable markets on Sussex and Goulburn Streets. The abundance of exotic fruits and vibrant colors is a feast for the senses.

Chinese Bakeries: Satisfy your sweet tooth at a hidden bakery tucked away on a side street. Try traditional treats like mooncakes, filled buns, and egg tarts – a delicious and affordable way to sample local delicacies.

Specialty Shops: Look beyond the tourist shops and discover stores catering to the local community. Find authentic Chinese ingredients, traditional teapots, and unique souvenirs that tell a story.

Experiences:

Dim Sum Lunch: Indulge in the quintessential Chinatown experience – a dim sum lunch. Sample a variety of small steamed dishes presented in bamboo baskets, perfect for sharing with friends and family.

Cooking Class: Learn the art of Chinese cuisine by taking a cooking class. Get hands-on experience and unlock the secrets to making delicious dishes like dumplings and stir-fries.

Chinese New Year Celebrations: If you visit during Chinese New Year, be mesmerized by the vibrant parades with lion dances and firecrackers. Immerse yourself in the festive atmosphere and experience the rich cultural traditions.

Tea Ceremony: Embrace tranquility with a traditional tea ceremony. Learn about the art of tea brewing and appreciate the delicate flavors and aromas of different teas.

Beyond the Tourist Trail:

For a truly immersive experience, go beyond the main streets and explore the back alleys and side streets. Strike up conversations with local shopkeepers and residents to discover their stories and hidden gems. Explore the neighborhood at night, when the neon lights illuminate the streets and a different energy takes hold.

Tips:

Cash is King at Some Stores: While many stores accept cards, some smaller shops may prefer cash. Be prepared to withdraw some money beforehand.

Don't be Afraid to Bargain: Bargaining is expected at Paddy's Markets and some smaller shops. It's part of the fun and can lead to great deals.

Learn a Few Basic Mandarin Phrases: A few simple Mandarin phrases like "in hao" (hello) and "Xie Xie" (thank you) can go a long way in showing respect and appreciation to the locals.

Kings Cross and Potts Point:

Kings Cross and Potts Point, nestled side-by-side in Sydney's inner-east, offer a captivating contrast. Kings Cross, once notorious for its nightlife, is evolving into a vibrant hub, while Potts Point retains a sophisticated charm. Let's delve into the characters, attractions, hidden gems, and experiences that await you in this dynamic duo.

Characters:

Kings Cross: Edgy, youthful, and undergoing a renaissance. You'll find backpackers, artists, and a mix of locals drawn to the late-night bars and alternative scene.

Potts Point: Chic, creative, and established. Expect fashionistas, art lovers, and professionals to enjoy the refined cafes and upscale boutiques.

Top Attractions (Kings Cross):

The Coca-Cola Sign: An iconic landmark and meeting point, this giant red sign has become synonymous with Kings Cross.

Australian Heritage Hotel: Step back in time at this grand pub, known for its ornate Victorian architecture and lively atmosphere.

Woods Wine Bar: A haven for wine lovers, this cozy bar boasts an extensive wine list and knowledgeable staff.

Street Art: Explore the back alleys and laneways to discover hidden gems of street art, reflecting the neighborhood's artistic spirit.

Top Attractions (Potts Point):

Elizabeth Bay House: This grand Georgian mansion, built in 1835, offers a glimpse into Sydney's colonial past.

Kink Street: A haven for art lovers, this street boasts a concentration of galleries showcasing contemporary Australian and international art.

Macleay Street: Indulge in some retail therapy at this fashionable strip, lined with designer boutiques and independent stores.

Art Deco Architecture: Admire the stunning Art Deco buildings that line many streets, a testament to the area's architectural heritage.

Hidden Gems:

Yellow Bar: Tucked away in a back alley, this intimate bar offers a relaxed atmosphere and expertly crafted cocktails. (Kings Cross)

Dao Restaurant: Experience authentic Vietnamese cuisine in this family-run restaurant, a local favorite. (Potts Point)

Mary's: This hidden gem serves up delicious burgers and a lively atmosphere, perfect for a casual meal. (Kings Cross)

Roslyn Packer Theatre: Catch a play or performance at this renowned theater company, known for its innovative productions. (Potts Point)

Unique Experiences:

Kings Cross Historical Walking Tour: Learn about the area's colorful past and transformation, from its red-light district days to its current artistic renaissance.

Rooftop Bar Hopping: Enjoy stunning city and harbor views while sipping on cocktails at some of the trendy rooftop bars popping up in Potts Point.

Art Gallery Crawl: Immerse yourself in the vibrant art scene by visiting the many galleries scattered throughout Potts Point, and maybe even meet some local artists.

Vintage Shopping Adventure: Hunt for unique treasures and one-of-a-kind finds in the vintage clothing stores and antique shops scattered around Kings Cross.

Considerations:

Nightlife: Kings Cross offers a variety of bars and clubs, while Potts Point has a more relaxed nightlife scene.

Accommodation: Both areas offer a range of accommodation options, from budget-friendly hostels in Kings Cross to chic boutique hotels in Potts Point.

Safety: While Kings Cross has seen significant improvement, it's always wise to be aware of your surroundings, especially at night.

Kings Cross and Potts Point offer a captivating blend of old and new, edgy and chic. With its diverse offerings, this dynamic duo caters to curious travelers seeking a taste of Sydney's undercurrent and artistic soul.

Barangaroo:

Barangaroo, Sydney's newest harborside district, is a vibrant fusion of modern architecture, world-class dining, public spaces, and a touch of history. Once an industrial port, it's transformed into a chic destination perfect for a luxurious escape or a day of casual exploration.

Characters:

The Affluent Aficionado: Barangaroo caters to those who appreciate the finer things. From the opulent Crown Sydney Hotel to high-end boutiques and Michelin-starred restaurants, it exudes an air of exclusivity.

The Culture Vulture: Art enthusiasts will find themselves drawn to Barangaroo's innovative architecture, like the geometric towers of Barangaroo South and the sculptural facades of Wulugul Walk. The precinct also hosts pop-up art installations and events throughout the year.

The Leisurely Explorer: Families and couples seeking relaxation will find solace in Barangaroo Reserve. Lush green spaces, playgrounds, and walking paths offer stunning city and harbor views, perfect for picnics, strolls, or simply soaking up the sunshine.

The Foodie: Barangaroo is a paradise for gourmands. Renowned chefs have set up shop here, offering everything from casual harborside dining to exquisite degustation experiences at acclaimed restaurants.

Top Attractions:

Crown Sydney Hotel: This architectural marvel, resembling a crown perched on the water's edge, houses a luxury hotel, high-end restaurants, a casino, and a stunning infinity pool overlooking the harbor.

Barangaroo Reserve: Escape the city buzz in this sprawling waterfront park. Featuring native plants, walking paths, playgrounds, and public art installations, it's a haven for relaxation and recreation.

Wulugul Walk: This scenic promenade stretches along the Barangaroo waterfront, offering stunning harbor views. Lined with cafes, restaurants, and bars, it's a vibrant hub for socializing and enjoying the outdoors.

The Cutaway: This heritage-listed sandstone building, once part of the original wharf complex, has been transformed into a multi-level dining and entertainment hub. Explore hidden bars, innovative restaurants, and unique retail stores.

Hidden Gems:

Barangaroo Point Cliff Walk: Take a short but rewarding hike along this hidden gem for breathtaking panoramic views of the Sydney Harbour Bridge, Opera House, and the city skyline.

Barangaroo House: Nestled amidst the skyscrapers, this three-level architectural gem houses award-winning venues like Smoke Bar (known for its innovative cocktails), Bea Restaurant (with a focus on sustainable seafood), and Rekodo, a vinyl bar with a Japanese twist.

Barangaroo Aboriginal Cultural Tour: Immerse yourself in the rich Indigenous history of the area with a guided tour led by Aboriginal storytellers. Learn about the traditional custodians of the land, their connection to the harbor, and the significance of the Barangaroo.

Experiences:

Dine with a View: Savor a delectable meal at one of Barangaroo's many waterfront restaurants, soaking in the stunning panorama of Sydney Harbour. From casual cafes to fine-dining experiences, there's something to suit every taste and budget.

Catch a Ferry: Experience Sydney from a different perspective with a scenic ferry ride from Barangaroo Wharf to Circular Quay. Take in the iconic landmarks and enjoy the cool sea breeze.

Attend a Special Event: Throughout the year, Barangaroo comes alive with various events, from art exhibitions and live music performances to food festivals and cultural celebrations. Check the calendar for upcoming events and immerse yourself in the vibrant atmosphere.

Luxury Shopping: Indulge in a spot of retail therapy at Barangaroo's high-end boutiques. Find designer clothing, luxury jewelry, and unique homewares from leading international brands.

Manly offers a perfect escape from the city's hustle and bustle, with its laid-back charm, stunning beaches, and diverse activities.

Best Places to Stay Based on Interests

Budget Travelers

Sydney, known for its beautiful harbor, iconic landmarks, and vibrant culture, can be an expensive destination. However, there are several areas in the city where budget travelers can find affordable accommodations without sacrificing convenience or comfort. Here are some of the best areas to stay in Sydney for budget travelers:

1. Kings Cross

Kings Cross, also known as "The Cross," is famous for its vibrant nightlife and eclectic mix of entertainment venues. It's a popular area for budget travelers due to its variety of hostels, budget hotels, and guesthouses.

- **Why Stay Here:** Affordable accommodations, close to the CBD, and vibrant nightlife.
- **Accommodation Options:** Hostels (e.g., Mad Monkey Backpackers), budget hotels, and guesthouses.
- **What to Do:** Visit the El Alamein Memorial Fountain, explore the nightlife, and enjoy cafes and restaurants.
- **Transportation:** Kings Cross Train Station provides easy access to other parts of Sydney.

2. Surry Hills

Surry Hills is known for its trendy cafes, restaurants, and artistic vibe. It's a great area for budget travelers who want to stay close to the city center while enjoying a unique local atmosphere.

- **Why Stay Here:** Proximity to the CBD, trendy and artistic vibe, and good food scene.
- **Accommodation Options:** Budget hotels, boutique hostels (e.g., Big Hostel), and guesthouses.
- **What to Do:** Explore Crown Street's cafes and boutiques, visit the Brett Whiteley Studio, and enjoy the Saturday Surry Hills Markets.
- **Transportation:** Well-connected by buses and within walking distance to Central Station.

3. Glebe

Glebe offers a bohemian and relaxed atmosphere with its cafes, bookstores, and markets. It's an excellent choice for budget travelers looking for a laid-back area close to the city.

- **Why Stay Here:** Bohemian vibe, close to the city, great food options, weekly markets.
- **Accommodation Options:** Hostels (e.g., Glebe Point YHA), budget inns, and guesthouses.

- **What to Do:** Visit the Glebe Markets, walk along the Glebe Foreshore, and explore the University of Sydney.
- **Transportation:** Well-served by buses, and a short walk to light rail stations.

4. Newtown

Newtown is a vibrant, eclectic neighborhood known for its alternative culture, street art, and diverse dining options. It's popular among students and budget-conscious travelers.

- **Why Stay Here:** Alternative culture, diverse dining, vibrant nightlife.
- **Accommodation Options:** Hostels (e.g., The Urban Newtown), budget hotels, and guesthouses.
- **What to Do:** Explore King Street's shops and cafes, visit Newtown's street art, and enjoy live music venues.
- **Transportation:** Easily accessible by train (Newtown Station) and buses.

5. Bondi Beach

While Bondi Beach is known for its iconic status and can be pricey, there are still budget-friendly options for travelers who want to stay near the beach.

- **Why Stay Here:** Iconic beach location, surf culture, relaxed atmosphere.
- **Accommodation Options:** Hostels (e.g., Bondi Backpackers), budget hotels, and surf lodges.
- **What to Do:** Enjoy Bondi Beach, walk the Bondi to Coogee coastal trail, and explore local markets and eateries.
- **Transportation:** Frequent buses connect Bondi Beach to the city center and Bondi Junction Train Station.

6. Central Business District (CBD)

Staying in the CBD might seem expensive, but there are budget options available, especially during off-peak seasons. Staying here offers the advantage of being close to major attractions and transport hubs.

- **Why Stay Here:** Proximity to major attractions, and excellent transportation links.
- **Accommodation Options:** Budget hotels, affordable hostels (e.g., Sydney Central YHA), and some budget-friendly apartments.

- **What to Do:** Visit the Sydney Opera House, Darling Harbour, and the Royal Botanic Garden.
- **Transportation:** Central Station, Town Hall Station, and numerous bus and light rail services provide easy access to the entire city.

7. Potts Point

Potts Point offers a mix of affordability and charm, with its tree-lined streets, historic buildings, and proximity to the harbor.

- **Why Stay Here:** This charming neighborhood, is close to the city, good dining options.
- **Accommodation Options:** Budget hotels, boutique hostels, guesthouses.
- **What to Do:** Stroll through Macleay Street, visit the Royal Botanic Garden, and enjoy the local cafes and restaurants.
- **Transportation:** Kings Cross Train Station and numerous bus routes make it easy to get around.

8. Redfern

Redfern is an up-and-coming area with a strong community feel and a mix of cultural influences. It's becoming increasingly popular with young travelers and offers affordable accommodation options.

- **Why Stay Here:** Up-and-coming area, diverse community, close to the city.
- **Accommodation Options:** Budget hotels, hostels, and guesthouses.
- **What to Do:** Explore Carriageworks, visit local cafes and bars, and enjoy Redfern Park.
- **Transportation:** Redfern Train Station provides excellent connectivity to the city and suburbs.

9. Ultimo

Ultimo is conveniently located near the CBD, Darling Harbour, and several educational institutions, making it a great spot for budget travelers.

- **Why Stay Here:** Central location, close to educational institutions, good transportation.
- **Accommodation Options:** Budget hotels, hostels (e.g., Sydney Railway Square YHA), and serviced apartments.

- **What to Do:** Visit the Powerhouse Museum, explore Darling Harbour, and enjoy the nearby Broadway Shopping Centre.
- **Transportation:** Well-connected by buses and a short walk to Central Station.

Backpackers and Solo Travelers

1. Kings Cross

Kings Cross, often referred to as "The Cross," is a vibrant and bustling area known for its nightlife, eclectic mix of restaurants, and budget-friendly accommodations. It has a reputation for being a hub for backpackers, offering numerous hostels and affordable hotels.

Highlights:

- Nightlife: Bars, clubs, and live music venues.
- Dining: Diverse range of restaurants and cafes.
- Convenience: Proximity to the CBD and public transport.

Why It's Great for Backpackers and Solo Travelers: Kings Cross provides a lively social atmosphere, making it easy to meet other travelers. The area is well-connected by public transport, allowing for easy exploration of Sydney's main attractions.

Popular Hostels:

- The Pod Sydney
- Mad Monkey Backpackers
- Blue Parrot Backpackers

2. Bondi Beach

Bondi Beach is an iconic Sydney destination famous for its stunning coastline, surfing culture, and relaxed vibe. It's a popular spot for backpackers and solo travelers who love the beach and outdoor activities.

Highlights:

- Beach Life: Surfing, sunbathing, and coastal walks.
- Community: Vibrant community events and markets.
- Fitness: Outdoor fitness classes and yoga on the beach.

Why It's Great for Backpackers and Solo Travelers: Bondi offers a laid-back atmosphere with plenty of opportunities to socialize and participate in group activities. The area is also home to several budget accommodations that cater specifically to backpackers.

Popular Hostels:

- Wake Up! Bondi Beach
- Noah's Backpackers
- Surfside Bondi Beach Backpackers

3. Surry Hills

Surry Hills is a trendy and artsy neighborhood known for its vibrant café culture, boutique shopping, and artistic vibe. It's an excellent area for solo travelers looking to experience Sydney's creative scene.

Highlights:

- Cafés and Restaurants: Numerous trendy eateries and coffee shops.
- Art and Culture: Art galleries, theaters, and creative spaces.
- Shopping: Unique boutiques and vintage stores.
- Why It's Great for Backpackers and Solo Travelers:

Surry Hills offers a more relaxed and culturally rich environment compared to the bustling CBD. It's a great place to meet like-minded travelers and immerse yourself in Sydney's artsy side.

Popular Hostels:

- Big Hostel
- Ady's Place Backpackers
- Railway Square YHA

4. Newtown

Newtown is a bohemian suburb known for its vibrant street art, eclectic dining scene, and alternative culture. It's ideal for solo travelers who enjoy a quirky and diverse atmosphere.

Highlights:

- Street Art: Colorful murals and graffiti art.
- Dining and Nightlife: A variety of international cuisines and lively bars.
- Music and Arts: Live music venues and independent theaters.

Why It's Great for Backpackers and Solo Travelers: Newtown's unique charm and welcoming community make it easy for solo travelers to feel at home. The area's diverse entertainment options ensure there's always something to do.

Popular Hostels:

- Sydney Park Hotel
- Summer House Newtown
- Billabong Gardens

5. The Rocks

The Rocks is a historic area located near Sydney Harbour, offering a mix of old-world charm and modern attractions. It's perfect for travelers interested in history, culture, and stunning harbor views.

Highlights:

- History: Cobblestone streets, heritage buildings, and museums.
- Markets: The Rocks Markets, offers crafts, food, and souvenirs.
- Views: Proximity to Sydney Harbour Bridge and Opera House.

Why It's Great for Backpackers and Solo Travelers: The Rocks offers a unique blend of historical and cultural experiences, making it a fascinating area to explore. The area is also well-connected to other parts of the city, providing easy access to major attractions.

Popular Hostels:

- Sydney Harbour YHA
- The Mercantile Hotel
- Sydney Central YHA

6. Darlinghurst

Darlinghurst is a lively inner-city suburb known for its cultural diversity, bustling nightlife, and LGBTQ+-friendly environment. It's a great area for solo travelers looking for a dynamic and inclusive atmosphere.

Highlights:

- Nightlife: Pubs, bars, and nightclubs.
- Dining: Diverse culinary options, from fine dining to street food.
- Cultural Events: Festivals, parades, and community events.

Why It's Great for Backpackers and Solo Travelers: Darlinghurst offers a vibrant social scene and a welcoming community, making it easy to connect with other travelers. Its central location also provides convenient access to Sydney's top attractions.

Popular Hostels:

- Cambridge Lodge
- Eva's Backpackers
- Sydney Star Backpackers

Families and Leisure Travelers

1. Circular Quay and The Rocks

Circular Quay and The Rocks are iconic areas known for their historical significance and proximity to Sydney's top attractions. Staying here puts you within walking distance of the Sydney Opera House, Sydney Harbour Bridge, and the bustling harbourfront. The Rocks is a charming, cobblestoned area with historic buildings, boutique shops, and vibrant weekend markets.

Why It's Great for Families and Leisure Travelers:

- Proximity to major attractions like the Opera House, Harbour Bridge, and Royal Botanic Garden.
- Plenty of family-friendly restaurants and cafes.
- Easy access to ferries, buses, and trains.
- Rich historical and cultural experiences.
- Regular events and markets, providing entertainment and shopping opportunities.

Accommodation Options:

- **Luxury:** Park Hyatt Sydney, Four Seasons Hotel Sydney.
- **Mid-range:** Sydney Harbour Marriott Hotel at Circular Quay, Rendezvous Hotel Sydney the Rocks.
- **Budget:** YHA Sydney Harbour, budget-friendly apartments.

2. Darling Harbour

Darling Harbour is a vibrant waterfront precinct filled with attractions, dining options, and entertainment venues. It's an ideal area for families and leisure travelers due to its lively atmosphere and range of activities, from the SEA LIFE Sydney Aquarium to the Australian National Maritime Museum.

Why It's Great for Families and Leisure Travelers:

- Numerous attractions suitable for all ages, including Wildlife Sydney Zoo and Darling Harbour Playground.
- Wide range of dining options from casual eateries to upscale restaurants.
- Regular events, fireworks display, and festivals.
- Easy access to public transport, including light rail and ferries.
- Proximity to the ICC Sydney for events and exhibitions.

Accommodation Options:

- **Luxury:** Sofitel Sydney Darling Harbour, The Darling at The Star.
- **Mid-range:** Novotel Sydney on Darling Harbour, Hyatt Regency Sydney.
- **Budget:** ibis Sydney Darling Harbour, budget-friendly serviced apartments.

3. Bondi Beach

Bondi Beach is one of Sydney's most famous beaches, offering a laid-back coastal vibe. It's perfect for families and leisure travelers who want to enjoy the sun, sand, and surf, along with a variety of beachside cafes, restaurants, and shops.

Why It's Great for Families and Leisure Travelers:

- Beautiful sandy beach ideal for swimming, surfing, and beach activities.
- Family-friendly Bondi to Coogee coastal walk with stunning views.
- Vibrant local scene with cafes, ice-cream shops, and weekend markets.
- Bondi Pavilion hosts cultural events and activities.
- Relaxed atmosphere with plenty of open spaces for kids to play.

Accommodation Options:

- **Luxury:** QT Bondi, Bondi Beach House.
- **Mid-range:** Adina Apartment Hotel Bondi Beach, Hotel Bondi.
- **Budget:** Bondi Backpackers, budget-friendly holiday rentals.

4. Manly

Manly is a charming beachside suburb accessible by a scenic ferry ride from Circular Quay. Known for its relaxed atmosphere and beautiful beaches, Manly offers a range of activities for families and leisure travelers, including surfing, snorkeling, and coastal walks.

Why It's Great for Families and Leisure Travelers:

- Family-friendly beaches like Manly Beach and Shelly Beach.
- Attractions such as Manly SEA LIFE Sanctuary and North Head Sanctuary.
- Lively promenade with shops, cafes, and restaurants.
- Scenic ferry ride to and from Circular Quay.
- Plenty of outdoor activities including kayaking, biking, and walking trails.

Accommodation Options:

- **Luxury:** The Sebel Sydney Manly Beach, Novotel Sydney Manly Pacific.
- **Mid-range:** Quest Manly, Manly Paradise Motel & Apartments.
- **Budget:** Manly Backpackers, budget-friendly beachside apartments.

5. Surry Hills

Surry Hills is a trendy and vibrant inner-city suburb known for its stylish cafes, restaurants, and boutique shops. It's a great area for leisure travelers who enjoy exploring urban culture and family-friendly parks and activities.

Why It's Great for Families and Leisure Travelers:

- Diverse dining options with many family-friendly restaurants and cafes.
- Proximity to attractions like the Sydney Cricket Ground and Moore Park.
- Tree-lined streets and parks such as Prince Alfred Park.
- Eclectic mix of boutiques, galleries, and vintage shops.
- Central location with easy access to public transport.

Accommodation Options:

- **Luxury:** Little Albion, a Crystalbrook Collection Boutique Hotel, ADGE Apartments.
- **Mid-range:** Rydges Sydney Central, 57 Hotel.
- **Budget:** Cambridge Hotel Sydney, budget-friendly guesthouses.

6. Coogee

Coogee is a relaxed coastal suburb with a family-friendly beach, beautiful parks, and a laid-back atmosphere. It's an ideal spot for families and leisure travelers looking for a quieter beach experience compared to Bondi.

Why It's Great for Families and Leisure Travelers:

- Safe swimming beach with lifeguards and gentle waves.
- Coogee to Bondi coastal walk with stunning ocean views.
- Family-friendly parks such as Grant Reserve and Goldstein Reserve.
- range of dining options from casual cafes to fine dining.
- Community events and outdoor activities.

Accommodation Options:

- **Luxury:** Crowne Plaza Sydney Coogee Beach, Coogee Bay Hotel.
- **Mid-range:** Adina Apartment Hotel Coogee Sydney, Coogee Sands Hotel & Apartments.
- **Budget:** Coogee Beach House, budget-friendly apartments.

For Couples

1. The Rocks

The Rocks is a historic precinct with cobblestone streets, charming cafes, and boutique shops. It's perfect for couples seeking a romantic and quaint atmosphere. With its proximity to the Sydney Harbour Bridge and Opera House, The Rocks offers iconic views and easy access to major attractions.

Highlights:

- Romantic walks along the harbour
- Historic pubs and fine-dining restaurants
- Boutique shopping and weekend markets

- Close to Circular Quay for ferry rides

Recommended Hotels:

- Park Hyatt Sydney: Luxurious with harbor views
- Harbour Rocks Hotel: Boutique charm with historical elements

2. Darling Harbour

Darling Harbour is a vibrant waterfront district with a variety of entertainment options. It's ideal for couples who enjoy dining out, nightlife, and waterfront activities. The area is home to many attractions like the SEA LIFE Sydney Aquarium, Madame Tussauds, and the Australian National Maritime Museum.

Highlights:

- Dining by the water at Cockle Bay Wharf
- Evening cruises and fireworks displays
- Entertainment venues and IMAX theatre
- Proximity to the Sydney CBD and Barangaroo

Recommended Hotels:

- Sofitel Sydney Darling Harbour: Modern luxury with harbor views
- Hyatt Regency Sydney: Centrally located with excellent amenities

3. Potts Point

Potts Point is an upscale neighborhood known for its art deco architecture, trendy cafes, and vibrant nightlife. It's perfect for couples seeking a stylish and cosmopolitan vibe. The area is also close to the Royal Botanic Garden, offering serene strolls.

Highlights:

- Trendy cafes and fine-dining restaurants
- Boutique shops and art galleries
- Nightlife and cozy wine bars
- Walkable distance to the Royal Botanic Garden

Recommended Hotels:

- Larmont Sydney by Lancemore: Chic and modern

- The Macleay Hotel: Comfortable with city views

4. Surry Hills

Surry Hills is a trendy inner-city suburb known for its creative vibe, eclectic dining scene, and vibrant nightlife. It's ideal for couples who love exploring unique cafes, bars, and boutiques. The area is also home to many galleries and theatres, adding to its cultural appeal.

Highlights:

- Diverse dining options from casual to gourmet
- Unique boutiques and vintage stores
- Art galleries and performance spaces
- Proximity to Central Station for easy transport

Recommended Hotels:

- Little Albion, a Crystalbrook Collection Boutique Hotel: Stylish and intimate
- ADGE Apartment Hotel: Spacious with a contemporary feel

5. Bondi Beach

Bondi Beach is perfect for couples who love the beach lifestyle. It's known for its stunning coastal views, vibrant café culture, and laid-back atmosphere. Bondi offers plenty of outdoor activities, including the famous Bondi to Coogee coastal walk.

Highlights:

- Beautiful beach and scenic coastal walk
- Beachfront cafes and restaurants
- Surfing, swimming, and outdoor fitness
- Markets and local events

Recommended Hotels:

- QT Bondi: Stylish with a beachy vibe
- Adina Apartment Hotel Bondi Beach: Comfortable and close to the beach

6. Manly

Manly offers a relaxed beach atmosphere with a range of dining, shopping, and outdoor activities. It's great for couples looking to escape the hustle and bustle of the city while still being close enough to enjoy all the major attractions via a scenic ferry ride.

Highlights:

- Beautiful beaches and coastal walks
- Surfing, kayaking, and other water sports
- Seaside cafes and restaurants
- Scenic ferry ride to Circular Quay

Recommended Hotels:

- The Sebel Manly Beach: Beachfront with excellent amenities
- Manly Pacific Sydney MGallery Collection: Modern with stunning views

7. Barangaroo

Barangaroo is a newer development that offers a sophisticated urban experience with waterfront dining, shopping, and parks. It's perfect for couples who enjoy modern amenities and a lively atmosphere.

Highlights:

- Waterfront dining and bars
- Contemporary art installations and cultural events
- Scenic walks along the harbour
- Close to Darling Harbour and the CBD

Recommended Hotels:

- Crown Towers Sydney: Ultra-luxurious with stunning views
- The Darling at The Star: Sophisticated and centrally located

8. Paddington

Paddington is known for its charming terrace houses, boutique shopping, and vibrant markets. It's perfect for couples who appreciate a more relaxed, village-like atmosphere with plenty of character.

Highlights:

- Boutique shopping on Oxford Street
- Cafes, pubs, and fine-dining restaurants
- Weekend Paddington Markets
- Close to Centennial Park for strolls

Recommended Hotels:

- Mrs Banks Hotel: Boutique with historical charm
- Arts Hotel: Quaint and centrally located

Luxury Travelers

For luxury travelers visiting Sydney, several neighborhoods offer exquisite accommodations, fine dining, proximity to attractions, and stunning views of the harbor or city skyline. Here are the best areas to stay in Sydney for luxury travelers:

1. Circular Quay

Circular Quay is Sydney's premier waterfront precinct, offering iconic views of the Sydney Opera House and Sydney Harbour Bridge. It's ideal for luxury travelers seeking convenience and spectacular harbor vistas.

Highlights:

- **Luxury Hotels:** The area boasts renowned hotels like the Park Hyatt Sydney and the Four Seasons Hotel Sydney, offering opulent suites with harbor views.
- **Fine Dining:** Enjoy upscale dining experiences at Quay Restaurant, Aria Sydney, and Bennelong Restaurant within the Opera House.
- **Attractions:** Walk to the Sydney Opera House for performances or tours, visit the Museum of Contemporary Art, and catch ferries to explore Sydney Harbour.

2. The Rocks

Adjacent to Circular Quay, The Rocks combines historical charm with luxury amenities, featuring cobblestone streets, heritage buildings, and vibrant markets.

Highlights:

- **Luxury Hotels:** Stay at the Park Hyatt Sydney or the InterContinental Sydney, offering heritage rooms and suites with harbor or city views.
- **Dining:** Experience fine dining at restaurants like Sails on Lavender Bay, The Dining Room at The Park Hyatt, and Quay Restaurant.
- **Attractions:** Explore The Rocks Markets, and Sydney Observatory, and enjoy scenic walks along the foreshore to Barangaroo Reserve.

3. Darling Harbour

Darling Harbour is a bustling waterfront precinct known for its entertainment venues, shopping, and luxury accommodations, perfect for luxury travelers seeking a vibrant atmosphere.

Highlights:

- **Luxury Hotels:** Choose from hotels like the Sofitel Sydney Darling Harbour or The Star Grand Hotel and Residences, offering modern amenities and harbor views.
- **Entertainment:** Visit the ICC Sydney for events, dine at upscale restaurants like Sepia and Tetsuya's, and enjoy cocktails at rooftop bars overlooking the harbor.
- **Attractions:** Explore SEA LIFE Sydney Aquarium, and WILD LIFE Sydney Zoo, and take harbor cruises departing from King Street Wharf.

4. Sydney CBD (Central Business District)

Highlights:

- **Luxury Hotels:** Stay at luxury hotels such as The Langham Sydney, The Westin Sydney, or the Shangri-La Hotel Sydney, offering upscale accommodations and city skyline views.
- **Shopping:** Explore luxury boutiques along Pitt Street Mall, and visit the Queen Victoria Building for designer shopping.
- **Cultural Attractions:** Visit the Art Gallery of New South Wales, and the Royal Botanic Garden Sydney, and attend performances at the Sydney Opera House.

Recommended Areas and Hotels

1. The Rocks:

Luxury Hotels

Park Hyatt Sydney (5 stars): Nestled beside Sydney Harbour with unparalleled views of the Opera House, Park Hyatt Sydney offers luxurious accommodations blending contemporary elegance with waterfront charm. Rooms and suites feature private balconies, marble bathrooms, and sophisticated decor. Phone Number: +61 2 9256 1234

InterContinental Sydney (5 stars): Located near Circular Quay, InterContinental Sydney blends heritage charm with modern luxury. The hotel features spacious rooms with panoramic views of Sydney Harbour or the city skyline, fine dining options, and a rooftop pool with stunning views. Phone Number: +61 2 9253 9000

Boutique Hotels

The Russell Boutique Hotel (4 stars): A charming boutique hotel in a restored 1887 heritage building, The Russell offers individually decorated rooms with antique furnishings and modern amenities. Enjoy a central location in The Rocks, close to shops, cafes, and historic sites. Phone Number: +61 2 9241 3543

Harbour Rocks Hotel Sydney - MGallery by Sofitel (4 stars): Set in a heritage-listed building, Harbour Rocks Hotel combines historic charm with contemporary comfort. Rooms feature elegant decor, some with exposed brick walls, and the hotel offers a cozy courtyard, a restaurant, and a bar. Phone Number: +61 2 8220 9999

Budget-Friendly Hotels

The Australian Heritage Hotel (3 stars): Known for its historic pub atmosphere and budget-friendly accommodations, The Australian Heritage Hotel offers simple rooms with shared bathrooms. It's a great choice for budget travelers looking to stay in the heart of The Rocks. Phone Number: +61 2 9247 2229

The Mercantile Hotel (3 stars): A traditional Irish pub with affordable accommodations, The Mercantile Hotel offers basic rooms with shared facilities. Located in The Rocks, it's popular among budget-conscious travelers seeking a lively atmosphere and central location. Phone Number: +61 2 9247 3570

2. Darling Harbour:

Luxury Hotels

Sofitel Sydney Darling Harbour (5 stars): Sofitel Sydney Darling Harbour offers luxurious accommodations with stunning views of the harbor and city skyline. Rooms are elegantly designed with modern amenities, and the hotel features a rooftop infinity pool, several dining options, and a spa. Phone Number: +61 2 8388 8888

The Star Grand Hotel and Residences (5 stars): Adjacent to The Star casino complex, The Star Grand Hotel and Residences offers spacious rooms and suites with contemporary decor and panoramic views. Guests can enjoy world-class dining, entertainment, and a rooftop pool. Phone Number: +61 1800 700 700

Boutique Hotels

Ovolo Darling Harbour (4 stars): Ovolo Darling Harbour is a boutique hotel known for its stylish and quirky design. Rooms feature vibrant decor, modern amenities, and complimentary minibars. The hotel also offers a social hour with free drinks and snacks. Phone Number: +61 2 8586 1888

Novotel Sydney Darling Square (4 stars): Located in Darling Square, Novotel Sydney Darling Square offers contemporary rooms with city views. The hotel features a rooftop fitness center, an outdoor pool, and a restaurant serving Australian cuisine. Phone Number: +61 2 8217 4000

Budget-Friendly Hotels

ibis Sydney Darling Harbour (3 stars): ibis Sydney Darling Harbour provides affordable accommodations within walking distance of Darling Harbour attractions. Rooms are simple yet comfortable, and guests have access to a restaurant, bar, and business center. Phone Number: +61 2 9563 0888

Metro Aspire Hotel Sydney (3 stars): Metro Aspire Hotel Sydney offers budget-friendly rooms near Darling Harbour. The hotel features modern amenities, a rooftop terrace with city views, and a restaurant serving breakfast and dinner. Phone Number: +61 2 9211 1499

3. Bondi Beach:

Luxury Hotels

QT Bondi (5 stars): QT Bondi offers luxurious beachfront accommodations with stylish interiors inspired by Bondi's surf culture. Rooms feature balconies with ocean views, plush furnishings, and modern amenities. The hotel also boasts a rooftop swimming pool and restaurant. Phone Number: +61 2 8362 3900

Bondi Beachouse YHA (4 stars): Located just steps from Bondi Beach, Bondi Beachouse YHA offers stylish and modern accommodations with private and dormitory rooms. Guests can enjoy rooftop views, communal kitchen facilities, and a relaxed beachside atmosphere. Phone Number: +61 2 9365 2088

Boutique Hotels

Adina Apartment Hotel Bondi Beach (4 stars): Adina Apartment Hotel combines the comfort of apartment-style living with boutique hotel amenities. Located near Bondi Beach, it offers spacious studios and apartments with kitchenettes, modern decor, and rooftop terrace views. Phone Number: +61 2 8362 3900

Hotel Bondi (3 stars): Overlooking Bondi Beach, Hotel Bondi offers boutique-style accommodations with a lively atmosphere. Rooms feature beach views, comfortable furnishings, and easy access to Bondi's vibrant cafes, bars, and nightlife. Phone Number: +61 2 9130 3271

Budget-Friendly Hotels

Noah's Bondi Beach (3 stars): Noah's Bondi Beach provides budget-friendly accommodations just moments from the sand. Rooms are simple and comfortable, with some offering ocean views. The hotel also features a rooftop terrace and is close to Bondi's shops and restaurants. Phone Number: +61 2 9365 2088

Bondi 38 Serviced Apartments (3 stars): Bondi 38 Serviced Apartments offers self-contained studios and apartments near Bondi Beach. Ideal for budget-conscious travelers, accommodations include kitchen facilities, comfortable furnishings, and a convenient location. Phone Number: +61 2 9130 3271

4. Surry Hills and Darlinghurst:

Luxury Hotels

The Old Clare Hotel, Chippendale (5 stars): Located in nearby Chippendale, The Old Clare Hotel blends contemporary luxury with historical charm. The hotel features stylish rooms, some with city views, and amenities include a rooftop pool, fine dining restaurant, and a vibrant bar. Phone Number: +61 2 8277 8277

Ovolo Woolloomooloo, Woolloomooloo (5 stars): Situated in the historic Finger Wharf at Woolloomooloo, Ovolo Woolloomooloo offers spacious, loft-style rooms with waterfront views. The hotel boasts a rooftop pool, a free minibar, and a complimentary happy hour for guests. Phone Number: +61 2 9331 9000

Boutique Hotels

57 Hotel, Surry Hills (4 stars): 57 Hotel offers boutique accommodations in Surry Hills, featuring modern rooms with unique designs and vibrant decor. The hotel provides a central location near cafes, restaurants, and galleries, ideal for exploring the trendy Surry Hills neighborhood. Phone Number: +61 2 9212 5666

Medusa Hotel, Darlinghurst (4 stars): A stylish boutique hotel in Darlinghurst, Medusa Hotel offers individually designed rooms with chic furnishings and modern amenities. The hotel is known for its intimate atmosphere and personalized service. Phone Number: +61 2 9331 1000

Budget-Friendly Hotels

Cambridge Hotel Sydney, Surry Hills (3 stars): Cambridge Hotel Sydney offers comfortable and affordable accommodations in Surry Hills. Rooms are well-appointed with modern amenities, and the hotel features a restaurant, bar, and fitness center. Phone Number: +61 2 9212 1111

Morgans Boutique Hotel, Darlinghurst (3 stars): Morgans Boutique Hotel provides budget-friendly accommodations with a focus on comfort and convenience. Rooms are cozy and well-equipped, and the hotel is located within walking distance of cafes, bars, and public transport. Phone Number: +61 2 9358 1588

5. The Inner West (Newtown, Glebe, Leichhardt):

Luxury Hotels

The Urban Newtown (4 stars): The Urban Newtown offers stylish accommodations with modern amenities in the vibrant suburb of Newtown. Rooms are well-appointed with contemporary decor, and the hotel features a rooftop terrace with city views. Phone Number: +61 2 9557 8333

Glebe Space (4 stars): Located in Glebe, Glebe Space provides luxury serviced apartments with spacious living areas, full kitchens, and designer furnishings. It's ideal for travelers seeking a home-away-from-home experience with easy access to cafes and shops. Phone Number: +61 2 9571 8600

Boutique Hotels

Cambridge Lodge Boutique Hotel (3 stars): Cambridge Lodge Boutique Hotel in Stanmore offers boutique accommodations with a cozy atmosphere. Rooms are individually decorated, and the hotel features a garden courtyard, a communal kitchen, and friendly service. Phone Number: +61 2 9569 2322

The Collectionist Hotel (4 stars): Situated in Camperdown, The Collectionist Hotel offers a unique boutique experience with individually themed rooms created by local artists. Guests can choose rooms based on their preferred design aesthetic, making each stay distinct. Phone Number: +61 2 8089 1045

Budget-Friendly Hotels

Quality Apartments Camperdown (3 stars): Quality Apartments Camperdown provides comfortable and affordable accommodations with self-contained studios and apartments. It's located near Newtown and offers easy access to public transport and dining options. Phone Number: +61 2 9557 8195

Westside Motor Inn (3 stars): Located in Leichhardt, Westside Motor Inn offers budget-friendly rooms with basic amenities. It's a convenient choice for travelers exploring the Inner West, with easy access to nearby cafes and public transport. Phone Number: +61 2 9569 1144

6. Paddington and Woollahra:

Luxury Hotels

The Hughenden Boutique Hotel, Woollahra (4 stars): The Hughenden Boutique Hotel offers a blend of Victorian charm and modern luxury. Located in Woollahra, this heritage-listed hotel features individually decorated rooms with antique furnishings and elegant decor. Guests can enjoy amenities such as a restaurant serving high tea, a cozy lounge bar, and a courtyard garden. Phone Number: +61 2 9363 4863

The Hughenden Boutique Hotel, Paddington (4 stars): Also, part of The Hughenden brand, this hotel in Paddington maintains the same Victorian charm and luxury. It features beautifully appointed rooms with period-style furnishings, a library, and an onsite restaurant serving gourmet cuisine. Phone Number: +61 2 9363 4863

Boutique Hotels

The Savoy Double Bay Hotel, Woollahra (4 stars): Situated in the elegant suburb of Double Bay, adjacent to Woollahra, The Savoy Double Bay Hotel offers boutique-style accommodations with a contemporary flair. Rooms are stylishly decorated and feature modern amenities. The hotel also boasts a rooftop pool with stunning views of Sydney Harbour. Phone Number: +61 2 8388 8388

The Hughenden Boutique Hotel, Paddington (4 stars): As mentioned above, The Hughenden Boutique Hotel in Paddington offers boutique accommodations with Victorian charm. Each room is uniquely decorated, blending historic elegance with modern comfort. The hotel features a library, a restaurant serving gourmet meals, and a cozy atmosphere. Phone Number: +61 2 9363 4863

Budget-Friendly Hotels

The Residences Centennial Park, Paddington (3 stars): Located near Centennial Parklands, The Residences Centennial Park offers budget-friendly apartment-style accommodations with kitchenettes and living areas. It's ideal for travelers looking for self-catering options and a residential atmosphere close to Paddington's attractions. Phone Number: +61 2 9326 8659

The Hughenden Boutique Hotel, Paddington (4 stars): Again, part of The Hughenden brand, this hotel in Paddington provides a mix of affordability and charm. With its historic ambiance and comfortable rooms, it's a great choice for budget-conscious travelers seeking a unique stay in Paddington. Phone Number: +61 2 9363 4863

7. Manly:

Luxury Hotels

Q Station Sydney Harbour National Park (4 stars): Located within Sydney Harbour National Park, Q Station offers luxury accommodations with historical charm. Set in heritage-listed buildings, rooms feature modern amenities, some with harbor views. The hotel also offers guided ghost tours and dining options. Phone Number: +61 2 9466 1500

Novotel Sydney Manly Pacific (4.5 stars): Situated right on Manly Beach, Novotel Sydney Manly Pacific offers luxurious rooms and suites with stunning ocean views. Guests can enjoy beachfront dining, an outdoor pool, and easy access to Manly's shops, cafes, and attractions. Phone Number: +61 2 9977 7666

Boutique Hotels

The Sebel Sydney Manly Beach (4 stars): A stylish boutique hotel overlooking Manly Beach, The Sebel Sydney Manly Beach offers contemporary suites with balconies and ocean views. Enjoy a rooftop pool, restaurant, and proximity to Manly Wharf and the Corso shopping district. Phone Number: +61 2 9977 8866

Manly Beach House (3.5 stars): A charming boutique guesthouse just steps from Manly Beach, Manly Beach House offers comfortable rooms with shared or private bathrooms. Guests can relax in the garden courtyard or explore nearby cafes and coastal walks. Phone Number: +61 2 9977 5799

Budget-Friendly Hotels

Boardrider Hostel/Backpacker & Budget Motel (2 stars): Located in the heart of Manly, Boardrider Hostel offers budget-friendly dormitory rooms and private motel rooms. Facilities include a communal kitchen, lounge area, and easy access to Manly's surf beaches and nightlife. Phone Number: +61 2 9977 3315

Manly Bunkhouse (1.5 stars): A budget-friendly hostel offering dormitory-style accommodation and private rooms with shared bathrooms.

Manly Bunkhouse is centrally located, close to Manly Beach, ferry wharf, and local shops and restaurants. Phone Number: +61 2 9977 2205

8. Chinatown:

Luxury Hotels

The Old Clare Hotel (5 stars): The Old Clare Hotel is a luxury boutique hotel located in the heart of Chippendale, close to Chinatown. It combines contemporary design with historic architecture, featuring stylish rooms, a rooftop pool, and acclaimed dining options. Phone Number: +61 2 8277 8277

The Darling at The Star (5 stars): Situated near Darling Harbour and Chinatown, The Darling at The Star offers luxury accommodations with modern amenities and panoramic views of the city skyline. The hotel features a spa, rooftop pool, and several dining venues. Phone Number: +61 1800 800 830

Boutique Hotels

Ovolo 1888 Darling Harbour (4 stars): Ovolo 1888 Darling Harbour blends historic charm with contemporary style, offering boutique accommodations near Chinatown. Rooms feature unique decor, high-tech amenities, and complimentary minibars. The hotel also includes a rooftop terrace and free happy-hour drinks. Phone Number: +61 2 8586 1888

The Ultimo Hotel (4 stars): Located in Ultimo, adjacent to Chinatown, The Ultimo Hotel offers boutique-style accommodations with modern design and comfortable amenities. It's known for its central location, stylish rooms, and friendly service. Phone Number: +61 2 9217 6666

Budget-Friendly Hotels

Sydney Hotel CBD (3 stars): Sydney Hotel CBD offers budget-friendly accommodations in the heart of Sydney's Chinatown. Rooms are simple and functional, suited for travelers looking for affordable lodging with easy access to dining, shopping, and transport. Phone Number: +61 2 9211 4600

Ibis Sydney World Square (3 stars): Situated near World Square in Sydney's CBD, Ibis Sydney World Square offers budget-friendly accommodations within walking distance of Chinatown. Rooms are comfortable and well-equipped, catering to budget-conscious travelers. Phone Number: +61 2 9280 9888

9. Kings Cross and Potts Point:

Luxury Hotels

Ovolo Woolloomooloo (5 stars): Located in Woolloomooloo Bay, adjacent to Kings Cross and Potts Point, Ovolo Woolloomooloo offers luxury accommodations with stylish interiors and stunning harbor views. Rooms feature modern amenities, vibrant decor, and complimentary minibars. Phone Number: +61 2 9331 9000

Larmont Sydney by Lancemore (5 stars): Situated in Potts Point, Larmont Sydney by Lancemore offers sophisticated rooms and suites with contemporary design and city views. The hotel features a rooftop terrace, a fitness center, and a chic restaurant serving modern Australian cuisine. Phone Number: +61 2 9295 8888

Boutique Hotels

Spicers Potts Point (5 stars): A boutique hotel in the heart of Potts Point, Spicers Potts Point blends historic charm with modern luxury. Rooms are elegantly appointed with luxurious amenities, and the hotel offers a courtyard garden, complimentary evening canapes, and personalized service. Phone Number: +61 1300 468 472

Hotel Challis (3.5 stars): Nestled in Potts Point, Hotel Challis offers boutique-style accommodations with a blend of heritage architecture and contemporary comforts. Rooms feature modern decor, some with balconies, and guests enjoy access to a shared courtyard. Phone Number: +61 2 8356 8300

Budget-Friendly Hotels

Springfield Lodge Sydney (3 stars): Located in Potts Point, Springfield Lodge Sydney offers budget-friendly accommodations with modern amenities. Rooms are comfortable and well-equipped, and the hotel provides a convenient base for exploring Kings Cross and nearby attractions. Phone Number: +61 2 9356 1000

Holiday Inn Potts Point - Sydney (3 stars): Situated in Potts Point, Holiday Inn Potts Point offers comfortable rooms with modern amenities at affordable rates. The hotel features a rooftop swimming pool, a fitness center, and a restaurant serving Australian cuisine. Phone Number: +61 2 9368 4000

10. Barangaroo:

Luxury Hotels

Crown Towers Sydney (5 stars): Crown Towers Sydney is a luxurious hotel offering spacious rooms and suites with modern amenities and stunning views of Sydney Harbour. Guests can enjoy fine dining options, a spa, and exclusive access to Crown Sydney's restaurants and entertainment facilities. Phone Number: +61 2 8871 8888

The Langham Sydney (5 stars): Located in The Rocks area near Barangaroo, The Langham Sydney exudes timeless elegance with spacious rooms featuring plush furnishings and marble bathrooms. The hotel offers a day spa, indoor pool, and dining options showcasing innovative cuisine. Phone Number: +61 2 9256 2222

Boutique Hotels

Ovolo 1888 Darling Harbour (4 stars): Ovolo 1888 Darling Harbour blends historic charm with contemporary design, offering boutique rooms with unique decor and modern amenities. The hotel features a rooftop terrace, free minibar, and complimentary social hour for guests. Phone Number: +61 2 8586 1888

The Darling Hotel (5 stars): Adjacent to The Star casino complex in Pyrmont, The Darling Hotel offers boutique luxury with spacious rooms, stylish decor, and views of the Sydney skyline. Guests can enjoy a rooftop pool, spa treatments, and fine dining experiences. Phone Number: +61 2 9777 9000

Budget-Friendly Hotels

ibis Sydney Darling Harbour (3 stars): Situated near Darling Harbour, ibis Sydney Darling Harbour offers affordable accommodations with comfortable rooms and convenient amenities. The hotel provides easy access to attractions like the Sydney Aquarium and dining options in Darling Harbour. Phone Number: +61 2 9563 0888

Metro Aspire Hotel Sydney (3 stars): Located in Ultimo near Darling Harbour, Metro Aspire Hotel Sydney offers budget-friendly rooms with modern furnishings and essential amenities. The hotel is close to public transport, making it convenient for exploring Sydney's attractions. Phone Number: +61 2 9211 1499

Chapter 8: Cultural Experiences

Art Galleries and Museums in Sydney

Art Gallery of New South Wales

The Art Gallery of New South Wales, located on Art Gallery Rd in The Domain, Sydney, is renowned for its extensive collection of Australian, European, and Asian art. Open daily with extended hours on Wednesdays, it offers free general entry with occasional ticketed exhibitions. Easily accessible from Circular Quay by bus or a short walk, the gallery features permanent exhibits like the Aboriginal and Torres Strait Islander art collection and hosts Art After Hours events weekly. Its picturesque setting and diverse art offerings make it a must-visit for both locals and tourists seeking cultural enrichment in Sydney.

- **Located:** Art Gallery Rd, The Domain NSW 2000
- **Opening Hours:** Daily 10 AM - 5 PM (Wednesdays until 10 PM)
- **Getting There:** Bus routes 311, 324, 325, or a 15-minute walk from Circular Quay
- **Admission:** Free for general entry; special exhibitions may have fees
- **Insider Tip:** Visit on Wednesdays for Art After Hours events; explore the Aboriginal and Torres Strait Islander art collection.

Museum of Contemporary Art Australia (MCA)

The Museum of Contemporary Art Australia (MCA), situated at 140 George St in The Rocks, Sydney, showcases contemporary art from Australia and around the world. Open daily with late hours on Thursdays, entry is free, though special exhibitions may require tickets. Accessible by ferry to Circular Quay or nearby buses, it's known for its innovative exhibitions, artist talks, and workshops. Visitors can enjoy panoramic views from the rooftop café and participate in guided tours exploring modern artistic expressions. The MCA's dynamic programming and prime location by Sydney Harbour make it a vibrant hub for contemporary art enthusiasts.

- **Located:** 140 George St, The Rocks NSW 2000
- **Opening Hours:** Daily 10 AM - 5 PM (Thursdays until 9 PM)
- **Getting There:** Ferry to Circular Quay or buses to nearby stops; 10-minute walk from Circular Quay
- **Admission:** Free for general entry; some exhibitions may require tickets
- **Insider Tip:** Enjoy the rooftop café with stunning views of Sydney Harbour; check out the regular guided tours and talks.

Australian Museum

The Australian Museum, located at 1 William St, Sydney NSW 2010, is a premier institution showcasing natural history and cultural heritage. It offers extensive exhibitions on Australian biodiversity, with highlights including interactive dinosaur displays and Indigenous Australia galleries. The museum's collections span anthropology, geology, and marine biology, featuring rare specimens and immersive learning experiences. Visitors can explore diverse ecosystems, participate in educational programs, and engage with ongoing research initiatives, making it a valuable resource for both education and conservation awareness.

- **Located:** 1 William St, Sydney NSW 2010
- **Opening Hours:** Daily 9:30 AM - 5 PM
- **Getting There:** Train to Museum Station or buses to nearby stops
- **Admission:** General entry fees apply; discounts for children and concessions
- **Insider Tip:** Don't miss the Dinosaurs exhibition; explore Indigenous Australia and Pacific culture exhibits.

Powerhouse Museum

The Powerhouse Museum, situated at 500 Harris St, Ultimo NSW 2007, is renowned for its innovative exhibitions in science, technology, design, and history.

It houses a vast collection ranging from interactive displays on space exploration to iconic Australian inventions. The museum offers engaging experiences for all ages, including hands-on workshops, live demonstrations, and rotating exhibitions that explore themes like transportation, communication, and sustainability.

- **Located:** 500 Harris St, Ultimo NSW 2007
- **Opening Hours:** Daily 10 AM - 5 PM
- **Getting There:** Light rail to Exhibition Centre or buses to nearby stops
- **Admission Fee:** General admission: Adults $15, Children (4-16 years) $8, Family (2 adults + 2 children) $38. Concessions available.
- **Insider Tip:** Explore The Wiggles exhibition for a family-friendly experience or attend one of the museum's themed nights with live music and special access to exhibitions.

Hyde Park Barracks Museum

A UNESCO World Heritage site, the Hyde Park Barracks Museum explores the history of convict transportation and the early days of Sydney's settlement. It features exhibitions on convict life, archaeological finds, and historical artifacts.

- **Opening Hours:** Daily 10:00 AM - 5:00 PM.
- **How to Get There:** Located in Hyde Park near Sydney's CBD. Accessible from St James or Museum train stations.
- **Admission Fee:** General admission for adults is AUD 15.

- **Insider Tip:** Join a guided tour for in-depth insights into convict history. The museum's cafe offers a tranquil setting amidst Hyde Park.

Australian National Maritime Museum

The Australian National Maritime Museum, located at 2 Murray St, Darling Harbour NSW 2000, celebrates Australia's maritime heritage and culture. Situated on Sydney's waterfront, it features extensive exhibitions on naval history, exploration, and maritime technology. Highlights include historic vessels such as HMAS Vampire and HMB Endeavour replica, interactive displays on maritime archaeology, and rotating exhibitions on contemporary maritime issues. The museum offers educational programs, guided tours, and special events, making it an immersive experience for visitors of all ages. Easily accessible by ferry, train, or bus, it's a prominent cultural destination that combines history, science, and adventure on the water.

- **Opening Hours:** Daily 9:30 AM - 5:00 PM.
- **How to Get There:** Located in Darling Harbour near Pyrmont. Accessible from Darling Harbour ferry wharf and a short walk from Town Hall or Wynyard train stations.
- **Admission Fee:** General admission for adults is AUD 32, including access to exhibitions and historic vessels.

- **Insider Tip:** Check the museum's website for special events, such as boat tours and live demonstrations aboard historic ships. Don't miss the outdoor playground and submarine tour for family-friendly activities.

Justice and Police Museum

The Justice and Police Museum, located at Corner Albert and Phillip Streets, Sydney NSW 2000, offers a unique glimpse into Australia's law enforcement and judicial history. Housed in a historic building, it features exhibits on crime, policing, and the justice system. Visitors can explore original holding cells, learn about famous cases, and view forensic artifacts. The museum's collection includes photographs, documents, and personal stories that highlight Sydney's criminal past and the evolution of law enforcement methods. Guided tours provide deeper insights into crime and punishment throughout history, making it a captivating destination for those interested in legal and social history.

- **Opening Hours:** Weekends only, 10:00 AM - 5:00 PM.
- **How to Get There:** Located in Circular Quay near The Rocks. Accessible from Circular Quay train station and ferry terminals.
- **Admission Fee:** General admission for adults is AUD 15.

- **Insider Tip:** Join guided tours for behind-the-scenes access to historical exhibits. Photography enthusiasts will enjoy capturing the atmospheric interiors and exhibits.

The Rocks Discovery Museum

The Rocks Discovery Museum, located at Kendall Lane, The Rocks NSW 2000, is a fascinating cultural hub showcasing the history and development of Sydney's iconic Rocks area. Housed in a restored 1850s sandstone building, the museum features interactive displays, artifacts, and multimedia presentations. Visitors can explore the area's Aboriginal heritage, colonial past, and evolution into a vibrant urban precinct. Highlights include archaeological finds, convict history exhibits, and stories of early settlers and contemporary residents. The museum offers free entry and is conveniently located near Circular Quay, making it an accessible and enriching experience for tourists and locals interested in Sydney's heritage.

- **Opening Hours:** Daily 10:00 AM - 5:00 PM.
- **How to Get There:** Located in The Rocks near Circular Quay. Accessible from Circular Quay train station and a short walk from Sydney CBD.
- **Insider Tip:** Visit the museum's terrace for panoramic views of Sydney Harbour. Combine your visit with a walking tour of The Rocks for a comprehensive historical experience.

Nicholson Museum

The Nicholson Museum, located at Quadrangle A14, The University of Sydney NSW 2006, is Australia's oldest university museum dedicated to antiquities. Founded in 1860, it houses a significant collection of artifacts from ancient Egypt, Greece, Rome, and the Near East. Visitors can explore a diverse array of archaeological treasures, including sculptures, pottery, and mummies, providing insights into ancient civilizations and their cultural achievements. The museum offers educational programs, research opportunities, and public lectures, making it a valuable resource for students, scholars, and enthusiasts of archaeology and classical studies.

- **Located:** Quadrangle A14, The University of Sydney NSW 2006
- **Opening Hours:** Mon-Fri 10 AM - 4 PM
- **Getting There:** Bus to Parramatta Rd or a short walk from Redfern Station
- **Admission:** Free
- **Insider Tip:** Australia's oldest university museum; features an extensive collection of antiquities from Egypt, Greece, and Rome.

White Rabbit Gallery

The White Rabbit Gallery, located at 30 Balfour St, Chippendale NSW 2008, stands out as a contemporary art space dedicated to showcasing Chinese contemporary art. Founded by Judith Neilson, it features a rotating collection of artworks that reflect diverse themes, techniques, and socio-political narratives from China's vibrant contemporary art scene. The gallery's exhibitions range from multimedia installations to traditional Chinese brush painting, providing a comprehensive view of modern Chinese artistic expressions. Visitors can also enjoy the tranquil tea house within the gallery, adding a cultural dimension to their experience. Entry is free, making it accessible to all art enthusiasts and curious visitors alike.

- **Located:** 30 Balfour St, Chippendale NSW 2008
- **Opening Hours:** Wed-Sun 10 AM - 5 PM
- **Getting There:** Short walk from Central Station; buses are also available
- **Admission:** Free
- **Insider Tip:** Focus on contemporary Chinese art; visit the tea house for a cultural experience.

Sydney Jewish Museum

The Sydney Jewish Museum, located at 148 Darlinghurst Rd, Darlinghurst NSW 2010, is a significant institution dedicated to preserving and educating about Jewish history, culture, and the Holocaust. Housed in a restored synagogue, the museum offers poignant exhibitions that chronicle Jewish life in Australia, the impact of the Holocaust, and contemporary Jewish identity. Visitors can explore artifacts, personal stories, and interactive displays that highlight resilience, remembrance, and human rights. The museum also hosts educational programs, guided tours, and special events, fostering understanding and dialogue about tolerance and diversity. It's a profound and educational experience for all who visit.

- **Opening Hours:** Sunday to Thursday, 10:00 AM - 4:00 PM; Friday, 10:00 AM - 2:00 PM (Closed on Jewish holidays).
- **How to Get There:** Located in Darlinghurst near Central Station. Accessible by bus or train from Sydney CBD.
- **Admission Fee:** General admission for adults is AUD 15.
- **Insider Tip:** Join guided tours to gain a deeper understanding of the museum's collections and personal narratives. The museum's gift shop offers books, jewelry, and crafts related to Jewish culture.

Macleay Museum

The Macleay Museum, located at Science Rd, The University of Sydney NSW 2006, is a hidden gem showcasing natural history and anthropology collections. Established in 1887, it houses a diverse array of specimens, artifacts, and cultural objects, including scientific instruments, Aboriginal tools, and fossils. The museum's exhibits explore evolutionary biology, Pacific cultures, and historical scientific discoveries. Visitors can engage with interactive displays, attend lectures, and participate in research activities. The museum's historic building and curated collections offer a unique opportunity to delve into the intersections of science, culture, and exploration, making it a valuable educational resource and cultural destination in Sydney.

- **Opening Hours:** Monday to Friday, 10:00 AM - 4:30 PM.
- **How to Get There:** Located on the university campus in Camperdown. Accessible by bus from Central Station or Newtown.
- **Insider Tip:** Visit the museum's special exhibitions and public lectures on natural history and anthropology. The museum's staff are knowledgeable and happy to share insights into the collections.

Susannah Place Museum

Susannah Place Museum, situated at 58-64 Gloucester St, The Rocks NSW 2000, provides a rare glimpse into the lives of working-class families in Sydney during the 19th and 20th centuries. Consisting of four terraced houses, the museum preserves the living conditions and daily experiences of its former residents through authentic period settings and artifacts. Visitors can explore furnished rooms, kitchens, and backyard privies, gaining insights into urban working-class life, immigration, and community dynamics. Guided tours offer deeper historical context, highlighting the resilience and diversity of Sydney's early settlers. The museum is a captivating window into Sydney's social history and architectural heritage.

- **Opening Hours:** Thursday to Sunday, 10:00 AM - 4:00 PM.
- **How to Get There:** Located in The Rocks near Circular Quay. Accessible by train or ferry to Circular Quay Station.
- **Admission Fee:** General admission for adults is AUD 12.
- **Insider Tip:** Join guided tours for detailed stories about the families who lived in Susannah Place. The museum also offers evening tours and special events, providing a unique perspective on Sydney's history after dark.

Brett Whiteley Studio

The Brett Whiteley Studio, located at 2 Raper Street, Surry Hills NSW 2010, is a preserved workspace and gallery dedicated to the renowned Australian artist Brett Whiteley (1939-1992). This intimate studio offers visitors a unique insight into Whiteley's creative process and personal life, surrounded by his artworks, easels, and personal belongings. The space itself, a converted warehouse, reflects Whiteley's eclectic style and artistic experimentation. Open to the public on weekends, the studio provides a contemplative environment to appreciate Whiteley's works spanning painting, sculpture, and prints, offering a poignant experience for art enthusiasts and those curious about Australian contemporary art history.

- **Opening Hours:** Friday to Sunday, 10:00 AM - 4:00 PM.
- **How to Get There:** Located in Surry Hills near Museum Station. Accessible by train or bus from Sydney CBD.
- **Admission Fee:** General admission for adults is AUD 10.
- **Insider Tip:** Visit during quieter times for a more intimate experience with Whiteley's artworks and personal memorabilia. The studio's rooftop offers views of Surry Hills and is a favorite spot for photography enthusiasts.

Museum of Sydney

The Museum of Sydney, located at the corner of Bridge and Phillip Streets, Sydney NSW 2000, offers a captivating journey through the city's history, from its Aboriginal beginnings to modern times. Built on the site of the First Government House, the museum showcases archaeological remains, multimedia exhibits, and interactive displays that explore Sydney's evolution and cultural diversity. Highlights include exhibitions on colonial life, architecture, and significant events that shaped the city. Visitors can enjoy guided tours, educational programs, and temporary exhibitions that delve into various aspects of Sydney's social, political, and architectural heritage, making it a must-visit for both locals and tourists alike.

- **Located:** Corner of Bridge and Phillip Streets, Sydney NSW 2000
- **Opening Hours:** Daily 10 AM - 5 PM
- **Getting There:** Train to Circular Quay or buses to nearby stops
- **Admission:** General entry fees apply; discounts for children and concessions
- **Insider Tip:** Learn about Sydney's history and architecture; visit the courtyard's Edge of the Trees sculpture.

Customs House

Customs House, located at 31 Alfred St, Circular Quay NSW 2000, is a historic building with a modern twist, serving as a cultural and architectural landmark in Sydney. Originally built in the 19th century, it now houses the City of Sydney Library and features contemporary exhibition spaces and event venues. Visitors can enjoy art, design, and history exhibitions, along with digital art installations in the foyer. The building's rooftop offers panoramic views of Sydney Harbour, making it a popular spot for events and gatherings. Customs House is easily accessible by ferry and public transport, welcoming locals and tourists to explore its cultural offerings.

- **Located:** 31 Alfred St, Circular Quay NSW 2000
- **Opening Hours:** Mon-Fri 8 AM - 8 PM, Sat-Sun 10 AM - 8 PM
- **Getting There:** Ferry to Circular Quay or buses to nearby stops
- **Admission:** Free
- **Insider Tip:** Visit the City of Sydney Library on the top floor; enjoy the digital artwork projections in the foyer.

Australian Centre for Photography (ACP

The Australian Centre for Photography (ACP), located at 72 Oxford St, Darlinghurst NSW 2010, is a leading institution dedicated to photography as a contemporary art form. Established in 1974, it hosts a dynamic program of exhibitions, workshops, and events that explore photography's cultural significance and evolving practices. The ACP showcases works by emerging and established photographers, fostering critical dialogue and artistic innovation. Visitors can engage with diverse photographic genres, from documentary to experimental, through curated exhibitions and public programs. The center also offers educational courses and artist residencies, contributing to the cultural landscape of Sydney as a hub for visual arts and photography enthusiasts.

- **Opening Hours:** Wednesday to Sunday, 10:00 AM - 5:00 PM.
- **How to Get There:** Situated in Paddington, accessible by bus from Sydney CBD or Bondi Junction.
- **Insider Tip:** Attend artist talks and photography workshops offered regularly. The ACP Bookshop offers a wide selection of photography books and prints for enthusiasts and collectors.

Theaters and Performing Arts

Sydney's theater and performing arts scene is vibrant and diverse, offering everything from world-class productions to intimate performances. Here's a detailed look at some of the key venues and performing arts organizations in the city:

1. Sydney Opera House

An iconic symbol of Sydney, the Sydney Opera House is renowned for its striking sail-like design and its world-class performances. It hosts a wide array of events including opera, ballet, theater, and concerts. With several performance spaces, the Opera House caters to various artistic expressions. The Joan Sutherland Theatre, the Drama Theatre, and the Forecourt are among the key venues within this cultural landmark.

Location: Bennelong Point, Sydney NSW 2000

Notable Programs: The Opera House presents productions from Opera Australia, The Australian Ballet, and Sydney Theatre Company, as well as a range of international performances and festivals.

2. Sydney Theatre Company (STC)

STC is one of Australia's leading theater companies, known for its bold and diverse programming. It operates from The Wharf, a converted industrial space on Sydney's waterfront. STC's productions range from classic plays to contemporary works and new Australian writing.

Location: The Wharf, Pier 4/5, Hickson Road, Walsh Bay, Sydney NSW 2000

Notable Programs: STC frequently collaborates with renowned playwrights and directors, and its season often includes Australian premiers and innovative adaptations.

3. Belvoir St Theatre

Belvoir St Theatre is celebrated for its commitment to new Australian work and reimagining classic texts. Located in a historic building, the theater is known for its intimate setting and bold productions.

Location: 25 Belvoir Street, Surry Hills, Sydney NSW 2010

Notable Programs: The theater's productions often explore social and cultural issues, with a focus on innovative storytelling and dynamic performances.

4. The Seymour Centre

The Seymour Centre is a hub for performing arts, hosting theater, music, dance, and comedy. It serves as a venue for both emerging and established artists. The center includes multiple performance spaces such as the Seymour Theatre, the Everest Theatre, and the Studio.

Location: Corner of City Road and Cleveland Street, Chippendale, Sydney NSW 2008

Notable Programs: The Seymour Centre often features productions from independent theater companies, as well as major festivals and cultural events.

5. Hayes Theatre Co

Hayes Theatre Co. specializes in musicals and contemporary theater, with a focus on high-quality, intimate productions. The venue offers an up-close experience with a capacity of around 200 seats, creating an immersive theatrical experience.

Location: 19 Greenknowe Avenue, Potts Point, Sydney NSW 2011

Notable Programs: Known for its innovative musicals and popular theatrical productions, Hayes Theatre Co frequently showcases Australian talent and new works.

6. The Ensemble Theatre

The Ensemble Theatre is one of Australia's oldest professional theater companies, with a reputation for presenting engaging and thought-provoking plays. Located with a view of Sydney Harbour, the theater offers a cozy and personal environment.

Location: 78 McDougall Street, Kirribilli, Sydney NSW 2061

Notable Programs: The Ensemble Theatre's programming includes a mix of classic plays, contemporary dramas, and comedies, often featuring established Australian actors and playwrights.

7. Dance and Physical Theater

Sydney Dance Company:

Overview: One of Australia's premier contemporary dance companies, Sydney Dance Company presents innovative performances and regularly collaborates with international choreographers.

Location: Pier 4, 15 Hickson Road, Walsh Bay, Sydney NSW 2000

Force Majeure:

Known for its interdisciplinary approach, Force Majeure combines theater with physical performance to explore contemporary themes and experiences.

Location: Various venues

8. Festivals and Events

Sydney Festival: Held annually in January, this festival showcases a wide range of performing arts, including theater, dance, music, and circus. It features both local and international artists, offering a rich array of performances across the city.

Sydney Writers' Festival: A major literary event that includes readings, discussions, and performances, often featuring theater adaptations of literary works.

9. Community and Independent Theater

Old Fitz Theatre: Located in Woolloomooloo, this venue is known for its intimate performances and focus on new and emerging playwrights.

Riverside Theatres: Situated in Parramatta, Riverside Theatres offers a range of performances including drama, comedy, and musical theater, serving the broader Sydney community.

Local Festivals and Events

Sydney, Australia, is renowned for its vibrant festivals and events that showcase the city's diverse culture and creativity. Here's a guide to the 10 best local festivals and events you should consider experiencing in Sydney:

1. Sydney New Year's Eve – When: December 31 – January 1

Sydney's New Year's Eve celebrations are world-famous for their spectacular fireworks display over Sydney Harbour. The event includes a range of activities, from family-friendly events in various parks to the glittering main fireworks display at midnight. The celebration also features live music, performances, and food stalls, making it a lively and festive occasion for all ages.

Tips: Arrive early to secure a good viewing spot, as prime locations fill up quickly. Consider booking a spot at a waterfront restaurant or cruise for a more exclusive experience.

2. Sydney Festival – When: January

The Sydney Festival is a major annual arts festival that transforms the city with performances, art installations, and cultural activities.

It features a diverse lineup of music, dance, theater, and visual arts, with both free and ticketed events. Highlights include open-air concerts, international acts, and local talent.

Tips: Check the festival's program in advance and book tickets early for popular shows. Many events are held in various locations across the city, so plan your itinerary to make the most of the festival.

3. Mardi Gras – When: February/March

Sydney's Mardi Gras is one of the world's largest and most vibrant LGBTQ+ pride festivals. The event features a colorful parade through the streets of Oxford and Flinders, showcasing flamboyant floats, costumes, and performances. The festival also includes parties, film screenings, and discussions on LGBTQ+ issues.

Tips: The parade route gets crowded, so arrive early to find a good viewing spot. Tickets for after-parties and events can sell out quickly, so secure them in advance.

4. Vivid Sydney – When: May – June

Vivid Sydney is a spectacular light, music, and ideas festival that illuminates the city's landmarks with stunning light installations and projections. The event also includes musical performances and thought-provoking talks. Key highlights are the light displays on the Sydney Opera House and Harbour Bridge.

Tips: Wear comfortable shoes for walking, as the event spans several areas of the city. Visiting during weekdays can help avoid weekend crowds.

5. Sydney Film Festival – When: June

The Sydney Film Festival is an annual event that showcases a wide range of films from around the world, including feature films, documentaries, and short films. The festival is known for its high-quality screenings and special guest appearances from filmmakers and actors.

Tips: Review the festival program ahead of time and book tickets early, especially for popular screenings. Consider attending some of the Q&A sessions with filmmakers for deeper insights into the films.

6. Australian Open Water Swimming Championships – When: February

Held at Bondi Beach, this event attracts top swimmers and enthusiasts from across the globe to compete in open-water swimming races. The competition includes a range of distances and categories, and spectators can enjoy the lively atmosphere and beachside activities.

Tips: Arrive early to get a good view of the swimming area and explore the beach. Check the event schedule to catch the races you're interested in.

7. Royal Easter Show – When: April

The Royal Easter Show is a traditional agricultural fair held at Sydney Olympic Park. It features livestock exhibits, carnival rides, food stalls, and live entertainment. The event celebrates Australian rural life and agriculture with activities for all ages, including animal shows and interactive exhibits.

Tips: Purchase tickets online to avoid long lines at the entrance. Wear comfortable clothing and prepare for a day of walking and exploring.

8. Sydney International Food Festival – When: October

The Sydney International Food Festival is a gastronomic event that highlights Sydney's diverse culinary scene. It includes food stalls, cooking demonstrations, and special events hosted by renowned chefs. The festival is a great opportunity to sample a wide variety of cuisines from around the world. Tips: Check the festival schedule for special events and book tickets in advance for any exclusive dinners or workshops. Bring an appetite and be prepared to explore different food options.

9. Sydney Writers' Festival – When: May

The Sydney Writers' Festival is a major literary event that brings together authors, poets, and thinkers from around the world.

It features author talks, panel discussions, and book signings. The festival offers a platform for engaging with contemporary literature and exploring new ideas.

Tips: Review the program and book tickets for popular sessions in advance. Attend some of the free events and book launches to discover new authors and books.

10. Sculpture by the Sea – When: October – November

Sculpture by the Sea is an outdoor exhibition held along the Bondi to Tamarama coastal walk. The event features a diverse range of sculptures by local and international artists, set against the stunning backdrop of the Sydney coastline. It's a unique opportunity to enjoy art and nature simultaneously. Tips: Wear comfortable walking shoes and check the weather forecast, as the event is outdoors. Visiting early in the morning or later in the afternoon can help avoid crowds and provide better lighting for viewing the sculptures.

General Tips:

Public Transport: Use Sydney's public transport system, including trains, buses, and ferries, to navigate the city and reach festival locations.

Accommodation: Book your accommodation well in advance, especially during peak festival times, to secure the best rates and locations.

Weather: Sydney's weather can vary, so check forecasts and dress accordingly for outdoor events.

Aboriginal Culture and Tours

Sydney, with its rich tapestry of modernity and history, is also home to one of Australia's oldest cultures—its Aboriginal heritage. For those interested in exploring this deep and vibrant culture, Sydney offers a range of immersive tours and experiences that provide insight into the traditions, stories, and connections to the land of its First Nations peoples.

1. Sydney Aboriginal Tours

Aboriginal Heritage Tour

This tour offers a deep dive into the history and culture of Sydney's Aboriginal people. Guided by Indigenous experts, participants gain firsthand knowledge of traditional practices, Dreamtime stories, and the spiritual connection between the land and its people.

Highlights: Visit significant sites like The Rocks, where you can learn about pre-colonial Sydney and its Indigenous inhabitants. The tour includes demonstrations of traditional art, music, and dance.

Duration: 3-4 hours

Contact: Aboriginal Heritage Tours, website

Koori Tours

Overview: Specializing in the cultural and historical narratives of the Koori people, these tours offer a personalized experience led by local Aboriginal guides.

Highlights: Experience a walk through the Botany Bay area, where Captain Cook first landed, but also hear about its significance to the Aboriginal people. Engage in activities such as traditional tool-making and storytelling sessions.

Duration: Half-day or full-day options

Contact: Koori Tours, website

2. Aboriginal Cultural Experiences

Barangaroo Reserve

Located on the western edge of Sydney's Central Business District, Barangaroo Reserve offers a unique opportunity to explore the rich Aboriginal heritage of the area. This cultural space is named after Barangaroo, a significant Cammeraygal woman who played a key role in early colonial history.

Highlights: The reserve features a cultural walk showcasing traditional rock carvings and significant sites. The Barangaroo Pavilion hosts exhibitions and events related to Aboriginal culture.

Duration: Self-guided or guided tours available

Location: Barangaroo Avenue, Barangaroo, Sydney

Contact: Barangaroo Reserve, website

The Royal Botanic Garden

This garden offers a variety of tours and workshops that delve into Aboriginal uses of plants, traditional bush foods, and medicine.

Highlights: Participate in guided walks that explain the significance of different plants to Aboriginal culture and learn about traditional techniques for using them.

Duration: 1-2 hours

Location: Mrs Macquaries Road, Sydney

Contact: The Royal Botanic Garden, website

3. Indigenous Art and Crafts

Art Galleries

Sydney is home to several galleries that showcase Aboriginal art, providing insights into the diverse artistic expressions of Indigenous Australians.

Highlights: The Art Gallery of New South Wales frequently features exhibitions of Aboriginal and Torres Strait Islander art. Another notable venue is the National Aboriginal Design Agency Gallery.

Duration: Variable, depending on exhibitions

Contact: Art Gallery of New South Wales, website

Galleries and Shops

For those interested in purchasing authentic Aboriginal art and crafts, local galleries and shops offer a range of traditional and contemporary pieces.

Highlights: Visit galleries such as the Gallery of Aboriginal Art or Koori Heritage Trust Shop for unique artworks and handcrafted items.

4. Cultural Workshops and Events

Cultural Workshops

Participate in workshops that focus on traditional Aboriginal skills such as dot painting, basket weaving, or didgeridoo playing.

Highlights: These workshops are often held in cultural centers or community spaces and are a great way to gain hands-on experience in Aboriginal art and traditions.

Duration: 1-3 hours

Contact: Cultural Workshops Sydney, website

Festivals and Events

Sydney hosts various cultural events throughout the year celebrating Aboriginal culture. Events like NAIDOC Week offer a rich program of activities, including performances, art exhibitions, and community gatherings.

Highlights: Check out events listings for seasonal festivals and community celebrations to experience live music, dance, and storytelling.

Contact: NAIDOC Week Sydney, website

Architectural and Historical Walking Tours

1. Sydney Architecture Walk

The Sydney Architecture Walk is a captivating journey through the city's architectural evolution, blending historical and modern design. Starting from Circular Quay, this tour takes you through the iconic buildings of Sydney, including the Sydney Opera House and the Sydney Harbour Bridge. As you explore, you'll learn about the city's architectural heritage, from colonial structures to contemporary marvels. The tour often includes insights into the design philosophies of renowned architects and the stories behind Sydney's landmark buildings.

- **Location/Meeting Point:** Circular Quay, near the Sydney Opera House
- **Highlights:** Sydney Opera House, Sydney Harbour Bridge, Customs House, The Rocks
- **Tour Providers:** Walks 101
- **Duration:** 2.5 hours
- **Contact Info:** +61 2 9265 1234, www.walks101.com

2. The Rocks Historical Walking Tour

This immersive tour delves into the rich history of The Rocks, Sydney's oldest neighborhood.

Starting at the historic Cadman's Cottage, the tour explores the cobblestone streets and early colonial buildings that tell the story of Sydney's beginnings. Highlights include the historic pubs, old warehouses, and the bustling markets that have shaped the area. Guides share fascinating anecdotes about convicts, settlers, and early Sydney life, providing a deep understanding of The Rocks' historical significance.

- **Location/Meeting Point:** Cadman's Cottage, 110 George Street, The Rocks
- **Highlights:** Cadman's Cottage, The Rocks Markets, The Argyle Cut, Old Colonial Buildings
- **Tour Providers:** Sydney Historical Tours
- **Duration:** 2 hours
- **Contact Info:** +61 2 9252 2727, www.sydneyhistoricaltours.com

3. Sydney Heritage Walk

The Sydney Heritage Walk offers an in-depth exploration of Sydney's historical landmarks and hidden gems. Starting at Town Hall, the tour weaves through the city's vibrant past, visiting landmarks such as the State Library of New South Wales and Hyde Park Barracks. The walk emphasizes colonial and early 20th-century architecture and includes insights into Sydney's development over the centuries. Expect to discover lesser-known historical sites that reveal the rich tapestry of Sydney's heritage.

- **Location/Meeting Point:** Sydney Town Hall, George Street
- **Highlights:** State Library of New South Wales, Hyde Park Barracks, St. Mary's Cathedral
- **Tour Providers:** Sydney Walking Tours
- **Duration:** 3 hours
- **Contact Info:** +61 2 9267 4699, www.sydneywalkingtours.com

4. Art Deco Sydney Walking Tour

Discover Sydney's Art Deco heritage on this specialized walking tour that highlights the city's most stunning Art Deco buildings. Starting from the iconic Sydney Town Hall, this tour guides you through the architectural splendor of the 1920s and 1930s. Key buildings include the Strand Arcade and the State Theatre. The tour provides a comprehensive look at Art Deco design elements, including geometric shapes, bold colors, and intricate detailing, offering a unique perspective on Sydney's architectural evolution.

- **Location/Meeting Point:** Sydney Town Hall, George Street
- **Highlights:** Sydney Town Hall, Strand Arcade, State Theatre, Chifley Tower
- **Tour Providers:** Deco Walks Sydney
- **Duration:** 2.5 hours
- **Contact Info:** +61 2 9221 0303, www.decowalkssydney.com

5. Sydney Convict Trail Walking Tour

The Sydney Convict Trail Walking Tour offers an engaging exploration of Sydney's convict past. Starting at the Australian National Maritime Museum, the tour takes you through significant convict sites, including the historic sites of The Rocks and Circular Quay. The tour highlights the experiences of early convicts and the impact of their labor on Sydney's development. Historical insights and storytelling provide a vivid picture of life in early Sydney, making it a compelling experience for history enthusiasts.

- **Location/Meeting Point:** Australian National Maritime Museum, Darling Harbour
- **Highlights:** The Rocks, Circular Quay, Hyde Park Barracks, Australian National Maritime Museum
- **Tour Providers:** Convict Heritage Tours
- **Duration:** 3 hours
- **Contact Info:** +61 2 9217 0111, www.convictheritagetours.com

6. Sydney Colonial Buildings Tour

This tour focuses on the architectural and historical significance of Sydney's colonial-era buildings. Starting at Macquarie Street, the tour explores important sites such as the First Government House, the Sydney Hospital, and St. James Church. It delves into the early settlement period, examining the architectural styles and the stories of the figures who influenced Sydney's early development. The tour offers a fascinating glimpse into the colonial past and its architectural legacy.

- **Location/Meeting Point:** Macquarie Street, near the Sydney Hospital
- **Highlights:** First Government House, Sydney Hospital, St. James Church, Hyde Park Barracks
- **Tour Providers:** Colonial Architecture Sydney
- **Duration:** 2 hours
- **Contact Info:** +61 2 9265 1256, www.colonialarchitecturesydney.com

7. Sydney Modernist Architecture Tour

The Sydney Modernist Architecture Tour provides a deep dive into the city's mid-20th-century architectural styles. Starting at the University of Sydney, the tour highlights buildings that exemplify the modernist movement, such as the Sirius Building and the Australian Museum. This tour explores the design principles of modernism, including functionalism and simplicity, and how they influenced Sydney's urban landscape during the post-war period.

- **Location/Meeting Point:** University of Sydney, Camperdown
- **Highlights:** Sirius Building, Australian Museum, University of Sydney Architecture, Sydney Town Hall
- **Tour Providers:** Modern Sydney Tours
- **Duration:** 2.5 hours
- **Contact Info:** +61 2 9518 4444, www.modernsydneytours.com

8. Sydney Harbour Historical Walk

This tour offers a unique perspective on Sydney's history by focusing on the development of the Harbour area. Starting at Circular Quay, the tour explores the historical evolution of Sydney's waterfront, including significant sites like Bennelong Point and the former docks. The tour provides insights into Sydney's maritime history and the role of the Harbour in shaping the city's growth and cultural identity.

- **Location/Meeting Point:** Circular Quay, near the Sydney Opera House
- **Highlights:** Bennelong Point, Sydney Harbour Bridge, The Rocks, Circular Quay
- **Tour Providers:** Harbour History Tours
- **Duration:** 2 hours
- **Contact Info:** +61 2 9252 1234, www.harbourhistorytours.com

9. Sydney Gardens and Green Spaces Tour

Explore Sydney's lush gardens and green spaces on this relaxing walking tour. Starting at the Royal Botanic Garden, the tour guides you through some of the city's most beautiful parks and gardens, including Hyde Park and the Domain. Learn about the history of these green spaces, their role in Sydney's urban planning, and the diverse flora they support. It's a perfect blend of natural beauty and historical context.

- **Location/Meeting Point:** Royal Botanic Garden, Mrs Macquaries Road
- **Highlights:** Royal Botanic Garden, Hyde Park, The Domain, Parramatta Park
- **Tour Providers:** Sydney Garden Tours
- **Duration:** 2 hours
- **Contact Info:** +61 2 9262 1122, www.sydneygardentours.com

10. Sydney Historical Pub Crawl

Combining history with a touch of nightlife, the Sydney Historical Pub Crawl explores the city's oldest and most storied pubs. Starting at The Australian Hotel in The Rocks, the tour visits several historic pubs, each with its unique history and character. Along the way, guides share tales of Sydney's past and the role these establishments played in the city's social life.

- **Location/Meeting Point:** The Australian Hotel, 100 Cumberland Street, The Rocks
- **Highlights:** The Australian Hotel, The Hero of Waterloo, The Rocks Pub, The Glenmore Hotel
- **Tour Providers:** Sydney Pub Tours
- **Duration:** 3 hours
- **Contact Info:** +61 2 9279 7878, www.sydneypubtours.com

Chapter 9: Cuisine and Dining Choices

Overview of Local Cuisine

Sydney's cuisine is a vibrant and diverse reflection of the city's multicultural population and its coastal location. It blends traditional Australian fare with influences from around the globe, creating a unique gastronomic landscape. Here's an in-depth look at the elements that define Sydney's cuisine:

Seafood

Given its coastal location, Sydney boasts an abundance of fresh seafood. The city's fish markets, particularly the Sydney Fish Market, are some of the largest in the Southern Hemisphere, offering a wide variety of seafood including:

Sydney Rock Oysters: Known for their distinctive taste and creamy texture, these oysters are a local delicacy.

Barramundi: A versatile and popular fish in Australian cuisine, often grilled or pan-fried.

Balmain Bugs and Moreton Bay Bugs: These shellfish are often served grilled or as part of seafood platters.

King Prawns: Frequently featured in barbecues and seafood dishes.

Blue Swimmer Crabs and Lobsters: Enjoyed in both casual and fine dining settings, often served with rich sauces or as part of elaborate seafood spreads.

Modern Australian Cuisine

Modern Australian cuisine, or "Mod Oz," is characterized by its innovative use of local ingredients and multicultural influences. Some notable aspects include:

Fusion Dishes: Combining elements from Asian, European, and Middle Eastern cuisines. Examples include kangaroo steak with an Asian-style marinade or lamb with Mediterranean spices.

Native Ingredients: Increasingly popular are native Australian ingredients like bush tomatoes, lemon myrtle, finger limes, and warragal greens, often used to add unique flavors to contemporary dishes.

Multicultural Influence

Sydney's multicultural population brings a wealth of global flavors to the city's food scene:

Asian Cuisine: Chinatown and areas like Haymarket offer a plethora of Chinese, Japanese, Korean, Thai, and Vietnamese restaurants. Popular dishes include dumplings, sushi, pho, and pad them

Italian Cuisine: Norton Street in Leichhardt is known as Little Italy, offering authentic pasta, pizza, and gelato.

Middle Eastern Cuisine: Suburbs like Lakemba and Auburn feature Lebanese, Turkish, and Persian eateries, serving dishes like kebabs, falafel, and baklava.

Indian and Sri Lankan Cuisine: Areas like Harris Park have a significant South Asian presence with a variety of curry houses, dosa restaurants, and sweet shops.

Café Culture and Brunch

Sydney has a thriving café culture, heavily influenced by European traditions. Brunch is particularly popular, with cafes serving a variety of dishes such as:

Avocado Toast: Often enhanced with poached eggs, feta, and dukkha.

Smashed Peas and Ricotta: A twist on the classic toast topping.

Acai Bowls: Made with blended acai berries and topped with fresh fruit, granola, and seeds.

Flat Whites and Piccolos: Coffee culture in Sydney is robust, with a preference for these smooth espresso-based drinks.

Fine Dining

Sydney is home to numerous fine dining establishments that are frequently recognized on international platforms. Renowned restaurants include:

Quay: Known for its innovative dishes and stunning views of the Sydney Opera House and Harbor Bridge.

Bennelong: Located within the Sydney Opera House, offering modern Australian cuisine with a focus on premium local produce.

Tetsuya's: A fusion of Japanese and French techniques, with dishes that highlight the best of both culinary traditions.

Street Food and Casual Dining

Sydney's street food and casual dining scenes are vibrant and varied:

Food Trucks: Offering everything from gourmet burgers to Asian street food, these mobile eateries are popular at events and markets.

Markets: Sydney's various markets, such as the Glebe Markets and the Carriage works Farmers Market, provide a range of street food options including golem, bao buns, and artisanal baked goods.

Fish and Chips: A classic Australian casual meal, best enjoyed at beachside locations like Bondi or Manly.

Wine and Craft Beer

Sydney's beverage scene complements its diverse cuisine:

Wine: Australia's wine regions, such as the Hunter Valley just north of Sydney, supply a variety of wines that are featured prominently in local restaurants and wine bars.

Craft Beer: The craft beer movement has taken off in Sydney, with numerous breweries and taprooms offering locally brewed ales, lagers, and stouts. Notable breweries include Young Henrys and Batch Brewing Company.

Desserts and Sweets

Sydney's dessert scene is as varied as its savory offerings:

Pavlova: A meringue-based dessert with a crisp crust and soft, light inside, usually topped with whipped cream and fresh fruits.

Lamingtons: Sponge cakes coated in chocolate and rolled in coconut, sometimes with a layer of cream or jam in the middle.

Tim Tams: Iconic Australian chocolate biscuits are often used in the "Tim Tam Slam" ritual with hot beverages.

Must-Try Dishes

1. Sydney Rock Oysters

Sydney Rock Oysters are a delicacy native to Australia's east coast, known for their smooth, silky texture and rich, briny flavor. Often served freshly shucked on the half shell with a squeeze of lemon, these oysters are a quintessential Sydney seafood experience. Many top restaurants, such as Sydney Cove Oyster Bar and The Morrison, offer premium oysters sourced from pristine waters around Sydney.

- **Where to Try:** Sydney Cove Oyster Bar, The Morrison Bar & Oyster Room

2. Barramundi

Barramundi is a popular Australian fish known for its mild flavor and flaky texture. It is often grilled, pan-fried, or baked, and served with various accompaniments such as vegetables, lemon butter sauce, or tropical fruit salsa. The dish showcases the fresh seafood that is abundant in Sydney's coastal waters.

- **Where to Try:** The Boathouse on Blackwattle Bay, The Fish Shop

3. Meat Pie

The classic Australian meat pie is a hearty pastry filled with minced meat, gravy, and sometimes onions and mushrooms. This beloved comfort food is often enjoyed with tomato sauce and is a staple in Australian bakeries, cafes, and sporting events. The flaky crust and savory filling make it a perfect snack or meal.

- **Where to Try:** Harry's Cafe de Wheels, Bourke Street Bakery

4. Lamingtons

Lamingtons are quintessential Australian sponge cakes coated in chocolate sauce and rolled in desiccated coconut. Often filled with jam or cream, these sweet treats are enjoyed with a cup of tea or coffee. Lamingtons are a beloved part of Australian baking culture and can be found in many cafes and bakeries across Sydney.

- **Where to Try:** Flour and Stone, The Grounds of Alexandria

5. Pavlova

Named after the Russian ballerina Anna Pavlova, this iconic Australian dessert features a crisp meringue shell with a soft, marshmallow-like center, topped with fresh fruit and whipped cream. Pavlova is a light and refreshing dessert that showcases Australia's love for meringue-based sweets.

- **Where to Try:** The Tea Room QVB, Bills

6. Smashed Avocado on Toast

A popular breakfast or brunch dish, smashed avocado on toast is a simple yet delicious meal featuring a ripe avocado spread on toasted sourdough bread, often garnished with feta, cherry tomatoes, poached eggs, and a drizzle of olive oil. This dish is a favorite among Sydneysiders and can be found in many trendy cafes.

- **Where to Try:** Three Blue Ducks, The Grounds of Alexandria

7. Kangaroo

Kangaroo meat is lean, high in protein, and uniquely Australian. It is often served as a steak, burger, or in gourmet dishes, prepared medium-rare to retain its tenderness and flavor. Kangaroo dishes are usually paired with native herbs and spices, showcasing the unique flavors of Australian bush tucker.

- **Where to Try:** The Glenmore Hotel, The Meat & Wine Co.

8. Green Chicken Curry Pie

A fusion of Australian and Thai cuisine, the green chicken curry pie combines the flavors of Thai green curry with the comforting appeal of a traditional meat pie. Filled with tender chicken, green curry paste, coconut milk, and vegetables, this pie offers a spicy and aromatic twist on the classic.

- **Where to Try:** Bourke Street Bakery, Infinity Bakery

9. Pho

Reflecting Sydney's vibrant multicultural food scene, pho is a Vietnamese noodle soup consisting of a fragrant broth, rice noodles, herbs, and meat, typically beef or chicken. This aromatic dish is a staple in Sydney's Vietnamese restaurants and is enjoyed for its depth of flavor and comforting qualities.

- **Where to Try:** Pho PHD, Pho An

10. Cronut

A hybrid of a croissant and a donut, the cronut features flaky, buttery layers of croissant dough fried like a donut and often filled with cream or custard. This decadent pastry has gained popularity in Sydney's bakeries and patisseries, offering a unique and indulgent treat.

- **Where to Try:** Brewton Newtown, Black Star Pastry

Seafood Restaurants

Sydney's coastal location makes it an ideal city for seafood lovers. From upscale dining to casual eateries, here are some of the best seafood restaurants in Sydney

Quay Restaurant

Quay is one of Sydney's most celebrated restaurants, known for its innovative cuisine and stunning views of Sydney Harbor, the Opera House, and the Harbor Bridge. Executive Chef Peter Gilmore crafts dishes that highlight Australia's finest seafood, such as the exquisite mud crab congee and the delicate sashimi of sea scallops. The restaurant offers a sophisticated dining experience with a focus on fresh, high-quality ingredients.

- **Location:** Overseas Passenger Terminal, The Rocks, Sydney
- **Opening Hours:** Tuesday to Sunday: 12:00 PM - 2:00 PM (Lunch), 6:00 PM - 10:00 PM (Dinner)
- **Phone Number:** +61 2 9251 5600

Sydney Cove Oyster Bar

Situated on the waterfront at Circular Quay, Sydney Cove Oyster Bar is renowned for its fresh seafood, especially oysters. Guests can enjoy a variety of oyster preparations, from natural to Kilpatrick, along with other seafood delights like prawn cocktails and seafood platters. The open-air setting provides breathtaking views of the harbor, making it an ideal spot for leisurely dining.

- **Location:** Circular Quay East, Sydney
- **Opening Hours:** Monday to Sunday: 11:30 AM - 9:00 PM
- **Phone Number:** +61 2 9247 2937

The Boathouse on Blackwattle Bay

The Boathouse on Blackwattle Bay offers a unique dining experience with its rustic charm and spectacular views of the Anzac Bridge. Specializing in premium seafood, the restaurant is famous for its signature dish, the Snapper Pie. The menu features a range of fresh, sustainably sourced seafood, ensuring a memorable meal for every guest.

- **Location:** 123 Ferry Road, Glebe, Sydney
- **Opening Hours:** Monday to Saturday: 6:00 PM - 10:00 PM, Sunday: 12:00 PM - 3:00 PM (Lunch), 6:00 PM - 10:00 PM (Dinner)
- **Phone Number:** +61 2 9518 9011

Flying Fish

Located at The Star Sydney, Flying Fish offers a refined dining experience with an emphasis on contemporary seafood dishes. The menu, crafted by Executive Chef Peter Robertson, features innovative creations like kingfish sashimi and roasted barramundi, complemented by an extensive wine list. The stylish, nautical-themed decor enhances the overall dining experience.

- **Location:** The Star, 80 Pyrmont Street, Pyrmont, Sydney
- **Opening Hours:** Monday to Sunday: 12:00 PM - 2:30 PM (Lunch), 6:00 PM - 10:30 PM (Dinner)
- **Phone Number:** +61 2 9900 9898

Catalina

Perched on the edge of Rose Bay, Catalina offers stunning waterfront views and a menu that celebrates the best of Australian seafood. The restaurant is known for its impeccable service and dishes like blue swimmer crab salad and grilled Tasmanian salmon. The elegant setting makes it perfect for special occasions and leisurely lunches.

- **Location:** Lyne Park, Rose Bay, Sydney
- **Opening Hours:** Monday to Sunday: 12:00 PM - 10:00 PM
- **Phone Number:** +61 2 9371 0555

Bondi Icebergs Dining Room and Bar

Bondi Icebergs Dining Room and Bar is an iconic restaurant located above Bondi Beach, offering panoramic ocean views. The menu features fresh seafood with an Italian twist, such as lobster spaghetti and seared scallops. The relaxed yet stylish atmosphere makes it a popular spot for both locals and tourists.

- **Location:** 1 Notts Avenue, Bondi Beach, Sydney

- **Opening Hours:** Tuesday to Sunday: 12:00 PM - 10:00 PM
- **Phone Number:** +61 2 9365 9000

Manta Restaurant & Bar

Situated on Woolloomooloo Wharf, Manta Restaurant & Bar specializes in fresh, locally sourced seafood. The menu includes standout dishes like Sydney Rock oysters and grilled barramundi. The chic waterfront setting and exceptional service make it a prime spot for dining in Sydney.

- **Location:** 6 Cowper Wharf Roadway, Woolloomooloo, Sydney
- **Opening Hours:** Monday to Sunday: 12:00 PM - 3:00 PM (Lunch), 6:00 PM - 10:00 PM (Dinner)
- **Phone Number:** +61 2 9332 3822

Nick's Seafood Restaurant

Nick's Seafood Restaurant is located at Darling Harbor, renowned for its vibrant atmosphere and extensive seafood menu. Dishes include fresh lobster, prawns, and seafood platters perfect for sharing. The outdoor seating offers picturesque views of the harbor, making it an excellent choice for casual and celebratory meals alike.

- **Location:** The Promenade, Cockle Bay Wharf, Darling Harbor, Sydney
- **Opening Hours:** Monday to Sunday: 12:00 PM - 10:30 PM
- **Phone Number:** +61 2 9264 1212

Doyles on the Beach

Doyles on the Beach is a historic seafood restaurant located at Watsons Bay, known for its fresh seafood and stunning beachside views. Established in 1885, it offers classic dishes such as seafood chowder, fish and chips, and a variety of fresh shellfish. The relaxed, family-friendly atmosphere adds to its charm.

- **Location:** 11 Marine Parade, Watsons Bay, Sydney
- **Opening Hours:** Monday to Sunday: 12:00 PM - 3:00 PM (Lunch), 6:00 PM - 9:00 PM (Dinner)
- **Phone Number:** +61 2 9337 2007

Cirrus Dining

Cirrus Dining at Barangaroo specializes in contemporary seafood cuisine with a focus on sustainability. The menu, crafted by renowned chefs Brent Savage and Nick Hildebrandt, features dishes like kingfish sashimi, grilled octopus, and whole-baked snapper. The sleek, modern decor and waterfront views make it a top choice for seafood lovers.

- **Location:** 10/23 Barangaroo Avenue, Barangaroo, Sydney
- **Opening Hours:** Monday to Sunday: 12:00 PM - 3:00 PM (Lunch), 5:30 PM - 10:00 PM (Dinner)
- **Phone Number:** +61 2 9220 0111

Best Cafés and Breakfast Spots

Sydney is home to a thriving café culture, with spots that range from cozy neighborhood cafés to chic brunch havens offering a variety of modern Australian, Mediterranean, and international fare. Here are some of the best cafés and breakfast spots in Sydney:

The Grounds of Alexandria

A famous destination for both locals and tourists, The Grounds of Alexandria is more than just a café—it's an experience. Located in an industrial warehouse turned vibrant garden, this café offers a farm-to-table approach with fresh produce, artisanal coffee, and a stunning rustic ambiance. There are numerous seating areas, including a bakery, a coffee roastery, a florist, and a garden with animals like chickens and goats for a charming experience. Their menu is known for hearty dishes such as avocado toast, eggs benedict, and seasonal bowls packed with flavor and nutrition. Perfect for brunch, with Instagram-worthy decor all around.

- **Location:** 7a/2 Huntley St, Alexandria NSW 2015

- **Opening hours:** Monday to Friday 7:00 AM – 9:00 PM, Saturday & Sunday 7:30 AM – 10:00 PM
- **Phone number:** +61 2 9699 2225

Single O

Known for its coffee excellence, Single O (formerly known as Single Origin Roasters) is a go-to for coffee enthusiasts in Sydney. Their house-roasted coffee beans are carefully sourced and brewed to perfection. The café serves up a creative breakfast menu that focuses on fresh, local ingredients. Some popular dishes include the Japanese-inspired brown rice bowl with avocado and poached eggs or the hearty ricotta pancakes. The café itself is small and cozy, offering an intimate breakfast or brunch experience. If you're into coffee, this place is a must-visit.

- **Location:** 60–64 Reservoir St, Surry Hills NSW 2010
- **Opening hours:** Monday to Friday 6:30 AM – 3:00 PM, Saturday & Sunday 7:30 AM – 3:00 PM
- **Phone number:** +61 2 9211 0665

Bills (Surry Hills)

Bills is a quintessential Sydney café with locations across the city, but the Surry Hills location is particularly popular. Owned by renowned chef Bill Granger, the café is known for its iconic dishes like the ricotta hotcakes with honeycomb butter and banana, and the creamy scrambled eggs with sourdough toast.

The light-filled interiors, paired with a simple yet chic design, make for a relaxed, breezy brunch experience. The menu leans towards fresh, clean flavors, with a mix of Mediterranean and modern Australian influences.

- **Location:** 359 Crown St, Surry Hills NSW 2010
- **Opening hours:** Monday to Friday 7:00 AM – 3:00 PM, Saturday & Sunday 7:30 AM – 3:00 PM
- **Phone number:** +61 2 9360 4762

Brewtown Newtown

Nestled in the bohemian heart of Newtown, Brewtown offers an industrial-chic setting with inventive brunch options and its specialty "brewnuts"—a hybrid pastry between a croissant and a doughnut. The café is known for its creative approach to classic breakfast fare, with a menu featuring items like smashed avocado on sourdough with feta, eggs benedict with pulled pork, and hearty grain bowls. Coffee lovers can indulge in their excellent brews made from their own roasted beans.

- **Location:** 6–8 O'Connell St, Newtown NSW 2042
- **Opening hours:** Monday to Sunday 8:00 AM – 3:00 PM
- **Phone number:** +61 2 9519 7880

Reuben Hills

Reuben Hills, located in the trendy Surry Hills district, is an industrial-style café with exposed brick walls and minimalist decor. It doubles as a coffee roastery, ensuring every cup of coffee is fresh and expertly brewed. The café's menu has a distinctly Latin American influence, with dishes like the famed Reuben sandwich, baleadas (Honduran breakfast tacos), and salted caramel milkshakes. The casual yet cool vibe makes it a perfect spot for a weekend brunch, especially if you're in the mood for something unique.

- **Location:** 61 Albion St, Surry Hills NSW 2010
- **Opening hours:** Monday to Sunday 7:30 AM – 3:00 PM
- **Phone number:** +61 2 9211 5556

Shuk

Shuk is a hidden gem in the beachside suburb of Bondi, offering a laid-back and friendly atmosphere. The café draws its influence from Israeli and Middle Eastern cuisine, serving dishes like shakshuka, hummus platters, and labneh. Their all-day breakfast menu also includes local favorites like smoked salmon and poached eggs, with freshly baked bread. The café has a charming outdoor seating area, perfect for enjoying Sydney's sunny weather.

- **Location:** 2 Mitchell St, North Bondi NSW 2026
- **Opening hours:** Monday to Sunday 7:00 AM – 3:00 PM
- **Phone number:** +61 2 7901 3949

Café Sydney

Located atop the iconic Customs House overlooking the Sydney Harbour, Café Sydney offers an elegant breakfast experience with stunning views of the Harbour Bridge and Opera House. Although it is more renowned for lunch and dinner, its weekend brunches are equally spectacular. Café Sydney serves up a modern Australian menu, with dishes like smoked trout, organic eggs benedict, and fresh fruit platters. The rooftop terrace is an ideal setting for a leisurely morning with breathtaking views.

- **Location:** 5th Floor, Customs House, 31 Alfred St, Sydney NSW 2000
- **Opening hours:** Sunday brunch 10:00 AM – 12:00 PM
- **Phone number:** +61 2 9251 8683

Three Blue Ducks (Bronte)

Three Blue Ducks have become a Sydney institution with multiple locations, but the Bronte café remains a favorite for beachgoers. The relaxed coastal atmosphere pairs beautifully with their farm-to-table ethos.

The menu emphasizes sustainable, locally sourced produce, with hearty breakfast dishes like signature poached eggs with greens, miso mushrooms, and sourdough. It's a great place to grab a meal after a morning swim at Bronte Beach, just a short walk away.

- **Location:** 141-143 Macpherson St, Bronte NSW 2024
- **Opening hours:** Monday to Sunday 7:00 AM – 3:00 PM
- **Phone number:** +61 2 9389 0010

The Paramount Coffee Project

Located in the hip neighborhood of Surry Hills, The Paramount Coffee Project is a trendy café that stands out for its commitment to exceptional coffee and inventive brunch dishes. The menu features both classic and unique offerings such as fried chicken waffles, Korean-style scrambled eggs, and green breakfast bowls. Their minimalist, industrial-style interiors are paired with plenty of natural light, creating a cozy and vibrant space. Known for working with different coffee roasters from around the world, this café is a haven for coffee connoisseurs looking to try something new.

- **Location:** 80 Commonwealth St, Surry Hills NSW 2010
- **Opening hours:** Monday to Friday 7:00 AM – 3:00 PM, Saturday & Sunday 8:00 AM – 3:00 PM
- **Phone number:** +61 2 9211 1122

Claires Kitchen at Le Salon

For something a little different, Claires Kitchen at Le Salon offers a French-inspired breakfast and brunch menu in an elegant setting. Located on Oxford Street, this Parisian-style bistro is known for its decadent and artistic décor. The menu includes French classics like croque monsieur, crepes, and freshly baked pastries, alongside hearty dishes such as truffle scrambled eggs and smoked salmon. Perfect for those seeking a refined and indulgent brunch experience, Claire's Kitchen also features beautiful chandeliers and a stylishly furnished interior.

- **Location:** 35 Oxford St, Surry Hills NSW 2010
- **Opening hours:** Brunch on weekends 11:00 AM – 3:00 PM
- **Phone number:** +61 2 9283 1891

Fine Dining and Michelin-starred Restaurants

Sydney boasts an impressive collection of fine dining and Michelin-starred restaurants that reflect the city's cosmopolitan culture and love for fresh, local ingredients. From iconic harborside establishments to hidden gems in chic neighborhoods, these restaurants offer unforgettable culinary experiences. Here are some of Sydney's best fine dining destinations, showcasing their distinct atmosphere, exceptional dishes, and commitment to excellence.

Quay Restaurant

Perched in a prime location overlooking Sydney Harbour, Quay is one of Australia's most acclaimed fine dining restaurants, often included in global rankings. Executive Chef Peter Gilmore leads the kitchen with his creative and innovative take on modern Australian cuisine. The restaurant's multi-course tasting menu is a journey of flavors and textures, featuring dishes like mud crab congee and the famous Snow Egg dessert. Quay is designed to highlight the beauty of Sydney's harbor with floor-to-ceiling windows, providing breathtaking views of the Sydney Opera House and Harbour Bridge.

Location: Overseas Passenger Terminal, The Rocks, Sydney NSW 2000

Opening Hours:

- **Lunch:** Friday–Sunday: 12:00 PM – 2:30 PM
- **Dinner:** Wednesday–Saturday: 5:30 PM – 9:30 PM

Phone Number: +61 2 9251 5600

Bennelong

Nestled inside the iconic Sydney Opera House, Bennelong offers diners the unique experience of enjoying a meal within one of Australia's most famous landmarks. Head Chef Peter Gilmore (who also leads Quay) delivers a menu that celebrates Australian produce and culinary tradition. Each dish at Bennelong showcases seasonal ingredients, with standouts such as the Wagyu beef and roasted Murray cod. The sleek, curved design of the restaurant reflects the architectural brilliance of the Opera House, making it a must-visit for visitors and locals alike.

Location: Sydney Opera House, Bennelong Point, Sydney NSW 2000

Opening Hours:

- **Lunch:** Thursday–Saturday: 12:00 PM – 2:00 PM
- **Dinner:** Wednesday–Saturday: 5:45 PM – 10:00 PM

Phone Number: +61 2 9240 8000

Sixpenny

Located in the quiet suburb of Stanmore, Sixpenny is a small, intimate restaurant offering an elegant take on Australian dining. The focus is on sustainability and local ingredients, with many of the vegetables and herbs grown in the restaurant's garden. Diners can expect a beautifully crafted seasonal tasting menu that changes regularly, with dishes like glazed Maremma duck and fresh scallops. Sixpenny's understated décor allows the food to take center stage, creating a warm and personal dining experience.

Location: 83 Percival Rd, Stanmore NSW 2048

Opening Hours:

- **Dinner:** Wednesday–Saturday: 6:00 PM – 9:00 PM
- **Lunch:** Saturday–Sunday: 12:00 PM – 3:00 PM

Phone Number: +61 2 9572 6666

Oncore by Clare Smyth

Oncore, the Sydney outpost of renowned British chef Clare Smyth's Core restaurant in London, is located in the Crown Sydney Tower. The restaurant offers an elegant and sophisticated dining experience with spectacular views of Sydney's skyline.

Oncore's menu is rooted in sustainable, seasonal ingredients, drawing inspiration from both Australian produce and European techniques. Signature dishes include the iconic "Potato and Roe" and exquisite desserts like the "Core Apple." Oncore's impeccable service and refined atmosphere ensure a world-class experience.

- **Location:** Level 26, Crown Sydney, 1 Barangaroo Ave, Barangaroo NSW 2000
- **Opening Hours: Dinner:** Tuesday–Saturday: 5:45 PM – 10:00 PM
- **Phone Number:** +61 2 8871 7171

Tetsuya's

Tetsuya's is a Sydney institution and one of the most revered fine dining restaurants in the country. Chef Tetsuya Wakuda blends French culinary techniques with Japanese flavors to create a sophisticated degustation menu. Signature dishes include the Confit of Ocean Trout and the famed wagyu beef. The serene setting, complete with a Japanese garden, offers an escape from the city's bustle. Tetsuya's also boasts an impressive wine cellar, ensuring the perfect pairing for each dish.

- **Location:** 529 Kent St, Sydney NSW 2000
- **Opening Hours:** Dinner: Tuesday–Saturday: 6:00 PM – 10:00 PM
- **Phone Number:** +61 2 9267 2900

Restaurant Hubert

Inspired by the bistros of Paris, Restaurant Hubert offers a romantic, old-world atmosphere paired with impeccable French cuisine. Located in a subterranean space, the restaurant features vintage décor, candle-lit tables, and live jazz performances. The menu showcases classic French dishes such as duck l'orange, escargots, and house-made pâté, all made with the finest ingredients. A carefully curated wine list complements the menu, featuring a wide selection of French and Australian wines.

- **Location:** 15 Bligh St, Sydney NSW 2000
- **Opening Hours:** Monday–Saturday: 12:00 PM – 12:00 AM
- **Phone Number:** +61 2 9232 0881

LuMi Dining

Overlooking the waterfront at Pyrmont Bay, LuMi Dining is a contemporary restaurant that merges Italian cuisine with Japanese influences. Chef Federico Zanellato's degustation menu is known for its creativity and innovation, with dishes like burnt miso pasta and Hokkaido scallops with shiso and radish. The restaurant's minimalistic design and floor-to-ceiling windows create a relaxed, airy atmosphere, perfect for enjoying a leisurely meal while taking in the beautiful views of the bay.

Location: 56 Pirrama Rd, Pyrmont NSW 2009

Opening Hours:

- **Dinner:** Thursday–Saturday: 6:30 PM – 10:30 PM
- **Lunch:** Saturday–Sunday: 12:00 PM – 3:00 PM

Phone Number: +61 2 9571 1999

Automata

Automata, located in Chippendale's trendy Kensington Street precinct, offers a sleek, industrial-chic setting with exposed brick walls and an open kitchen. Head Chef Clayton Wells has crafted a multi-course tasting menu that reflects his bold approach to flavor, with an emphasis on seasonality and sustainability. Dishes change frequently but often include standout items such as black Angus beef, cured kingfish, and inventive vegetable dishes. The casual yet refined atmosphere makes Automata a favorite for those seeking something modern and unique.

Location: 5 Kensington St, Chippendale NSW 2008

Opening Hours:

- **Dinner:** Wednesday–Saturday: 6:00 PM – 9:00 PM

- **Lunch:** Friday–Saturday: 12:00 PM – 3:00 PM

Phone Number: +61 2 8277 8555

Est.

Est. is a mainstay in Sydney's fine dining scene, consistently delivering high-end, modern Australian cuisine in an elegant setting. Located in the historic Establishment building, this restaurant features soaring white columns, plush seating, and refined décor that exudes sophistication. Chef Jacob Davey's degustation menu emphasizes seasonal ingredients, with dishes that balance flavor and texture beautifully. Signature plates include fresh seafood options like rock lobster and barramundi, paired with inventive sauces and accompaniments. Est. is renowned for its impeccable service and a well-curated wine list that enhances the dining experience.

Location: Level 1, Establishment, 252 George St, Sydney NSW 2000

Opening Hours:

- **Lunch:** Friday: 12:00 PM – 2:00 PM
- **Dinner:** Monday–Saturday: 6:00 PM – 10:00 PM

Phone Number: +61 2 9240 3000

Bentley Restaurant + Bar

Located in Sydney's bustling CBD, Bentley Restaurant + Bar combines industrial-chic design with an innovative approach to modern Australian cuisine. Known for pushing the boundaries of flavor, Head Chef Brent Savage creates dishes that are as visually stunning as they are delicious, with a focus on bold pairings and unique ingredients. Expect plates like Moreton Bay bugs with native spices or lamb rump with fermented grains. Bentley's extensive wine list, curated by award-winning sommelier Nick Hildebrandt, complements the inventive menu, offering over 1,000 choices of international and Australian wines.

Location: 27 O'Connell St, Sydney NSW 2000

Opening Hours:

- **Lunch:** Monday–Friday: 12:00 PM – 3:00 PM
- **Dinner:** Monday–Saturday: 6:00 PM – 10:00 PM

Phone Number: +61 2 8214 0505

Food Trucks and Food Halls

Sydney offers an exciting and diverse food scene, with food trucks and food halls providing a chance to experience the city's culinary culture in a more casual and often creative setting. These places combine vibrant street food with gourmet offerings, often emphasizing global flavors and local ingredients. Here are some of the most notable food trucks and food halls in Sydney.

1. Cantina Mobil

Cantina Mobil is one of Sydney's most beloved Mexican food trucks, delivering bold flavors and street-style Mexican cuisine. Specializing in tacos and burritos, this food truck serves up tender slow-cooked meats like pork and beef, or a vegetarian option with black beans and guacamole. Their signature dish, the "Cantina Bowl," combines all these elements in a fresh and filling salad. You'll often find Cantina Mobil popping up at various events or parked in popular city spots. The bright green truck is easy to spot, and its friendly atmosphere keeps locals and visitors coming back.

Location: Various locations (usually Circular Quay, Darling Harbour, or Surry Hills). Check social media for exact locations.

Hours: Typically 11 AM – 3 PM (lunch hours), but this can vary depending on the event or location.

2. Mr. Gee's Burger Truck

For burger enthusiasts, Mr. Gee's Burger Truck is a must-visit. Known for its juicy, flavorful burgers made from quality Australian beef, this food truck serves burgers with a twist, such as their famed "Truffle Burger" or the mouthwatering "Cheeseburger Royale." Mr. Gee's is all about indulgence, offering crispy fries and milkshakes as perfect companions to the burgers. The truck roams around the inner-city suburbs and CBD, offering a gourmet twist on the classic burger experience.

Location: Various locations (often found at festivals, pop-ups, or around the Inner West). Check their Instagram for the latest updates.

Hours: Wednesday to Saturday, 5 PM – 10 PM.

3. Eat Art Truck

The Eat Art Truck is a food truck with a modern twist on BBQ, serving dishes like slow-cooked pork belly buns, crispy fried chicken, and beef brisket. What sets this truck apart is its commitment to art and creativity—local street artists are often invited to paint the truck while customers enjoy their meals. It's a perfect fusion of visual and culinary art.

Location: Typically roams around central locations like the Sydney CBD or Darlinghurst. Follow their website or social media for updates.

Hours: Thursday to Saturday, 12 PM – 9 PM.

4. Tramsheds Harold Park

Tramsheds Harold Park is a trendy food hall located in a beautifully restored tram depot. It is home to a variety of eateries and offers a mix of cuisines from around the world, including modern Australian, Mediterranean, and Asian influences. Some of the highlights include Gelato Messina, a local favorite for artisan gelato, and Bodega 1904, known for Spanish-inspired tapas and fresh seafood. Tramsheds is a perfect destination for a casual yet upscale dining experience.

Location: 1 Dalgal Way, Forest Lodge NSW 2037

Hours: Open daily from 7 AM – 10 PM (individual restaurant hours may vary).

5. The Cannery Rosebery

The Cannery in Rosebery is another food hall that celebrates Sydney's dynamic food scene. It houses several artisan food outlets, offering everything from fresh seafood at Fish Butchery to Italian specialties at Da Mario. The space also has specialty coffee shops, bakeries, and organic grocers, making it a hub for both dining and shopping. The industrial-chic atmosphere adds a trendy touch, making it popular among locals and tourists alike.

Location: 61 Mentmore Ave, Rosebery NSW 2018

Hours: Open daily from 7 AM – 9 PM (hours may differ for individual stores).

6. Sydney Fish Market Food Hall

The Sydney Fish Market is renowned for its fresh seafood, and the food hall inside provides visitors with an unparalleled opportunity to enjoy this bounty right on site. From freshly shucked oysters to grilled fish and sushi, the variety of seafood here is incredible. The market is bustling with energy, and visitors can sample gourmet seafood dishes while overlooking the harbor. It's a must for seafood lovers looking for a fresh and flavorful meal in a relaxed setting.

Location: Bank St, Pyrmont NSW 2009

Hours: Open daily from 7 AM – 4 PM (food hall hours may vary).

7. Gateway Sydney

Located right by Circular Quay, Gateway Sydney is a multi-level food hall offering a variety of high-end fast-casual dining options. The space is sleek and modern, with an array of international and local cuisines, ranging from Italian pasta and pizza at Fratelli Fresh to Thai street food at Chat Thai. It's the perfect spot for a quick lunch or dinner with a view of the Sydney Opera House or the Harbour Bridge.

Location: 1 Macquarie Place, Circular Quay, Sydney NSW 2000

Hours: Open daily from 7 AM – 10 PM.

8. The Streets of Barangaroo

Barangaroo has become one of Sydney's trendiest waterfront precincts, and its food hall offers a wide array of dining options, from grab-and-go sandwiches and salads to sit-down meals at restaurants like Ume Burger and Banksii Vermouth Bar & Bistro. The modern and sophisticated atmosphere makes it ideal for after-work drinks or casual dining with stunning views of the harbor.

Location: Barangaroo Avenue, Barangaroo NSW 2000

Hours: Open daily from 8 AM – 9 PM.

Vegan and Vegetarian Restaurants

Bodhi Restaurant & Bar

Bodhi Restaurant & Bar is a renowned vegan restaurant located in the heart of Sydney. It offers a diverse menu featuring Asian-inspired vegan dishes, including dim sum, salads, and noodles. The outdoor garden setting under fig trees provides a tranquil dining atmosphere. Bodhi is particularly famous for its plant-based yum cha, which is served during the day, and its creative à la carte menu in the evening.

- **Location:** 2-4 College Street, Sydney NSW 2000

Opening Hours:

- Monday to Friday: 12:00 PM – 10:00 PM
- Saturday: 11:00 AM – 10:00 PM
- Sunday: 11:00 AM – 4:00 PM

Phone Number: +61 2 9360 2523

Yellow

Yellow is a sophisticated vegetarian bistro located in Potts Point. The restaurant is known for its innovative vegetarian and vegan dishes, created using seasonal produce. The menu features a range of beautifully plated dishes that highlight the flavors and textures of vegetables. Yellow offers both à la carte and tasting menus, providing an exquisite dining experience for vegetarians and vegans.

- **Location:** 57 Macleay Street, Potts Point NSW 2011

Opening Hours:

- Wednesday to Saturday: 6:00 PM – 10:00 PM
- Sunday: 12:00 PM – 2:30 PM, 6:00 PM – 10:00 PM

Phone Number: +61 2 9332 2344

Yule's

Yule's is a vibrant vegetarian restaurant in Surry Hills, offering a diverse menu with influences from various cuisines. The menu includes a range of small plates, mains, and desserts, all designed to be shared. Yule's also features an extensive selection of house-brewed vegan beers and cocktails, making it a great spot for a relaxed meal with friends.

- **Location:** 417 Crown Street, Surry Hills NSW 2010
- **Opening Hours:** Monday to Sunday: 12:00 PM – 12:00 AM
- **Phone Number:** +61 2 9319 6609

Gigi Pizzeria

Gigi Pizzeria in Newtown is famous for its authentic Neapolitan-style pizzas, which are entirely plant-based. The menu features a variety of creative vegan pizzas made with fresh, high-quality ingredients. Gigi Pizzeria's commitment to traditional pizza-making techniques ensures a delicious and authentic dining experience.

- **Location:** 379 King Street, Newtown NSW 2042
- **Opening Hours:** Monday to Sunday: 5:00 PM – 10:00 PM
- **Phone Number:** +61 2 9557 2224

Soul Burger

Soul Burger is a popular vegan burger joint with several locations in Sydney. The restaurant offers a wide range of plant-based burgers that are both delicious and environmentally friendly. The menu includes classic burger options as well as unique creations, all made with house-made vegan patties, fresh vegetables, and flavorful sauces.

- **Location:** 111 Belmore Road, Randwick NSW 2031

- **Opening Hours:** Monday to Sunday: 11:30 AM – 9:00 PM
- **Phone Number:** +61 2 9398 4393

Shift Eatery

Shift Eatery in Surry Hills is Sydney's first vegan deli café. It offers a variety of plant-based sandwiches, salads, and breakfast items. The menu also includes delicious vegan pastries, coffee, and smoothies. The cozy and welcoming atmosphere makes it a great spot for a casual meal or coffee break.

- **Location:** 4/241 Commonwealth Street, Surry Hills NSW 2010

Opening Hours:

- Monday to Friday: 7:00 AM – 3:30 PM
- Saturday to Sunday: 8:00 AM – 4:00 PM

Phone Number: +61 2 9281 7000

Lentil As Anything

Lentil As Anything in Newtown is a unique, pay-as-you-feel vegan restaurant that aims to make healthy and delicious food accessible to everyone. The menu features a variety of global vegan dishes, made with fresh, locally sourced ingredients. The community-focused ethos and inclusive atmosphere make it a standout dining experience.

- **Location:** 391 King Street, Newtown NSW 2042
- **Opening Hours:** Monday to Sunday: 12:00 PM – 3:30 PM, 6:00 PM – 9:00 PM
- **Phone Number:** +61 2 7226 9389

Alibi Bar & Kitchen

Alibi Bar & Kitchen is a chic vegan restaurant located within the Ovolo Woolloomooloo Hotel. The menu, curated by renowned plant-based chef Matthew Kenney, offers innovative and beautifully presented dishes that highlight fresh, seasonal ingredients. The stylish setting and waterfront views make it an ideal spot for a special night out.

- **Location:** 6 Cowper Wharf Roadway, Woolloomooloo NSW 2011
- **Opening Hours:** Monday to Sunday: 5:30 PM – 10:00 PM
- **Phone Number:** +61 2 9331 9000

Loving Hut

Loving Hut in Northbridge is part of a global chain of vegan restaurants offering a diverse menu of Asian-inspired dishes. The extensive menu includes vegan versions of popular dishes such as pho, fried rice, and curries, all made with plant-based ingredients. The casual dining atmosphere and friendly service make it a great spot for a relaxed meal.

- **Location:** 377 Pacific Highway, Northbridge NSW 2063
- **Opening Hours:** Tuesday to Sunday: 12:00 PM – 3:00 PM, 5:00 PM – 9:00 PM
- **Phone Number:** +61 2 9967 3368

Eden Bondi

Eden Bondi is a trendy vegan restaurant located near Bondi Beach. The menu features a variety of plant-based dishes, including bowls, burgers, and share plates, all made with fresh, organic ingredients. The vibrant decor and beachside location create a relaxed and inviting dining experience, perfect for enjoying healthy and delicious food.

- **Location:** 1/144-148 Glenarm Avenue, Bondi Beach NSW 2026

Opening Hours:

- Monday to Friday: 5:00 PM – 9:00 PM

- Saturday to Sunday: 8:00 AM – 9:00 PM

Phone Number: +61 2 9130 4298

Cooking Classes and Food Tours

Sydney offers a rich array of cooking classes and food tours that showcase the city's diverse culinary scene. Here's a comprehensive guide to some of the top options:

Sydney Seafood School

Located at the Sydney Fish Market, Sydney Seafood School is renowned for its hands-on cooking classes focusing on seafood. Classes cover a range of topics from selecting fresh seafood to mastering techniques like filleting and cooking. Each session includes a guided market tour and practical cooking experience, where participants prepare a variety of dishes under the guidance of expert chefs. The classes are suitable for all skill levels and provide insights into local seafood varieties and preparation methods.

- **Location:** Sydney Fish Market, Pyrmont, Sydney
- **Duration:** 3-4 hours
- **Contact:** +61 2 9004 1100, info@sydneyseafoodschool.com.au

Savor Australia Food Tours

Savor Australia offers a range of food tours that explore Sydney's vibrant food scene. Popular tours include the Taste of Sydney tour, which takes you through key culinary hotspots and hidden gems in neighborhoods like Surry Hills, Darlinghurst, and Newtown. These tours include visits to specialty food stores, gourmet cafes, and local markets, along with tastings of artisanal products, street foods, and chef-created dishes. Tours are guided by food enthusiasts who provide local insights and culinary stories.

- **Location:** Various starting points across Sydney
- **Duration:** 4-5 hours
- **Contact:** +61 2 9280 2277, info@savor.com.au

The Spice Lab

The Spice Lab offers immersive cooking classes and spice-themed experiences focused on global cuisines.

Participants learn how to use spices and herbs to create dishes from different culinary traditions, including Indian, Middle Eastern, and Southeast Asian cuisines. The classes are interactive and provide hands-on experience in blending spices, preparing flavorful dishes, and understanding the cultural significance of various ingredients. The Spice Lab also hosts private classes and team-building events.

- **Location:** Bondi Junction, Sydney
- **Duration:** 2-3 hours
- **Contact:** +61 2 8065 1111, info@thespicelab.com.au

Authentic Italian Cooking School

Authentic Italian Cooking School offers a range of classes focusing on traditional Italian cuisine. Led by experienced Italian chefs, these classes cover pasta making, pizza baking, and crafting classic Italian dishes like risotto and tiramisu. Participants learn authentic techniques and recipes, using high-quality ingredients. The classes are interactive and include a meal where students enjoy the dishes they've prepared, accompanied by Italian wines and local specialties.

- **Location:** Surry Hills, Sydney
- **Duration:** 3-4 hours
- **Contact:** +61 2 9211 0899, info@authenticitaliancookingschool.com.au

Sydney Food Tours

Sydney Food Tours provides guided culinary adventures exploring the diverse food culture of Sydney. Their tours include the Ultimate Food Tour, which covers a variety of local eateries, food markets, and specialty shops in neighborhoods such as Chinatown, Glebe, and Paddington. Each tour offers a blend of tastings, local insights, and historical context, showcasing Sydney's multicultural food scene. Participants enjoy a range of foods from gourmet to street level, with an emphasis on fresh, local ingredients.

- **Location:** Various locations across Sydney
- **Duration:** 3-4 hours
- **Contact:** +61 2 9380 4053, info@sydneyfoodtours.com.au

The Cooking School at Pyrmont

The Cooking School at Pyrmont offers a variety of classes, from basic cooking skills to advanced culinary techniques. Classes focus on different aspects of cooking, including modern Australian cuisine, baking, and international dishes. The school provides a hands-on experience with professional chefs guiding participants through each recipe. The classes are designed for home cooks of all levels and include practical tips, ingredient insights, and cooking techniques.

- **Location:** Pyrmont, Sydney
- **Duration:** 3-4 hours
- **Contact:** +61 2 9552 1633, info@cookingpyrmont.com.au

Sydney Gourmet Food Tour

The Sydney Gourmet Food Tour offers a comprehensive exploration of Sydney's gourmet food scene. This tour takes you to high-end food markets, boutique food producers, and fine dining establishments. Highlights include tastings of gourmet cheeses, artisanal chocolates, and locally produced wines. The tour provides insights into the culinary trends in Sydney, focusing on quality ingredients and innovative cooking techniques. It's an ideal tour for food lovers interested in exploring Sydney's upscale food offerings.

- **Location:** Various upscale neighborhoods in Sydney
- **Duration:** 4-5 hours
- **Contact:** +61 2 9231 5523, info@sydneygourmetfoodtour.com.au

Chapter 10: Shopping in Sydney

Shopping Districts and Malls

Pitt Street Mall

Pitt Street Mall is Sydney's premier shopping destination, located in the heart of the CBD. This pedestrianized street is home to a variety of international and Australian retail stores, including flagship stores of major brands such as Zara, H&M, and Uniqlo. It's surrounded by major shopping centers like Westfield Sydney and the Strand Arcade, making it a hub for fashion, accessories, and lifestyle shopping.

- **Location:** Pitt Street, Sydney CBD
- **Opening Hours:** Monday to Wednesday, Friday: 9:30 AM - 7:00 PM; Thursday: 9:30 AM - 9:00 PM; Saturday: 9:30 AM - 6:00 PM; Sunday: 10:00 AM - 6:00 PM

Westfield Sydney

Westfield Sydney is a large, upscale shopping center located on Pitt Street Mall. It features over 300 retail stores, including luxury brands like Gucci, Prada, and Louis Vuitton, as well as popular high-street labels. The mall also offers a wide range of dining options, from casual eateries to fine dining restaurants. Its central location makes it a convenient shopping spot for both locals and tourists.

- **Location:** 188 Pitt Street, Sydney CBD
- **Opening Hours:** Monday to Wednesday, Friday, Saturday: 9:30 AM - 7:00 PM; Thursday: 9:30 AM - 9:00 PM; Sunday: 10:00 AM - 7:00 PM

The Strand Arcade

The Strand Arcade is a historic shopping arcade dating back to 1891, offering a unique shopping experience with its Victorian-era architecture and boutique stores. It hosts a range of specialty shops, designer boutiques, and Australian brands such as Akira Isogawa and Dinosaur Designs. The Strand Arcade is known for its charming atmosphere and personalized shopping service.

- **Location:** 412-414 George Street, Sydney CBD
- **Opening Hours:** Monday to Wednesday, Friday: 9:00 AM - 5:30 PM; Thursday: 9:00 AM - 9:00 PM; Saturday: 9:00 AM - 5:00 PM; Sunday: 11:00 AM - 4:00 PM

Queen Victoria Building (QVB)

The Queen Victoria Building, commonly known as QVB, is a grand, historic shopping complex featuring over 180 boutiques and specialty stores spread across four levels. With its stunning architecture, stained glass windows, and intricate tilework, QVB offers a luxurious shopping experience. It houses a mix of fashion, jewelry, homewares, and unique gifts, alongside cafes and restaurants.

- **Location:** 455 George Street, Sydney CBD
- **Opening Hours:** Monday to Saturday: 9:00 AM - 6:00 PM; Sunday: 11:00 AM - 5:00 PM

World Square Shopping Centre

World Square Shopping Centre is a bustling retail and dining precinct located in the heart of Sydney. It features over 90 stores, including fashion retailers, electronics, beauty services, and a diverse range of dining options. World Square is popular for its convenient location, offering a mix of everyday essentials and trendy fashion items.

- **Location:** 644 George Street, Sydney CBD
- **Opening Hours:** Monday to Wednesday, Friday: 10:00 AM - 7:00 PM; Thursday: 10:00 AM - 9:00 PM; Saturday: 10:00 AM - 6:00 PM; Sunday: 11:00 AM - 6:00 PM

The Galleries

The Galleries is a contemporary shopping complex that caters to a young, trendy crowd. It offers a mix of fashion, art, and lifestyle stores, as well as popular eateries. The Galleries is known for its unique blend of local and international brands, art installations, and a creative atmosphere that attracts shoppers looking for something different.

- **Location:** 500 George Street, Sydney CBD
- **Opening Hours:** Monday to Wednesday, Friday: 10:00 AM - 7:00 PM; Thursday: 10:00 AM - 9:00 PM; Saturday: 10:00 AM - 6:00 PM; Sunday: 11:00 AM - 6:00 PM

Broadway Shopping Centre

Located just outside the CBD, Broadway Shopping Centre is a popular retail destination featuring over 140 stores, including major retailers like Coles, Target, and Kmart. It also has a Hoyts cinema and a variety of dining options. The center is known for its convenient layout and family-friendly amenities, making it a favorite among locals.

- **Location:** 1 Bay Street, Ultimo
- **Opening Hours:** Monday to Wednesday, Friday: 9:00 AM - 7:00 PM; Thursday: 9:00 AM - 9:00 PM; Saturday: 9:00 AM - 6:00 PM; Sunday: 10:00 AM - 6:00 PM

Paddington Markets

Paddington Markets is a vibrant outdoor market held every Saturday, offering a wide array of unique, handmade items including fashion, accessories, homewares, and artworks. It is an ideal place to find one-of-a-kind pieces from emerging designers and artisans. The market has a lively atmosphere with live music and food stalls, attracting both locals and tourists.

- **Location:** 395 Oxford Street, Paddington
- **Opening Hours:** Saturday: 10:00 AM - 4:00 PM

Birkenhead Point Outlet Centre

Birkenhead Point Outlet Centre is Sydney's largest outlet mall, offering discounted prices on a wide range of brands including Nike, Ralph Lauren, and Calvin Klein. Located on the waterfront in Drummoyne, the center features over 140 stores, a marina, and a selection of dining options. It's a great spot for bargain hunters looking for quality goods at reduced prices.

- **Location:** 19 Roseby Street, Drummoyne
- **Opening Hours:** Monday to Wednesday, Friday: 10:00 AM - 6:00 PM; Thursday: 10:00 AM - 8:00 PM; Saturday: 9:00 AM - 6:00 PM; Sunday: 10:00 AM - 6:00 PM

Chatswood Chase Sydney

Chatswood Chase Sydney is a premium shopping center located in the North Shore suburb of Chatswood. It features high-end fashion brands, specialty stores, and gourmet food outlets. With over 200 retailers including David Jones, Tiffany & Co., and Apple, Chatswood Chase offers a luxurious shopping experience with a focus on quality and style.

- **Location:** 345 Victoria Avenue, Chatswood
- **Opening Hours:** Monday to Wednesday, Friday: 9:30 AM - 5:30 PM; Thursday: 9:30 AM - 9:00 PM; Saturday: 9:00 AM - 5:00 PM; Sunday: 10:00 AM - 5:00 PM

Local Markets and Artisanal Shops

The Rocks Markets

The Rocks Markets are a bustling weekend market offering a mix of artisanal goods, unique fashion, handcrafted jewelry, and gourmet food. Located in the historic Rocks precinct, the market stalls are set up along cobblestone streets, providing a charming atmosphere for shoppers. Visitors can find a variety of handmade crafts, local art, and delicious street food. The markets are a great place to discover local talent and enjoy live entertainment.

- **Location:** George Street, The Rocks, Sydney, NSW 2000
- **Opening Hours:** Saturday and Sunday, 10:00 AM - 5:00 PM

Paddington Markets

Paddington Markets has been a Sydney institution since 1973, featuring over 150 stalls with a focus on local designers, artisans, and food producers. The market is known for its eclectic mix of fashion, accessories, homewares, and art. Shoppers can also enjoy fresh produce, gourmet treats, and international cuisine. The market supports small businesses and is a hub for discovering unique, handcrafted items.

- **Location:** 395 Oxford Street, Paddington, NSW 2021
- **Opening Hours:** Saturday, 10:00 AM - 4:00 PM

Glebe Markets

Glebe Markets is one of Sydney's most vibrant and eclectic markets, offering an array of vintage clothing, handmade crafts, jewelry, and fresh produce. Set in Glebe Public School's grounds, the market has a laid-back vibe with live music and a variety of food stalls. It's a great spot for finding unique fashion pieces and artisanal goods and enjoying a relaxed weekend outing.

- **Location:** Glebe Public School, Glebe Point Road, Glebe, NSW 2037
- **Opening Hours:** Saturday, 10:00 AM - 4:00 PM

Carriage works Farmers Market

Carriage works Farmers Market is a popular destination for fresh, seasonal produce and artisanal products. Held in the historic Carriage works building, the market features over 70 stalls from local farmers, producers, and artisans. Visitors can find organic fruits and vegetables, gourmet meats, dairy products, and freshly baked goods. The market also hosts cooking demonstrations and offers a variety of ready-to-eat foods.

- **Location:** 245 Wilson Street, Eveleigh, NSW 2015
- **Opening Hours:** Saturday, 8:00 AM - 1:00 PM

Bondi Farmers Market

Bondi Farmers Market offers fresh produce, artisanal foods, and handmade crafts in a beachside setting. Held on the grounds of Bondi Beach Public School, the market features stalls with organic fruits and vegetables, farm-fresh dairy, homemade jams, and baked goods. Shoppers can also enjoy hot food stalls, coffee, and live music, making it a perfect spot for a relaxed Saturday morning.

- **Location:** Bondi Beach Public School, Campbell Parade, Bondi Beach, NSW 2026
- **Opening Hours:** Saturday, 9:00 AM - 1:00 PM

Mauriceville Organic Food and Farmers Markets

Mauriceville Organic Food and Farmers Markets are known for their wide variety of organic and sustainably produced food. The market features fresh fruits and vegetables, free-range meats, dairy products, and artisanal bread. Shoppers can also find handmade crafts, clothing, and eco-friendly products. With live music and a friendly community atmosphere, it's a favorite among locals for a Sunday outing.

- **Location:** Addison Road Community Centre, 142 Addison Road, Mauriceville, NSW 2204
- **Opening Hours:** Sunday, 9:00 AM - 3:00 PM

Kirribilli Markets

Kirribilli Markets is one of Sydney's oldest and most popular markets, offering a diverse range of fashion, accessories, art, and antiques. Located under the iconic Sydney Harbor Bridge, the markets feature stalls selling vintage clothing, handmade jewelry, homewares, and gourmet food. With a backdrop of stunning harbor views, it's a great place to find unique items and enjoy a day out.

- **Location:** Burton Street Tunnel, Milsons Point, NSW 2061
- **Opening Hours:** 4th Saturday of each month, 8:30 AM - 3:00 PM; 2nd Sunday of each month (Art and Design Market), 9:00 AM - 3:00 PM

Sydney Fish Market

Sydney Fish Market is a seafood lover's paradise, offering a wide variety of fresh seafood, including fish, shellfish, and crustaceans. The market also features a range of specialty shops selling gourmet products, including deli items, wines, and baked goods. Visitors can dine on-site at various seafood restaurants or enjoy takeaway meals. The market also offers cooking classes and tours.

- **Location:** Bank Street and Pyrmont Bridge Road, Pyrmont, NSW 2009
- **Opening Hours:** Daily, 7:00 AM - 4:00 PM

Rozelle Collectors Market

Rozelle Collectors Market is a treasure trove for antique and vintage enthusiasts, offering a wide range of collectibles, retro fashion, vinyl records, and second-hand goods. Set on the grounds of Rozelle Public School, the market has a relaxed, community feel with food stalls, live music, and plenty of unique finds. It's a great place to hunt for rare items and enjoy a nostalgic shopping experience.

- **Location:** Rozelle Public School, 663 Darling Street, Rozelle, NSW 2039
- **Opening Hours:** Saturday, 9:00 AM - 3:00 PM

Balmain Market

Balmain Market is one of Sydney's oldest markets, offering a charming mix of handmade crafts, fashion, antiques, and gourmet food. Located in the historic St. Andrews Congregational Church grounds, the market has a village atmosphere with a focus on locally made products. Shoppers can find unique gifts, enjoy delicious food, and listen to live music in a picturesque setting.

- **Location:** St. Andrews Congregational Church, Darling Street, Balmain, NSW 2041
- **Opening Hours:** Saturday, 8:30 AM - 4:00 PM

Boutique Stores and Designer Labels

Zimmermann

Zimmermann is an iconic Australian fashion label known for its feminine and sophisticated designs. Founded by sisters Nicky and Simone Zimmermann, the brand features beautiful dresses, swimwear, and ready-to-wear collections characterized by delicate prints, high-quality fabrics, and intricate detailing. Zimmermann has gained a global following and is a staple for fashion-forward women seeking elegant and modern pieces.

- **Location:** 79 Elizabeth Street, Paddington, Sydney, NSW 2021
- **Opening Hours:** Mon-Sat: 10:00 AM - 6:00 PM, Sun: 11:00 AM - 5:00 PM

Basile

Basile is renowned for its minimalist and sustainable fashion. The brand focuses on high-quality, organic fabrics and timeless designs. Basile offers a range of wardrobe essentials, from casual T-shirts and jeans to tailored pieces, all embodying effortless style and comfort. The store's modern, clean aesthetic reflects its commitment to simplicity and sustainability.

- **Location:** 132 Oxford Street, Paddington, Sydney, NSW 2021
- **Opening Hours:** Mon-Sat: 10:00 AM - 6:00 PM, Sun: 11:00 AM - 5:00 PM

Dinosaur Designs

Dinosaur Designs creates unique and artistic homewares and jewelry. Known for their resin pieces, the brand's products are handcrafted in Sydney and feature bold colors and organic shapes. Dinosaur Designs offers an array of items including vases, bowls, and statement jewelry, each piece a work of art blending function and aesthetics.

- **Location:** 339 Oxford Street, Paddington, Sydney, NSW 2021
- **Opening Hours:** Mon-Sat: 10:00 AM - 6:00 PM, Sun: 11:00 AM - 5:00 PM

Camilla

Camilla is famous for its vibrant and luxurious resort wear. Founded by designer Camilla Franks, the brand offers colorful kaftans, dresses, and accessories featuring elaborate prints and embellishments.

Camilla's collections are inspired by travel and culture, creating a bohemian-chic aesthetic perfect for those seeking bold and exotic fashion.

- **Location:** 84 William Street, Paddington, Sydney, NSW 2021
- **Opening Hours:** Mon-Sat: 10:00 AM - 6:00 PM, Sun: 11:00 AM - 5:00 PM

Aje

Aje is a contemporary Australian fashion brand known for its distinctive blend of raw beauty and effortless style. Co-founded by Adrian Norris and Edwina Forest, Aje's collections feature sculptural silhouettes, hand-painted prints, and artisanal details. The brand offers a range of ready-to-wear pieces that are both edgy and feminine.

- **Location:** 5-7 Heeley Street, Paddington, Sydney, NSW 2021
- **Opening Hours:** Mon-Sat: 10:00 AM - 6:00 PM, Sun: 11:00 AM - 5:00 PM

Incur

Incur is a curated boutique offering a mix of international and local designer labels. The store features a wide range of apparel, footwear, and accessories from brands like Acne Studios, APC, and Common Projects. Incur is known for its contemporary and trendy selection, catering to both men and women who appreciate stylish and high-quality fashion.

- **Location:** The Galleries, 500 George Street, Sydney, NSW 2000
- **Opening Hours:** Mon-Wed & Fri: 10:00 AM - 7:00 PM, Thu: 10:00 AM - 9:00 PM, Sat: 10:00 AM - 6:00 PM, Sun: 11:00 AM - 5:00 PM

Ginger & Smart

Ginger & Smart combines sophisticated design with sustainability. Founded by sisters Alexandra and Genevieve Smart, the brand offers luxurious ready-to-wear collections featuring bold prints, vibrant colors, and innovative fabrics. Ginger & Smart's designs are elegant yet modern, perfect for the contemporary woman who values both style and ethics.

- **Location:** 5/23-25 Bay Street, Double Bay, Sydney, NSW 2028
- **Opening Hours:** Mon-Sat: 10:00 AM - 6:00 PM, Sun: 11:00 AM - 5:00 PM

Kubi

Kubi is an iconic Australian streetwear brand known for its edgy and rebellious style. The brand offers a range of denim, apparel, and accessories with a distinctive aesthetic characterized by distressed details, bold graphics, and a rock-and-roll attitude. Kubi is popular among fashion enthusiasts who seek unique and statement-making pieces.

- **Location:** Shop 4/11-13 Knox Street, Double Bay, Sydney, NSW 2028
- **Opening Hours:** Mon-Sat: 10:00 AM - 6:00 PM, Sun: 11:00 AM - 5:00 PM

The Strand Arcade

The Strand Arcade is a heritage-listed shopping destination in Sydney, housing a variety of boutique stores and designer labels. It offers a unique shopping experience with its Victorian architecture and an eclectic mix of fashion, jewelry, and specialty stores. Notable boutiques include Dion Lee, Lover, and Scanlan Theodore, making it a must-visit for fashion enthusiasts.

- **Location:** 412-414 George Street, Sydney, NSW 2000
- **Opening Hours:** Mon-Wed & Fri: 9:00 AM - 5:30 PM, Thu: 9:00 AM - 9:00 PM, Sat: 9:00 AM - 5:00 PM, Sun: 11:00 AM - 5:00 PM

Parlor X

Parlor X is a high-end boutique located in a beautiful heritage-listed church in Paddington. It offers an exquisite selection of international and Australian designer labels, including Balenciaga, Chloe, and Saint Laurent. Parlor X is known for its curated collections and personalized shopping experience, catering to fashion-forward clients seeking exclusive and luxury fashion pieces.

- **Location:** 261 Oxford Street, Paddington, Sydney, NSW 2021
- **Opening Hours:** Mon-Sat: 10:00 AM - 6:00 PM, Sun: Closed

Aboriginal Art and Souvenirs

The Rocks Aboriginal Dreaming Centre

The Rocks Aboriginal Dreaming Centre showcases authentic Aboriginal art and cultural artifacts. It offers a range of traditional and contemporary artworks, including paintings, didgeridoos, boomerangs, and handcrafted jewelry.

Visitors can also learn about Aboriginal culture through guided tours and cultural workshops.

- **Location:** 33 Playfair St, The Rocks, Sydney
- **Opening Hours:** Daily, 10:00 AM - 5:00 PM

Kate Owen Gallery

Kate Owen Gallery specializes in contemporary Aboriginal art from across Australia, featuring works by established and emerging Indigenous artists. The gallery showcases paintings that depict Dreamtime stories, landscapes, and cultural motifs, offering a diverse selection of artworks for collectors and enthusiasts.

- **Location:** 680 Darling St, Rozelle, Sydney
- **Opening Hours:** Tuesday - Sunday, 10:00 AM - 6:00 PM

Coo-eel Aboriginal Art Gallery

Coo-eel Aboriginal Art Gallery is one of Australia's oldest Aboriginal art galleries, offering a comprehensive collection of artworks, including paintings, sculptures, and artifacts. The gallery promotes Aboriginal artists and their cultural heritage, providing a platform for both established and emerging talents.

- **Location:** 31 LaRock Ave, Bondi Beach, Sydney
- **Opening Hours:** Monday - Saturday, 10:00 AM - 5:00 PM

The Artery Aboriginal Art Gallery

The Artery Aboriginal Art Gallery specializes in contemporary Aboriginal art, showcasing paintings, sculptures, and artifacts that reflect diverse Indigenous cultures and artistic expressions. The gallery supports Aboriginal artists and communities, offering a curated selection of authentic artworks.

- **Location:** 35 Queen St, Woollahra, Sydney
- **Opening Hours:** Tuesday - Saturday, 11:00 AM - 5:00 PM

Outlandish Aboriginal Art Gallery

Outlandish Aboriginal Art Gallery features a diverse range of Aboriginal art, including paintings, didgeridoos, boomerangs, and cultural artifacts.

The gallery highlights artworks from various Aboriginal communities across Australia, offering a unique insight into Indigenous art and culture.

- **Location:** 121 Beach St, Coo gee, Sydney
- **Opening Hours:** Monday - Friday, 9:00 AM - 5:00 PM; Saturday, 10:00 AM - 4:00 PM

The Aboriginal Art Gallery

The Aboriginal Art Gallery at The Royal Botanic Garden Sydney showcases a collection of authentic Aboriginal artworks, including paintings, prints, and sculptures. The gallery collaborates with Aboriginal artists and communities to promote cultural heritage and artistic traditions.

- **Location:** The Royal Botanic Garden, Mrs. Macquarie's Rd, Sydney
- **Opening Hours:** Daily, 10:00 AM - 4:00 PM

Boomaler Aboriginal Artists Co-operative

Boomaler Aboriginal Artists Co-operative is an artist-run gallery that supports Aboriginal artists from diverse cultural backgrounds. The gallery features exhibitions of contemporary Aboriginal art, including paintings, prints, and mixed-media works that explore themes of identity and cultural heritage.

- **Location:** 55-59 Flood St, Leichhardt, Sydney
- **Opening Hours:** Wednesday - Saturday, 11:00 AM - 4:00 PM

Tali Gallery

Tali Gallery specializes in Aboriginal and Pacific art, showcasing a collection of paintings, prints, and artifacts. The gallery collaborates with Aboriginal artists and communities, offering ethically sourced artworks that celebrate Indigenous cultures and traditions.

- **Location:** 667 Darling St, Rozelle, Sydney
- **Opening Hours:** Tuesday - Sunday, 10:00 AM - 5:00 PM

Aboriginal Bush Traders

Aboriginal Bush Traders offers a range of authentic Aboriginal art and handicrafts, including paintings, textiles, and souvenirs.

The store supports Aboriginal artists and communities from remote regions of Australia, promoting sustainable practices and cultural preservation.

- **Location:** 412 Darling St, Balmain, Sydney
- **Opening Hours:** Monday - Saturday, 10:00 AM - 5:00 PM; Sunday, 10:00 AM - 4:00 PM

Better World Arts

Better World Arts collaborates with Aboriginal artists and fair-trade artisans to create a range of ethically sourced art and gifts. The store offers Aboriginal paintings, textiles, homewares, and accessories that celebrate Indigenous artistry and cultural traditions.

- **Location:** Shop 10, 3 Gladstone St, Newtown, Sydney
- **Opening Hours:** Monday - Friday, 10:00 AM - 5:00 PM; Saturday, 10:00 AM - 4:00 PM

Chapter 11: Nightlife and Entertainment

Bars and Rooftop Lounges

Opera Bar

Nestled beside the iconic Sydney Opera House, the Opera Bar offers breathtaking views of Sydney Harbor, the Harbor Bridge, and the Opera House itself. This vibrant bar is known for its extensive cocktail menu, local wines, and craft beers. With live music and a diverse food menu featuring fresh seafood, charcuterie, and seasonal dishes, Opera Bar provides a quintessential Sydney experience, perfect for both daytime and evening relaxation.

- **Location:** Lower Concourse, Sydney Opera House, Bennelong Point, Sydney NSW 2000
- **Opening Hours:** Mon-Fri: 11:30 AM - Late, Sat-Sun: 10:30 AM - Late
- **Phone Number:** +61 2 9247 1666

The Glenmore Hotel

The Glenmore Hotel, located in The Rocks, is famed for its rooftop bar that offers panoramic views of Sydney Harbor and the city skyline. Established in 1921, this historic pub retains its old-world charm while providing a modern pub experience. The rooftop bar is perfect for casual drinks, with a menu featuring classic cocktails, craft beers, and pub fare like burgers, salads, and seafood platters.

- **Location:** 96 Cumberland St, The Rocks NSW 2000
- **Opening Hours:** Mon-Sat: 11:00 AM - 12:00 AM, Sun: 11:00 AM - 10:00 PM
- **Phone Number:** +61 2 9247 4794

Zeta Bar

Located on the rooftop of the Hilton Sydney, Zeta Bar is a sophisticated cocktail lounge with a chic ambiance. Renowned for its innovative cocktail creations and stylish decor, Zeta Bar attracts a trendy crowd. The outdoor terrace provides stunning views of the city skyline, making it an ideal spot for evening drinks and socializing. The menu features a range of artisanal cocktails, premium spirits, and a selection of fine wines.

- **Location:** Level 4, Hilton Sydney, 488 George St, Sydney NSW 2000
- **Opening Hours:** Thu-Sat: 5:00 PM - Late
- **Phone Number:** +61 2 9265 6070

Ivy Pool Club

Ivy Pool Club is a glamorous rooftop bar and poolside oasis located in the heart of Sydney. Known for its luxurious setting, complete with cabanas, a pool, and a vibrant atmosphere, Ivy Pool Club offers an exclusive nightlife experience.

The bar serves a wide range of cocktails, champagnes, and light bites, perfect for sipping by the pool or dancing under the stars.

- **Location:** Level 4, Ivy, 320 George St, Sydney NSW 2000
- **Opening Hours:** Fri: 12:00 PM - 10:00 PM, Sat: 12:00 PM - 11:00 PM
- **Phone Number:** +61 2 9254 8088

Smoke Bar at Barangaroo House

Smoke Bar, situated atop Barangaroo House, offers stunning views of Darling Harbor and the city skyline. This rooftop bar features a sleek, contemporary design and a sophisticated menu of cocktails, wines, and craft beers. Smoke Bar is known for its relaxed yet upscale vibe, making it a great spot for sunset drinks and evening gatherings. The food menu includes delicious bar snacks, charcuterie, and small plates.

- **Location:** Level 3, Barangaroo House, 35 Barangaroo Ave, Barangaroo NSW 2000
- **Opening Hours:** Mon-Thu: 4:00 PM - Late, Fri-Sun: noon - Late
- **Phone Number:** +61 2 8587 5400

The Rook

The Rook is a hidden rooftop bar located in the CBD, known for its laid-back atmosphere and delicious lobster rolls. The bar offers a diverse menu of craft cocktails, beers, and wines, with a focus on fresh, seasonal ingredients. The Rook's relaxed vibe and industrial-chic decor make it a popular spot for after-work drinks and casual gatherings.

- **Location:** Level 7, 56-58 York St, Sydney NSW 2000
- **Opening Hours:** Mon-Sat: noon - Late
- **Phone Number:** +61 2 9262 2505

Henry Deane at Hotel Palisade

Henry Deane is a sophisticated cocktail bar located on the top two floors of Hotel Palisade in Millers Point. Offering panoramic views of Sydney Harbor, the bar features a contemporary design and a stylish atmosphere. The menu includes expertly crafted cocktails, premium spirits, and a selection of fine wines, complemented by a range of gourmet bar snacks and small plates.

- **Location:** Level 4, 35 Betting ton St, Millers Point NSW 2000
- **Opening Hours:** Mon-Sun: 12:00 PM - 10:00 PM
- **Phone Number:** +61 2 9018 0123

Old Mate's Place

Old Mate's Place is a cozy, speakeasy-style rooftop bar hidden in the CBD. Known for its intimate setting and expertly crafted cocktails, the bar offers a warm and welcoming atmosphere. The rooftop terrace provides a charming escape from the city's hustle and bustle, with a menu featuring classic cocktails, craft beers, and a curated selection of wines.

- **Location:** Level 4, 199 Clarence St, Sydney NSW 2000
- **Opening Hours:** Tue-Thu: 4:00 PM - 12:00 AM, Fri-Sat: 4:00 PM - 2:00 AM
- **Phone Number:** +61 2 9267 6959

The Light Brigade Rooftop

The Light Brigade Rooftop, located in Woollahra, offers stunning views of the Sydney skyline and a relaxed, casual atmosphere. The rooftop bar serves a variety of craft beers, wines, and cocktails, along with a menu of pub classics and gourmet pizzas. The Light Brigade is a popular spot for after-work drinks, weekend gatherings, and enjoying the sunset over the city.

- **Location:** 2A Oxford St, Woollahra NSW 2025
- **Opening Hours:** Mon-Sun: noon - Late
- **Phone Number:** +61 2 9357 0888

Hyde Hacienda Sydney Bar + Lounge

Hyde Hacienda Sydney Bar + Lounge is a chic, Cuban-inspired bar located in Circular Quay, offering stunning views of Sydney Harbor and the Opera House. The bar features a stylish, tropical decor and a vibrant atmosphere. The menu includes a variety of signature cocktails, premium spirits, and a selection of South American-inspired dishes and tapas.

- **Location:** Level 3, 61 Macquarie St, Sydney NSW 2000
- **Opening Hours:** Wed-Thu: 5:00 PM - 10:00 PM, Fri-Sat: 3:00 PM - 12:00 AM, Sun: 3:00 PM - 10:00 PM
- **Phone Number:** +61 2 9256 4000

Nightclubs and Live Music Venues

Marquee Sydney

Located in The Star casino complex, Marquee Sydney is one of the city's premier nightclubs. Known for its glamorous atmosphere and international DJ line-ups, Marquee offers an unforgettable nightlife experience. The club features multiple rooms with distinct vibes, including the Main Room with a large dance floor and the Boombox Room for a more intimate setting.

- **Location:** The Star, 80 Pyrmont Street, Pyrmont, NSW 2009
- **Opening Hours:** Friday - Saturday: 10:00 PM - 4:00 AM
- **Phone Number:** +61 2 9657 7737

The Basement

The Basement is a legendary live music venue in Sydney, hosting a diverse range of artists from jazz and blues to rock and soul. With an intimate setting and excellent acoustics, it's the perfect spot for music lovers to enjoy live performances. The venue also offers a restaurant and bar, making it a great place for dinner and a show.

- **Location:** 7 Macquarie Place, Circular Quay, NSW 2000
- **Phone Number:** +61 2 9251 2797

Oxford Art Factory

Inspired by Andy Warhol's Factory, Oxford Art Factory is a dynamic live music venue and club that supports emerging and established artists. It features two performance spaces and regularly hosts live bands, DJs, and art installations. The venue's eclectic programming and vibrant atmosphere make it a favorite among locals and tourists alike.

- **Location:** 38-46 Oxford Street, Darlinghurst, NSW 2010
- **Opening Hours:** Monday - Sunday: 6:00 PM - Late (varies by event)
- **Phone Number:** +61 2 9332 3711

Home the Venue

Home The Venue is a multi-level nightclub located on Darling Harbor, offering stunning water views and a variety of music genres across its different rooms. From electronic dance music to hip-hop, Home the Venue attracts a diverse crowd. The rooftop terrace is a highlight, providing a picturesque setting for dancing under the stars.

- **Location:** 101/1-5 Wheat Road, Darling Harbor, NSW 2000
- **Opening Hours:** Friday - Saturday: 9:00 PM - 4:00 AM
- **Phone Number:** +61 2 9274 5499

The Metro Theatre

The Metro Theatre is an iconic live music venue in Sydney's CBD, known for hosting a wide range of artists from indie bands to international acts. With a capacity of over 1,200, it offers an intimate yet energetic concert experience. The venue's central location makes it easily accessible and a popular choice for music enthusiasts.

- **Location:** 624 George Street, Sydney, NSW 2000
- **Phone Number:** +61 2 9550 3666

The Lansdowne Hotel

The Lansdowne Hotel is a beloved institution in Sydney's music scene, offering live performances from up-and-coming and established bands. The venue features a casual pub atmosphere with a focus on good music, good food, and good times. It has become a go-to spot for those looking to discover new talent in a relaxed setting.

- **Location:** 2-6 City Road, Chippendale, NSW 2008
- **Opening Hours:** Monday - Sunday: noon - Late
- **Phone Number:** +61 2 8586 1139

Ivy

Ivy is a sophisticated nightlife complex in Sydney, featuring multiple bars, restaurants, and a famous rooftop pool bar. Known for its chic ambiance and exclusive events, Ivy offers a mix of house, R&B, and pop music. The complex includes Ivy Pool Club, a Mediterranean-inspired oasis perfect for daytime lounging and nighttime partying.

- **Location:** 320 George Street, Sydney, NSW 2000
- **Opening Hours:** Wednesday - Sunday: 12:00 PM - 2:00 AM
- **Phone Number:** +61 2 9240 3000

Mary's Underground

Located beneath the iconic Mary's in Circular Quay, Mary's Underground is a premier live music venue offering an eclectic range of performances. The venue combines an intimate jazz club atmosphere with rock and roll energy, making it a unique destination for music fans. Enjoy delicious food and drinks while experiencing top-tier live acts.

- **Location:** 29 Reify Place, Circular Quay, NSW 2000
- **Opening Hours:** Wednesday - Sunday: 6:00 PM - Late
- **Phone Number:** +61 2 9247 6744

The Argyle

Situated in a historic sandstone building in The Rocks, The Argyle offers a blend of nightlife and live music with multiple bars and dance floors. The venue hosts a variety of events, from DJ nights to themed parties, catering to diverse musical tastes. Its stylish interiors and lively atmosphere make it a popular nightlife destination.

- **Location:** 18 Argyle Street, The Rocks, NSW 2000
- **Opening Hours:** Thursday - Saturday: 5:00 PM - Late
- **Phone Number:** +61 2 9247 5500

The Encore Theatre

The Encore Theatre is a historic live music venue in Newtown, renowned for its excellent acoustics and diverse lineup of performers. From rock and indie bands to comedians and theatrical performances, the Encore hosts a wide range of events. Its rich history and vibrant atmosphere make it a cornerstone of Sydney's entertainment scene.

- **Location:** 118-132 Encore Road, Newtown, NSW 2042
- **Phone Number:** +61 2 9550 3666

Theater and Performing Arts

Sydney Opera House

The Sydney Opera House is one of the world's most iconic performing arts venues, known for its distinctive sail-like design. It hosts a diverse range of performances, including opera, ballet, classical concerts, contemporary music, theater, and more. The venue is home to several resident companies, including Opera Australia and the Sydney Symphony Orchestra. Guided tours offer a behind-the-scenes look at this architectural masterpiece.

- **Location:** Bennelong Point, Sydney NSW 2000
- **Opening Hours:** Daily 9:00 AM - 5:00 PM (Box Office), performance times vary
- **Phone Number:** +61 2 9250 7111

Capitol Theatre

The Capitol Theatre is a historic theater known for hosting major musical productions and theatrical performances. The beautifully restored venue, originally built in the 1920s, features a grand auditorium with opulent decor. It regularly stages popular musicals, ballets, and other large-scale performances, offering an immersive cultural experience.

- **Location:** 13 Campbell Street, Haymarket NSW 2000
- **Opening Hours:** Box Office: Monday - Friday 9:00 AM - 5:00 PM, performance times vary
- **Phone Number:** +61 2 9320 5000

Sydney Theatre Company (STC)

The Sydney Theatre Company is one of Australia's leading theater companies, known for producing a wide array of plays, from classic to contemporary works. The STC operates out of The Wharf Theatres at Walsh Bay, offering stunning views of the harbor. The company is renowned for its high-quality productions and commitment to fostering new talent.

- **Location:** The Wharf, Pier 4/5 Hickson Road, Walsh Bay NSW 2000
- **Opening Hours:** Monday - Friday 9:00 AM - 5:00 PM, performance times vary
- **Phone Number:** +61 2 9250 1777

Belvoir St Theatre

Belvoir St Theatre, located in Surry Hills, is a prominent venue for innovative and engaging theater productions. The theater is known for its intimate setting and commitment to new Australian works.

Belvoir has a reputation for staging bold and thought-provoking productions that challenge audiences and foster artistic expression.

- **Location:** 25 Belvoir Street, Surry Hills NSW 2010
- **Opening Hours:** Box Office: Monday - Friday 9:00 AM - 5:00 PM, performance times vary
- **Phone Number:** +61 2 9699 3444

Encore Theatre

Encore Theatre is Sydney's oldest and longest-running live theater, located in the vibrant inner-west suburb of Newtown. It hosts a diverse range of performances, including comedy, music, theater, and dance. The venue is renowned for its eclectic programming and intimate atmosphere, making it a favorite among locals and visitors alike.

- **Location:** 118-132 Encore Road, Newtown NSW 2042
- **Opening Hours:** Box Office: Monday - Friday 9:00 AM - 5:00 PM, performance times vary
- **Phone Number:** +61 2 9550 3666

6. The Seymour Centre

The Seymour Centre is a cultural hub located at the University of Sydney, offering a variety of performances, including theater, music, dance, and festivals. The venue is dedicated to fostering new talent and promoting innovative and experimental works. It features several performance spaces, each providing a unique and engaging audience experience.

- **Location:** City Road & Cleveland Street, Chippendale NSW 2008
- **Opening Hours:** Box Office: Monday - Friday 9:00 AM - 5:00 PM, performance times vary
- **Phone Number:** +61 2 9351 7940

Riverside Theatres

Riverside Theatres in Parramatta is a major performing arts venue in Western Sydney, offering a diverse program of theater, dance, music, and film. The complex includes three performance spaces, each catering to different types of productions. Riverside Theatres is committed to community engagement and supports local and international artists.

- **Location:** Corner of Church and Market Streets, Parramatta NSW 2150
- **Opening Hours:** Box Office: Monday - Friday 9:00 AM - 5:00 PM, performance times vary
- **Phone Number:** +61 2 8839 3399

The Ensemble Theatre

The Ensemble Theatre, located in Kirribilli, is Australia's longest continuously running professional theater company. It offers a diverse program of contemporary plays, classics, and new Australian works. The intimate venue provides a close-up theater experience, enhancing the connection between the audience and performers.

- **Location:** 78 McDougall Street, Kirribilli NSW 2061
- **Opening Hours:** Box Office: Monday - Friday 9:00 AM - 5:00 PM, performance times vary
- **Phone Number:** +61 2 9929 0644

The State Theatre

The State Theatre is a historic and opulent theater located in the heart of Sydney's CBD. Known for its grand architecture and luxurious interiors, it hosts a wide range of performances, including concerts, film screenings, and theatrical productions. The venue is a cultural landmark and a testament to Sydney's rich performing arts heritage.

- **Location:** 49 Market Street, Sydney NSW 2000
- **Opening Hours:** Box Office: Monday - Friday 9:00 AM - 5:00 PM, performance times vary
- **Phone Number:** +61 2 9373 6852

Griffin Theatre Company

Griffin Theatre Company is dedicated to the production of new Australian plays. Located at the SBW Stables Theatre in Kings Cross, Griffin has a reputation for fostering emerging writers and presenting innovative and challenging works. The intimate venue allows for a close and engaging theater experience, making it a vital part of Sydney's cultural landscape.

- **Location:** 10 Nimrod Street, Kings Cross NSW 2010

- **Opening Hours:** Box Office: Monday - Friday 9:00 AM - 5:00 PM, performance times vary
- **Phone Number:** +61 2 9361 3817

Sydney Harbor Dinner Cruises

Captain Cook Cruises - Sydney Harbor Dinner Cruise

Captain Cook Cruises offers an exceptional dining experience aboard their Sydney Harbor Dinner Cruise. Guests enjoy a luxurious 3-course meal featuring fresh, locally sourced ingredients while taking in panoramic views of the Sydney Opera House, Harbor Bridge, and city skyline. The cruise includes live entertainment and a selection of fine wines and cocktails, making it perfect for a romantic evening or special celebration.

- **Location:** Circular Quay Wharf No.6, Sydney, NSW 2000
- **Opening Hours:** Daily departures at 7:00 PM
- **Phone Number:** +61 2 9206 1111

Manistic Sydney Harbor Dinner Cruise

The Manistic Sydney Harbor Dinner Cruise provides a premium dining experience aboard a modern catamaran. The cruise features a freshly prepared buffet with seafood, meats, and vegetarian options, complemented by stunning night views of Sydney's landmarks. Guests can relax on the expansive outdoor decks or enjoy the indoor dining areas with panoramic windows.

- **Location:** King Street Wharf No.5, Darling Harbor, Sydney, NSW 2000
- **Opening Hours:** Daily departures at 7:30 PM
- **Phone Number:** +61 2 8296 7354

Sydney Showboats - Dinner Cruise with Show

Sydney Showboats offer a unique dinner cruise experience that includes a 3-course meal and a dazzling cabaret show. The show features talented performers, including dancers and magicians, providing guests with an unforgettable evening of entertainment. The vessel itself is a classic paddle-wheeler, adding to the charm and elegance of the experience.

- **Location:** King Street Wharf No.9, Darling Harbor, Sydney, NSW 2000
- **Opening Hours:** Tuesday to Sunday, departures at 7:00 PM
- **Phone Number:** +61 2 8296 7296

Clearview Glass Boat Dinner Cruise

The Clearview Glass Boat Dinner Cruise offers a sophisticated dining experience aboard an all-glass vessel, providing uninterrupted views of Sydney Harbor. The cruise includes a 4-course meal with premium beverages, live music, and an exclusive adults-only environment. This is an ideal choice for those seeking a refined and intimate evening on the water.

- **Location:** Circular Quay Wharf No.6, Sydney, NSW 2000
- **Opening Hours:** Daily departures at 7:00 PM
- **Phone Number:** +61 2 8296 7354

Starship Sydney Dinner Cruise

Starship Sydney offers a modern, luxurious dinner cruise experience aboard a sleek vessel with multiple decks and expansive glass windows. Guests enjoy a 3-course contemporary Australian meal while taking in 360-degree views of Sydney Harbor. The cruise also features a dance floor and live DJ, making it perfect for both dining and dancing.

- **Location:** King Street Wharf No.4, Darling Harbor, Sydney, NSW 2000
- **Opening Hours:** Friday and Saturday, departures at 7:00 PM
- **Phone Number:** +61 2 9279 3433

Harbor Spirit Dinner Cruise

The Harbor Spirit Dinner Cruise offers an elegant dining experience with a 3-course meal served in a stylish setting. Guests can choose from a range of gourmet dishes while enjoying live entertainment and stunning views of Sydney's iconic landmarks. The cruise provides both indoor and outdoor seating options, ensuring a memorable evening in the harbor.

- **Location:** King Street Wharf No.8, Darling Harbor, Sydney, NSW 2000
- **Opening Hours:** Thursday to Sunday, departures at 7:30 PM
- **Phone Number:** +61 2 9002 5778

MV Sydney 2000 Dinner Cruise

The MV Sydney 2000 Dinner Cruise by Captain Cook Cruises offers a premier dining experience aboard one of the most prestigious vessels on Sydney Harbor. The cruise features a 3-course à la carte menu with options including seafood, meats, and vegetarian dishes, complemented by fine wines. The vessel's multiple decks and panoramic windows provide spectacular views of the harbor.

- **Location:** Circular Quay Wharf No.6, Sydney, NSW 2000
- **Opening Hours:** Daily departures at 7:00 PM
- **Phone Number:** +61 2 9206 1111

Vivid Sydney Dinner Cruise

The Vivid Sydney Dinner Cruise is a special event cruise offered during the annual Vivid Sydney festival. Guests enjoy a gourmet dinner while witnessing the city's iconic landmarks illuminated in vibrant colors and light installations. The cruise offers a unique perspective of the festival's light shows, making it a highlight of Sydney's winter calendar.

- **Location:** King Street Wharf No.7, Darling Harbor, Sydney, NSW 2000
- **Opening Hours:** May - June, daily departures at 7:30 PM
- **Phone Number:** +61 2 8296 7354

Tall Ship Dinner Cruise

The Tall Ship Dinner Cruise provides a historic and romantic experience aboard an authentic 19th-century sailing ship. Guests enjoy a buffet dinner featuring a variety of dishes while sailing under the stars and taking in the views of Sydney Harbor. The cruise includes live music and opportunities to help hoist the sails, adding to the unique maritime experience.

- **Location:** Campbell's Cove, The Rocks, Sydney, NSW 2000
- **Opening Hours:** Thursday to Sunday, departures at 7:00 PM
- **Phone Number:** +61 2 8015 5571

Sydney Harbor Dinner and Latino Show Cruise

The Sydney Harbor Dinner and Latino Show Cruise offer a lively evening of dining and entertainment with a Latin flair. Guests enjoy a 3-course meal while being entertained by a vibrant Latino dance show, featuring salsa, samba, and other Latin American dance styles. The cruise provides a fun and festive atmosphere, perfect for a night out with friends or family.

- **Location:** King Street Wharf No.6, Darling Harbor, Sydney, NSW 2000
- **Opening Hours:** Friday and Saturday, departures at 7:30 PM

- **Phone Number:** +61 2 8296 7354

Best Craft Beer and Wine Bars

Sydney has a thriving craft beer and wine scene, with a variety of venues catering to enthusiasts seeking unique brews and exquisite wines. Below are some of the best craft beer and wine bars in the city:

The Lord Nelson Brewery Hotel

The Lord Nelson Brewery Hotel is Sydney's oldest continually licensed pub and one of the city's most iconic spots for craft beer. Located in the historic Rocks district, it has been brewing its range of beers since the 1980s. The bar features a rustic, old-world charm with stone walls and wooden beams. Its flagship beer, "Three Sheets," is a pale ale, but it offers a variety of brews, from malty stouts to refreshing lagers. The Lord Nelson's in-house brewery ensures every pint is fresh, and it's a must-visit for both history buffs and beer lovers.

- **Location:** 19 Kent St, The Rocks, Sydney, NSW 2000
- **Opening Hours:** Monday to Sunday, 12:00 PM – 12:00 AM
- **Phone Number:** +61 2 9251 4044

The Noble Hops

Located in the inner-west suburb of Redfern, The Noble Hops is a hidden gem for craft beer lovers. The bar is intimate yet lively, with a rotating tap list that features the best of Australian craft beer alongside rare international brews. The industrial decor, relaxed vibe, and knowledgeable staff make it the perfect spot to explore new and exciting beers. Whether you're into sour beers, hoppy IPAs, or rich porters, you'll find something new and interesting on tap here. They also have a small but curated selection of snacks to complement the drinks.

- **Location:** 125 Redfern St, Redfern, NSW 2016
- **Opening Hours:** Tuesday to Sunday, 3:00 PM – 12:00 AM (Closed Monday)
- **Phone Number:** +61 2 9319 0123

Love Tilly Devine

A sophisticated yet cozy wine bar, Love Tilly Devine is tucked away in a narrow laneway in Darlinghurst. The bar is renowned for its extensive wine list, showcasing a selection of organic, biodynamic, and natural wines from Australia and around the world.

The small, intimate space, dim lighting, and attentive service create a romantic atmosphere, perfect for wine aficionados. Love Tilly Devine also offers a carefully crafted menu of cheese, charcuterie, and small plates to pair with their wines.

- **Location:** 91 Crown Ln, Darlinghurst, NSW 2010
- **Opening Hours:** Monday to Saturday, 5:00 PM – 12:00 AM; Sunday, 5:00 PM – 10:00 PM
- **Phone Number:** +61 2 9326 9297

The Taphouse

The Taphouse in Darlinghurst is a multi-level craft beer haven with 60 different taps spread across its three floors. The beer selection changes frequently, with an emphasis on local brewers and seasonal varieties. Whether you're a fan of IPAs, stouts, sours, or pilsners, The Taphouse's knowledgeable staff can guide you through their extensive selection. In addition to its impressive beer list, The Taphouse boasts an inviting rooftop bar with views over the Sydney skyline, offering an excellent spot for afternoon drinks.

- **Location:** 122 Flinders St, Darlinghurst, NSW 2010
- **Opening Hours:** Monday to Saturday, 12:00 PM – 12:00 AM; Sunday, 12:00 PM – 10:00 PM
- **Phone Number:** +61 2 9360 0088

Odd Culture

Odd Culture is an experimental bar in Newtown that serves a wide selection of wild ales, sour beers, and natural wines. The bar specializes in fermented drinks, with a heavy focus on craft beers that have unusual and unique flavor profiles. Their wine list also leans toward minimal intervention and natural winemaking processes. The décor is eclectic and modern, and their food menu emphasizes fermented ingredients and seasonal produce, creating an adventurous pairing experience for both beer and wine lovers.

- **Location:** 266 King St, Newtown, NSW 2042
- **Opening Hours:** Monday to Saturday, 12:00 PM – 12:00 AM; Sunday, 12:00 PM – 10:00 PM
- **Phone Number:** +61 2 9060 9690

Barrelhouse Bar and Dining

For those seeking a laid-back vibe with quality local brews and boutique wines, Barrelhouse Bar and Dining in Circular Quay is an excellent choice. The venue has a relaxed, open-air atmosphere with a stylish interior and offers a diverse range of craft beers from Sydney's best breweries alongside carefully selected wines from Australian vineyards. Barrelhouse's food menu is also noteworthy, with a focus on modern Australian cuisine that pairs well with its drink offerings.

- **Location:** Shop 5, 7 Macquarie St, Circular Quay, NSW 2000
- **Opening Hours:** Monday to Friday, 11:00 AM – 10:00 PM; Saturday and Sunday, 12:00 PM – 10:00 PM
- **Phone Number:** +61 2 9251 5244

Pumphouse Sydney Bar & Restaurant

Located in the bustling Darling Harbour area, Pumphouse Sydney Bar & Restaurant has long been a go-to spot for beer lovers. The Pumphouse is known for its impressive range of craft beers, including its specialty brews. With over 60 beers on offer, both local and international, there's something for every taste. The spacious, industrial-chic venue has a warm atmosphere, perfect for catching up with friends or enjoying a leisurely drink after a day of exploring Darling Harbour. They also have a diverse wine list and a menu of modern Australian cuisine to match.

- **Location:** 17 Little Pier St, Darling Harbour, NSW 2000
- **Opening Hours:** Monday to Thursday, 11:30 AM – 10:00 PM; Friday and Saturday, 11:30 AM – 12:00 AM; Sunday, 11:30 AM – 10:00 PM
- **Phone Number:** +61 2 8217 4100

The Grifter Brewing Co.

For a true craft beer experience in a casual setting, head to The Grifter Brewing Co. in Marrickville. This independent brewery has made a name for itself with its creative and high-quality brews. Their tasting room is a comfortable space with a vintage-industrial vibe, and you can sample a wide range of their beers, including crowd favorites like the "Serpent's Kiss" watermelon pilsner and "The Omen" oatmeal stout. The Grifter is a favorite among locals and those looking to explore the ever-growing craft beer scene in Sydney's inner west.

- **Location:** 1/391-397 Enmore Rd, Marrickville, NSW 2204
- **Opening Hours:** Monday to Wednesday, 12:00 PM – 8:00 PM; Thursday to Saturday, 12:00 PM – 10:00 PM; Sunday, 12:00 PM – 8:00 PM
- **Phone Number:** +61 2 9565 1195

The Wild Rover

The Wild Rover is a quirky and lively Irish-themed bar in Surry Hills that's famous for its fantastic cocktail selection and impressive list of craft beers. The bar offers a blend of local craft beers alongside rare international imports, including rotating taps with seasonal selections. In addition to the beers, they offer a great range of natural wines, making it a versatile venue for groups with diverse tastes. The lively atmosphere, rustic decor, and friendly service make it a great spot for after-work drinks or weekend catch-ups.

- **Location:** 75 Campbell St, Surry Hills, NSW 2010
- **Opening Hours:** Monday to Friday, 4:00 PM – 12:00 AM; Saturday, 2:00 PM – 12:00 AM; Sunday, Closed
- **Phone Number:** +61 2 9280 2235

Batch Brewing Co.

Another Marrickville gem, Batch Brewing Co. focuses on small-batch brewing, offering beer lovers a constantly evolving lineup of interesting and experimental brews. Their tasting room is a relaxed and informal space where you can enjoy a pint or a tasting flight while learning more about the brewing process. The laid-back vibe, community feel and focus on quality make Batch Brewing Co. a must-visit for craft beer enthusiasts. Popular beers include the "American Pale Ale" and "Elsie the Milk Stout," but they're always brewing something new and creative.

- **Location:** 44 Sydenham Rd, Marrickville, NSW 2204
- **Opening Hours:** Monday to Wednesday, 12:00 PM – 8:00 PM; Thursday to Sunday, 12:00 PM – 10:00 PM
- **Phone Number:** +61 2 9550 5433

Casino and Entertainment Complexes

Sydney offers a range of casino and entertainment complexes where you can enjoy gaming, dining, and a variety of other activities. Here are some of the top options:

The Star Sydney

The Star Sydney is the city's premier casino and entertainment complex located in Pyrmont. It features a vast gaming floor with a variety of table games, electronic gaming machines, and VIP gaming rooms. The complex includes multiple fine-dining restaurants, casual eateries, bars, and a luxury hotel. The Star Event Centre hosts concerts, theater performances, and special events. With its luxurious facilities and prime waterfront location, The Star Sydney offers an all-encompassing entertainment experience.

- **Location:** 80 Pyrmont Street, Pyrmont, NSW 2009
- **Opening Hours:** 24/7
- **Phone Number:** +61 2 9777 9000

Crown Sydney

Crown Sydney is a luxury casino and hotel complex located in Barangaroo. This architectural marvel offers high-end gaming facilities, including VIP gaming salons, a wide range of table games, and electronic gaming machines. The complex boasts world-class restaurants by renowned chefs, luxury retail boutiques, and a lavish spa. Crown Sydney provides a sophisticated entertainment and leisure experience with stunning views of Sydney Harbor.

- **Location:** 1 Barangaroo Avenue, Barangaroo, NSW 2000
- **Opening Hours:** 24/7
- **Phone Number:** +61 2 8871 8871

City Tattersalls Club

City Tattersalls Club is a historic club in the heart of Sydney CBD, offering a variety of entertainment options including gaming, dining, and fitness facilities. The gaming floor includes a selection of poker machines and electronic table games. The club features multiple dining options, from casual cafes to fine dining, and hosts regular social events and entertainment nights. It also has a fitness center and a range of member services.

- **Location:** 198 Pitt Street, Sydney, NSW 2000
- **Opening Hours:** 24/7
- **Phone Number:** +61 2 9267 9421

Coo gee Bay Hotel

Coo gee Bay Hotel is a vibrant beachfront entertainment complex in Coo gee. The venue includes a hotel, several bars, a beer garden, and a gaming lounge with a variety of poker machines. It is a popular spot for both locals and visitors, offering live music, sports screenings, and beachside dining. The hotel provides comfortable accommodations with stunning ocean views, making it an ideal destination for relaxation and entertainment.

- **Location:** 253 Coo gee Bay Road, Coo gee, NSW 2034
- **Opening Hours:** 10:00 AM - 4:00 AM
- **Phone Number:** +61 2 9665 0000

Rooty Hill RSL

Rooty Hill RSL is a large entertainment complex in Western Sydney, featuring a casino-style gaming lounge with poker machines and electronic table games. The complex also includes several dining options, a nightclub, a live performance venue, and a hotel. Rooty Hill RSL is known for hosting major events, concerts, and shows, offering a comprehensive entertainment experience for visitors of all ages.

- **Location:** 55 Sherbrooke Street, Rooty Hill, NSW 2766
- **Opening Hours:** 10:00 AM - 6:00 AM
- **Phone Number:** +61 2 9625 5500

Club Burwood RSL

Club Burwood RSL is a modern club in the Inner West of Sydney, offering a range of entertainment and dining facilities. The gaming lounge features a variety of poker machines and electronic table games. The club has multiple dining options, including a bistro and a café, and regularly hosts live entertainment, trivia nights, and special events. The venue provides a friendly and relaxed atmosphere for members and guests.

- **Location:** 96 Shaftesbury Road, Burwood, NSW 2134
- **Opening Hours:** 10:00 AM - 4:00 AM
- **Phone Number:** +61 2 8741 2888

The Juniors Kingsford

The Juniors Kingsford is a lively club in the Eastern Suburbs, offering extensive entertainment and gaming facilities. The gaming lounge includes a variety of poker machines and electronic table games. The club features multiple dining venues, live entertainment, and sports screenings. The Juniors is known for its friendly community atmosphere and diverse range of activities for members and visitors.

- **Location:** 558A Anzac Parade, Kingsford, NSW 2032
- **Opening Hours:** 10:00 AM - 6:00 AM
- **Phone Number:** +61 2 9349 7555

South Sydney Graphic Arts Club

South Sydney Graphic Arts Club is a social club located in Mascot, offering gaming, dining, and entertainment options. The gaming lounge features a selection of poker machines and electronic games. The club has a bistro serving a variety of dishes, and it hosts regular events such as live music, trivia nights, and social gatherings. It is a popular spot for locals looking for a relaxed and friendly environment.

- **Location:** 182 Coward Street, Mascot, NSW 2020
- **Opening Hours:** 10:00 AM - 2:00 AM
- **Phone Number:** +61 2 9667 4321

Dooleys Lidcombe Catholic Club

Dooleys Lidcombe Catholic Club is a large, family-friendly entertainment complex in Lidcombe. The gaming lounge includes poker machines and electronic table games. The club offers multiple dining options, including a café, bistro, and fine dining restaurant. It also features a range of entertainment options, such as live music, sports screenings, and special events. The club provides a welcoming atmosphere for members and their families.

- **Location:** 24-28 John Street, Lidcombe, NSW 2141
- **Opening Hours:** 9:00 AM - 4:00 AM
- **Phone Number:** +61 2 8745 6100

Chapter 12: Outdoor Activities and Recreation

Top-Rated Beaches in Sydney

Bondi Beach

Bondi Beach is one of Sydney's most iconic beaches, renowned for its golden sands, clear waters, and vibrant atmosphere. Located in the eastern suburbs, Bondi offers a lively beach culture with surfers, sunbathers, and beachside cafes lining the promenade. The Bondi Pavilion hosts art exhibitions and events, adding to the cultural vibrancy of the area. Visitors can enjoy swimming in the designated areas, surfing at the southern end, or taking coastal walks to Tamayama and Bronte beaches.

- **Location:** Bondi Beach, Bondi, NSW 2026
- **Season:** Bondi Beach is enjoyable year-round, but the peak season is during summer (December to February) when the weather is warmest for swimming and sunbathing.
- **Facilities:** Bondi Beach offers facilities such as lifeguards, toilets, showers, picnic areas, BBQ facilities, and a playground. Nearby cafes and restaurants provide dining options, and there are shops for beach essentials and souvenirs.

Manly Beach

Manly Beach is a popular destination accessible by ferry from Circular Quay, offering a relaxed beach experience with a laid-back atmosphere. The beach stretches along the peninsula, providing ample space for swimming, surfing, and beach volleyball. Manly's Corso is a bustling pedestrian street lined with shops, cafes, and restaurants, making it ideal for a post-beach meal or shopping.

- **Location:** Manly Beach, Manly, NSW 2095
- **Season:** Manly Beach is enjoyable throughout the year, with peak season during summer (December to February) for swimming and water sports.
- **Facilities:** Facilities at Manly Beach include surfboard rentals, showers, toilets, picnic areas, BBQ facilities, and playgrounds. There are also beachside cafes and restaurants offering a variety of cuisines.

Coo gee Beach

Coo gee Beach is a family-friendly beach known for its calm surf and beautiful coastal walks. Located in Sydney's eastern suburbs, Coo gee Beach offers a relaxed atmosphere with grassy picnic areas and a promenade lined with cafes and shops. The Coo gee Pavilion is a popular spot for dining and socializing, offering beachside views and a rooftop bar.

- **Location:** Coo gee Beach, Coo gee, NSW 2034
- **Season:** Coo gee Beach is enjoyable year-round, with summer (December to February) being the busiest for swimming and sunbathing.
- **Facilities:** Coo gee Beach provides amenities such as lifeguards, toilets, showers, picnic shelters, BBQ facilities, and children's playgrounds. There are also volleyball courts and rock pools for additional recreation.

Tamayama Beach

Tamayama Beach, also known as "Glamorama," is a small but stunning beach nestled between Bondi and Bronte beaches. It's famous for its strong surf breaks and is popular among experienced surfers. The beach is surrounded by cliffs and parklands, offering picturesque views and a secluded atmosphere compared to its neighboring beaches.

- **Location:** Tamayama Beach, Tamayama, NSW 2026
- **Season:** Tamayama Beach is best enjoyed during summer (December to February) when the weather is warm and the surf conditions are suitable for experienced surfers.
- **Facilities:** Tamayama Beach has limited facilities, including toilets and showers. Visitors often use the facilities at nearby Bondi Beach or Bronte Beach for amenities such as cafes, picnic areas, and shops.

Bronte Beach

Bronte Beach is a family-friendly beach located south of Bondi Beach, known for its sheltered rock pools and a large grassy parkland perfect for picnics. The beach offers good swimming conditions with a natural pool created by rock formations at the southern end. Bronte's ocean pool is popular among swimmers looking for a safe and scenic swim.

- **Location:** Bronte Beach, Bronte, NSW 2024
- **Season:** Bronte Beach is enjoyable year-round, with summer (December to February) being popular for swimming and sunbathing.
- **Facilities:** Bronte Beach provides facilities such as lifeguards, toilets, showers, picnic areas with BBQ facilities, and a children's playground. There are cafes along the beachfront offering refreshments and meals.

Palm Beach

Palm Beach is a picturesque northern beach known for its golden sands, clear waters, and stunning views. Located on a peninsula, Palm Beach offers a tranquil escape from the city with a mix of surf beaches and calm bay areas. The Barrenjoey Lighthouse walk provides panoramic views of the coastline and Pittwater, making it a popular spot for nature enthusiasts.

- **Location:** Palm Beach, Palm Beach, NSW 2108
- **Season:** Palm Beach is enjoyable year-round, with summer (December to February) attracting beachgoers for swimming and water activities.
- **Facilities:** Palm Beach offers facilities such as toilets, showers, picnic areas, BBQ facilities, and parking. There are cafes and restaurants nearby for dining options, and shops for beach essentials.

Shelly Beach (Manly)

Shelly Beach is a tranquil cove nestled between Manly Beach and North Head, offering calm waters ideal for snorkeling and swimming. The beach is surrounded by lush vegetation and rocky headlands, providing a secluded atmosphere away from the bustling crowds of Manly.

- **Location:** Shelly Beach, Manly, NSW 2095
- **Season:** Shelly Beach is enjoyable year-round, with summer (December to February) being popular for water activities due to warm weather.
- **Facilities:** Facilities at Shelly Beach include toilets, showers, picnic tables, and a kiosk for snacks and drinks. The nearby cafes at Manly Beach provide additional dining options.

Dee Why Beach

Dee Why Beach is a long sandy beach in Sydney's northern suburbs, popular for its surf breaks and family-friendly atmosphere. The beachfront promenade offers cafes, restaurants, and shops, making it a convenient spot for beachgoers seeking dining and leisure options.

- **Location:** Dee Why Beach, Dee Why, NSW 2099

- **Season:** Dee Why Beach is enjoyable year-round, with summer (December to February) attracting surfers and families for swimming and beach activities.
- **Facilities:** Dee Why Beach provides facilities such as toilets, showers, picnic areas, BBQ facilities, and children's playgrounds. There are also beach volleyball courts and nearby cafes for refreshments.

Cronulla Beach

Cronulla Beach is a popular surfing beach in Sydney's southern suburbs, known for its consistent waves and vibrant beach culture. The beach is divided into several sections, including North Cronulla Beach and South Cronulla Beach, each offering different surf conditions and amenities.

- **Location:** Cronulla Beach, Cronulla, NSW 2230
- **Season:** Cronulla Beach is enjoyable year-round, with summer (December to February) being the peak season for surfing and beach activities.
- **Facilities:** Cronulla Beach provides facilities such as lifeguards, toilets, showers, picnic areas, BBQ facilities, and cafes along the foreshore. There are also shops for beach equipment and snacks.

Maroubra Beach

Maroubra Beach is a large surfing beach in Sydney's eastern suburbs, popular among surfers for its consistent swells and expansive sandy shore. The beach is known for its relaxed atmosphere and is less crowded compared to Bondi and Coo gee beaches, making it ideal for surf enthusiasts and families alike.

- **Location:** Maroubra Beach, Maroubra, NSW 2035
- **Season:** Maroubra Beach is enjoyable year-round, with summer (December to February) attracting surfers and beachgoers.
- **Facilities:** Maroubra Beach offers facilities such as lifeguards, toilets, showers, picnic areas, BBQ facilities, and a skate park. There are cafes and restaurants nearby for dining options, catering to both locals and visitors.

Harbor Cruises and Sailing

Sydney, renowned for its stunning harbor and iconic landmarks like the Sydney Opera House and Sydney Harbor Bridge, offers a plethora of options for harbor cruises and sailing adventures. Here's an extensive guide to exploring Sydney's harbor by boat:

Harbor Cruises

Types of Cruises

- **Sydney Harbor Sightseeing:** Explore iconic landmarks such as the Sydney Opera House, Sydney Harbor Bridge, and Fort Denison.
- **Lunch and Dinner Cruises:** Enjoy meals while cruising the harbor, often with live entertainment.
- **Sunset Cruises:** Witness stunning sunset views over the city skyline and harbor.

Operators

- **Captain Cook Cruises:** Offers a variety of sightseeing, lunch, and dinner cruises.
- **Fantasea Cruising:** Provides sightseeing and specialty cruises, including trips to Taranga Zoo.
- **Manistic Cruises:** Known for luxury dining cruises with panoramic views.

Highlights

- **Sydney Opera House:** View the iconic sails from the water.
- **Sydney Harbor Bridge:** Pass under or alongside this engineering marvel.
- **Fort Denison:** Visit this historic island fort in the middle of the harbor.

Sailing Experiences

Private Charters

- Yacht and Sailboat Charters: Hire a private yacht or sailboat for a customizable experience.
- Skippered Charters: Includes a skipper for those without sailing experience.

Sailing Schools

- **Courses:** Learn to sail or improve your skills with lessons and courses.
- **Locations:** Several schools operate around Sydney Harbor and beyond.

Popular Areas

- Middle Harbor: Explore quieter waters with scenic bushland and coves.
- Pittwater: Northern beaches area with sheltered bays and sailing clubs.
- Botany Bay: Historic area with sailing options and coastal views.

Tips for Harbor Cruises and Sailing

Booking

- **Advance Reservations:** Book cruises and charters in advance, especially during peak seasons.
- **Special Events:** Consider cruises during fireworks displays or special events for enhanced experiences.

Clothing and Gear

- **Sun Protection:** Bring sunscreen, hats, and sunglasses for protection against the Australian sun.
- **Warm Layers:** Evenings on the water can be cool, so bring layers.

Photography

- **Camera Ready:** Capture iconic views of Sydney Harbor and its landmarks from unique angles on the water.

Environmental Considerations

Conservation Efforts

- **Respect Wildlife:** Adhere to guidelines for observing marine life such as dolphins and whales.
- **Waste Disposal:** Dispose of waste responsibly to protect Sydney's pristine waters.

5. Safety Guidelines

Onboard Safety

- **Life Jackets:** Ensure availability and proper fit of life jackets, especially for children.
- **Emergency Procedures:** Familiarize yourself with onboard safety procedures and emergency contacts.

Whale Watching Tours

Whale watching in Sydney is a thrilling seasonal activity that attracts nature enthusiasts and tourists alike. From May to November, humpback whales migrate along the east coast of Australia, passing close to Sydney's coastline on their journey between Antarctica and warmer waters to the north. Here's a comprehensive guide to Sydney whale-watching tours:

Overview of Whale Watching in Sydney

Sydney offers excellent opportunities to witness these majestic creatures in their natural habitat. Humpback whales are the most commonly sighted species, known for their acrobatic breaches and tail slaps. During the migration season, these whales often travel close to the shore, providing spectacular views from coastal lookouts and dedicated whale-watching boats.

Types of Whales Watching Tours

1. Boat Tours:

Boat tours offer the best vantage points to observe whales up close. These tours are led by experienced guides who provide insights into whale behavior and conservation efforts. Many tours include hydrophones to listen to whale songs underwater.

- **Duration:** Tours typically last 2-4 hours, depending on the operator and whale sightings.
- **Vessels:** Choose from large catamarans to smaller, more intimate boats, ensuring a comfortable and personalized experience.
- **Departure Points:** Tours depart from various locations including Circular Quay, Darling Harbor, and Manly.

2. Tall Ship Cruises:

Some tours offer the unique experience of whale watching aboard traditional tall ships, adding a historical and picturesque element to the excursion.

- **Duration:** Similar to boat tours, typically lasting a few hours.
- **Experience:** Enjoy the thrill of sailing while searching for whales along Sydney's coastline.

3. Jet Boat Tours:

For an adrenaline-filled experience, jet boat tours combine high-speed thrills with whale watching. These tours provide close encounters with whales while enjoying the speed and agility of a jet boat.

- **Duration:** Shorter tours, usually around 1-2 hours.
- **Departure Points:** Mainly depart from Circular Quay and Darling Harbor.

4. Eco Tours:

Eco-friendly tours focus on sustainable practices and educational experiences. Guides provide information on marine life and conservation efforts.

- **Duration:** Similar to standard boat tours, emphasizing environmental stewardship and responsible whale-watching practices.

Best Time for Whale Watching

Season: The peak whale watching season in Sydney is from May to November, with the highest concentration of whales passing by in June and July.

Weather: Clear, calm days provide optimal viewing conditions, although tours operate in various weather conditions, ensuring safety and comfort.

What to Expect

Sightings: While sightings are never guaranteed, humpback whales are frequently spotted during the migration season, often breaching and displaying playful behavior.

Wildlife: In addition to whales, tours may encounter dolphins, seals, seabirds, and other marine life.

Guides: Knowledgeable guides provide commentary on whale behavior, migration patterns, and marine conservation efforts, enhancing the educational value of the tour.

Booking Tips

Advance Booking: Tours can book up quickly during peak season, so it's advisable to book in advance.

Weather Considerations: Check the weather forecast and sea conditions before booking to ensure a comfortable and enjoyable experience.

What to Bring: Sunscreen, sunglasses, a hat, and layered clothing are recommended, along with a camera or binoculars for capturing wildlife sightings.

Conservation and Responsible Tourism

Respect Wildlife: Follow guidelines for observing marine wildlife, and maintaining a safe distance from whales to minimize disturbance.

Environmental Awareness: Support operators committed to sustainable practices and marine conservation initiatives.

Surfing and Water Sports

Sydney, with its stunning coastline and favorable weather conditions, is a paradise for water sports enthusiasts. Whether you're into surfing, snorkeling, kayaking, or diving, Sydney offers a diverse range of activities to enjoy. Here’s an extensive guide to exploring surfing and water sports in Sydney:

1. Surfing at Bondi Beach

Bondi Beach is one of Sydney's most iconic surf spots, renowned for its consistent waves suitable for surfers of all levels. Beginners can take lessons with local surf schools while experienced surfers can challenge themselves on famous breaks like Bondi Point and South Bondi. The beach has a vibrant atmosphere with cafes, shops, and a bustling promenade.

2. Manly Beach Surfing

Manly Beach offers excellent surf conditions with waves that cater to both beginners and advanced surfers. The beach hosts several surf schools providing lessons in a safe and scenic environment. The beach is also a hub for beach volleyball, snorkeling, and stand-up paddleboarding.

3. Stand-up paddleboarding (SUP) in Sydney Harbor

Sydney Harbor provides a picturesque setting for stand-up paddleboarding (SUP). Paddle along the shoreline and enjoy views of iconic landmarks such as the Sydney Opera House and Harbor Bridge. SUP rentals and guided tours are available at various locations including Rose Bay, Manly, and Watsons Bay.

4. Kayaking in Middle Harbor

Middle Harbor, part of the expansive Sydney Harbor, offers serene waters ideal for kayaking adventures. Paddle through secluded coves, mangrove forests, and under towering sandstone cliffs. Kayak rentals and guided tours are available, allowing participants to explore the harbor's natural beauty and marine life.

5. Snorkeling at Shelly Beach, Manly

Shelly Beach, located near Manly, is a popular spot for snorkeling due to its calm waters and abundant marine life. Explore underwater rock formations and swim alongside colorful fish in the protected marine reserve. Snorkeling gear can be rented from local shops or brought along for a day of underwater exploration.

6. Scuba Diving at Bare Island

Bare Island, located in Botany Bay near La Perouse, is a renowned scuba diving site offering diverse underwater landscapes and marine biodiversity. Dive among kelp forests, rocky reefs, and historic shipwrecks while encountering sea turtles, octopuses, and various fish species. Guided dives and scuba equipment rentals are available from dive shops in the area.

7. Whale Watching Tours

Sydney offers whale-watching opportunities during the annual migration season (May to November).

Join guided boat tours departing from Circular Quay, Darling Harbor, or Manly to witness humpback whales, southern right whales, and occasionally orcas, as they journey along the coast. Experienced guides provide insights into whale behavior and conservation efforts.

8. Jet Skiing in Sydney Harbor

Experience the thrill of jet skiing in Sydney Harbor, zooming past iconic landmarks and enjoying scenic views of the city skyline. Jet ski rentals and guided tours are available, allowing participants to explore the harbor's hidden bays, beaches, and waterfront attractions.

9. Wind Surfing at Botany Bay

Botany Bay, located south of Sydney, is a popular destination for windsurfing enthusiasts due to its consistent winds and flat-water conditions. Beginners can take lessons to learn the basics of windsurfing while experienced surfers can enjoy freestyle maneuvers and long-distance cruising along the bay.

10. Deep Sea Fishing Charters

Join a deep-sea fishing charter departing from Sydney Harbor or nearby marinas to experience offshore fishing adventures. Target species such as snapper, kingfish, and tuna while enjoying panoramic views of the coastline and ocean. Fishing charters provide all necessary equipment, and experienced crew members offer tips and guidance for a successful fishing expedition.

Botanical Gardens and Parks

Sydney is blessed with a multitude of beautiful botanical gardens and parks, each offering unique landscapes, diverse flora and fauna, and recreational opportunities. Here are the most notable gardens and parks in Sydney:

Royal Botanic Garden Sydney

The Royal Botanic Garden Sydney is one of the oldest and most iconic botanical gardens in Australia, located near the Sydney Opera House and Circular Quay. Established in 1816, it spans 30 hectares of meticulously landscaped gardens, showcasing a stunning array of native and exotic plants. Highlights include the Calyx, a contemporary glasshouse for changing exhibitions, the Palace Rose Garden, and the iconic Mrs. Macquarie's Chair lookout with panoramic views of the harbor.

Centennial Parklands

Centennial Parklands is a vast urban oasis spanning 360 hectares in the eastern suburbs of Sydney, comprising Centennial Park, Moore Park, and Queens Park. It features expansive lawns, lakes, ponds, and diverse plantings, providing a haven for picnicking, cycling, jogging, and horse riding. The parklands host various events and activities throughout the year, including outdoor concerts, food festivals, and family-friendly events.

The Domain

Adjacent to the Royal Botanic Garden, The Domain is a sprawling green space used for recreational activities, concerts, and cultural events. It offers walking paths, open lawns, and mature trees, providing a tranquil retreat in the heart of Sydney's CBD. The Domain also houses the Art Gallery of New South Wales and hosts events such as Symphony in The Domain and Tropes, the world's largest short film festival.

Shakespeare's Point Reserve

Shakespeare's Point Reserve is a hidden gem located in the northern suburb of Castle Cove, offering breathtaking views of Middle Harbor. The park features native bushland, sandstone cliffs, and walking trails that lead to secluded beaches and rocky coves. It's a peaceful spot for bushwalking, birdwatching, and enjoying panoramic vistas of Sydney's harbor and surrounding natural beauty.

Bicentennial Park

Situated in Sydney Olympic Park, Bicentennial Park is a large recreational area with wetlands, meadows, and playgrounds, perfect for family outings and outdoor activities. The park offers cycling paths, BBQ facilities, and picnic areas amidst landscaped gardens and scenic waterways. It's also home to the Waterview in The Park restaurant, offering dining with views of the parklands and nearby Olympic venues.

Wendy Whiteley's Secret Garden

Tucked away in Lavender Bay, Wendy Whiteley's Secret Garden is a hidden sanctuary created by artist Wendy Whiteley on abandoned railway land. The garden features winding paths, native plants, and secluded nooks overlooking Sydney Harbor. It's a whimsical and artistic space where visitors can relax, explore sculptures, and enjoy stunning views of the harbor and Sydney Harbor Bridge.

Hyde Park

Hyde Park, located in the heart of Sydney, is the city's oldest public park and a treasured green space. Spanning 40 acres, it features lush lawns, tree-lined pathways, and historic monuments. Key attractions include the Archibald Fountain, a beautiful centerpiece, and the Anzac Memorial, a tribute to Australian war veterans. The park is divided into two sections: the northern area with formal gardens and fountains, and the southern area with open lawns and recreational spaces. It's easily accessible by train, bus, and foot, with Museum Station located nearby. Hyde Park is a perfect spot for relaxation, picnics, and cultural events, offering a serene retreat amidst the bustling city.

Blues Point Reserve

Blues Point Reserve is a waterfront park located in McMahons Point, offering panoramic views of Sydney Harbor, the Opera House, and the Harbor Bridge. The park features grassy slopes, shady trees, and a harborside promenade perfect for picnicking, relaxing, and watching ferries glide across the harbor. It's a popular spot for photography, especially during sunrise and sunset.

Camperdown Memorial Rest Park

Camperdown Memorial Rest Park is a historic parkland located in Newtown, known for its mature trees, wide open spaces, and Victorian-era memorials.

The park offers walking paths, playgrounds, and a dog-friendly area, making it a favorite destination for residents and families. It provides a peaceful retreat from urban life while retaining its heritage charm and community atmosphere.

Chinese Garden of Friendship

Located in Darling Harbor, the Chinese Garden of Friendship is a tranquil oasis designed in the style of a traditional Chinese garden. It features serene waterfalls, lakes, pavilions, and lush vegetation, including rare plants and native Chinese species. Visitors can explore winding pathways, admire ornate sculptures, and participate in tea ceremonies at the garden's Teahouse, offering a peaceful escape amidst the bustling city.

Botany Bay National Park

Botany Bay National Park, located in Kernel and La Perouse, offers a blend of natural beauty and historical significance. The park features stunning coastal cliffs, sandy beaches, and diverse ecosystems. It's the site where Captain James Cook first landed in 1770, marked by monuments and interpretive signs. Visitors can explore walking trails, enjoy picnics, and observe native wildlife. Key attractions include Cape Solander Lookout, popular for whale watching, and the historic Bare Island Fort. Easily accessible by car and public transport, Botany Bay National Park provides a scenic escape and a chance to delve into Australia's rich heritage.

Chapter 13: Sydney with Families

Family-Friendly Attractions

1. Taranga Zoo Sydney

Taranga Zoo Sydney is one of Australia's most iconic zoos, located on the shores of Sydney Harbor. It houses over 4,000 animals from native Australian wildlife to exotic species. Families can explore exhibits like the Wild Australia precinct, which showcases kangaroos and koalas, and the African Safari trail featuring giraffes and lions. The zoo offers interactive experiences such as animal encounters and shows, as well as stunning views of Sydney Harbor from its elevated location.

2. SEA LIFE Sydney Aquarium

SEA LIFE Sydney Aquarium is located in Darling Harbor and showcases Australia's diverse marine life. Families can explore themed zones like the Great Barrier Reef exhibit, Shark Walk, and Penguin Expedition. The aquarium offers interactive experiences such as touch pools, shark dives, and behind-the-scenes tours. Kids can learn about marine conservation and participate in educational programs during their visit.

3. Darling Harbor

Darling Harbor is a vibrant waterfront precinct offering a range of family-friendly attractions. Families can visit attractions like WILD LIFE Sydney Zoo, where they can see native Australian animals up close, and Madame Tussauds Sydney, featuring lifelike wax figures of celebrities and historical figures. Darling Harbor also offers playgrounds, water fountains, and regular family events and festivals throughout the year.

4. Sydney Harbor Bridge Climb

Sydney Harbor Bridge Climb offers families a thrilling adventure with panoramic views of Sydney Harbor and the city skyline. Participants can climb to the summit of the iconic bridge while learning about its history and engineering marvels from knowledgeable guides. The experience is suitable for children aged 8 and above (minimum height requirements apply) and provides a unique perspective of Sydney's landmarks.

5. Powerhouse Museum

The Powerhouse Museum is a science and technology museum located in Ultimo. It features interactive exhibits on space exploration, robotics, transport, and Australian history.

Families can enjoy hands-on activities such as building structures, experimenting with light and sound, and exploring the museum's extensive collection of artifacts and inventions. The museum also hosts special exhibitions and workshops for children of all ages.

6. Bondi Beach

Bondi Beach is Sydney's most famous beach, known for its golden sands, surf culture, and family-friendly atmosphere. Families can swim and sunbathe on the beach, take surf lessons, or explore coastal walks to nearby beaches like Bronte and Tamayama. Bondi also offers playgrounds, skate parks, and beachside cafes, making it a perfect spot for a day of relaxation and outdoor activities with kids.

7. Australian Museum

The Australian Museum is Australia's oldest natural history museum, located in the heart of Sydney's CBD. Families can explore exhibits on dinosaurs, fossils, indigenous cultures, and Australian wildlife. The museum offers interactive displays, educational programs, and daily shows such as live animal feedings and talks by museum experts. It's a great place for children to learn about natural history and science in a fun and engaging way.

8. Feather dale Wildlife Park

Feather dale Wildlife Park is located in Western Sydney and offers families the chance to encounter native Australian wildlife up close. The park features kangaroos, koalas, wombats, and a variety of bird species. Families can hand-feed kangaroos, cuddle koalas (extra fee applies), and attend daily keeper talks and animal feeding sessions. Feather dale provides educational experiences about conservation and the importance of protecting Australia's unique wildlife.

9. The Rocks Discovery Museum

The Rocks Discovery Museum offers families a glimpse into Sydney's colonial history through interactive exhibits and artifacts. Located in The Rocks precinct, the museum explores the area's indigenous heritage, convict history, and development as Sydney's oldest neighborhood. Families can learn about early settlers, archaeological finds, and the transformation of The Rocks into a vibrant cultural hub. The museum also hosts guided tours and family-friendly activities.

10. Centennial Parklands

Centennial Parklands is a vast urban green space located near Sydney's CBD, offering families opportunities for outdoor recreation and nature exploration. The parklands feature playgrounds, BBQ areas, ponds, and gardens. Families can hire bicycles or take horse-drawn carriage rides to explore the park's diverse landscapes. Centennial Parklands also hosts family events, nature walks, and educational programs focused on conservation and biodiversity.

Kids-friendly Beaches and Parks

Beaches

Manly Beach

Manly Beach is a popular family-friendly destination with its calm waters, perfect for swimming and water activities. The beachfront promenade offers playgrounds, picnic areas, and cafes, making it ideal for a day out with kids. The nearby Manly Sea Life Sanctuary (now SEA LIFE Sydney Aquarium) provides educational marine exhibits.

Balmoral Beach

Balmoral Beach in Mossman is renowned for its calm waters, making it a safe swimming spot for children. The beach is surrounded by shady parks with picnic areas and playgrounds, including the popular Balmoral Playground. Families can enjoy fish and chips from nearby cafes while taking in views of Sydney Harbor.

Coo gee Beach

Coo gee Beach features a family-friendly atmosphere with its protected swimming area, gentle waves, and adjacent grassy parklands. The northern end of the beach has a fenced playground, BBQ facilities, and shaded picnic tables, offering a relaxing spot for families to enjoy a beach day together.

Shelly Beach

Located in Manly, Shelly Beach is a sheltered bay known for its calm waters and abundant marine life, making it ideal for snorkeling with children. The beach is surrounded by the Cabbage Tree Bay Eco-Sculpture Walk, a family-friendly coastal trail showcasing sculptures and marine habitats.

Dee Why Beach

Dee Why Beach offers a wide stretch of sand and gentle waves, suitable for families with children of all ages. The beachfront promenade features playgrounds, BBQ facilities, and shaded picnic areas. The nearby Dee Why Lagoon provides opportunities for birdwatching and nature walks.

Parks

Centennial Parklands

Centennial Parklands is a vast urban oasis in Sydney's eastern suburbs, offering playgrounds, ponds, and wide-open spaces for families to explore. The park features bike paths, horse riding, and the popular Ian Potter Children's WILD PLAY Garden, designed for interactive nature-based play.

Darling Harbor Playground

Darling Harbor Playground is a large, themed playground located near the Australian National Maritime Museum. It features climbing structures, swings, slides, and water play areas, providing hours of entertainment for children of all ages. The playground is surrounded by cafes and attractions such as SEA LIFE Sydney Aquarium and WILD LIFE Sydney Zoo.

Blaxland Riverside Park

Blaxland Riverside Park in Sydney Olympic Park is one of the largest playgrounds in Sydney, offering expansive play areas, water features, climbing structures, and sandpits. The park overlooks the Parramatta River and includes BBQ facilities, picnic shelters, and bike paths, making it perfect for a family day out.

Pirrama Park

Pirrama Park in Pyrmont features a modern playground with climbing nets, slides, and water jets, providing interactive play experiences for children. The park offers BBQ facilities, picnic areas, and waterfront views of Sydney Harbor, making it a relaxing spot for families to enjoy outdoor activities.

Bradfield Park

Bradfield Park, located near Milsons Point in North Sydney, offers stunning views of the Sydney Harbor Bridge and Opera House. The park features grassy areas for picnics, playgrounds, and a popular ferry wharf. Families can take scenic walks along the foreshore or enjoy a picnic while watching ferries pass by.

Chapter 14: Sydney Itinerary

5 Days in Sydney: The Perfect Sydney Itinerary

Planning a 5-day itinerary for Sydney allows you to experience the city's vibrant culture, stunning landscapes, and iconic landmarks. Here's a comprehensive plan to make the most of your time:

Day 1: Explore Sydney's Iconic Landmarks

Your first day in Sydney is dedicated to immersing yourself in the city's most iconic landmarks, with plenty of time to savor its culinary delights and experience its vibrant nightlife. From the architectural marvel of the Sydney Opera House to the historic charm of The Rocks, this itinerary ensures you experience the best of Sydney in comprehensive detail.

7:30 AM - Breakfast at The Grounds of the City

Begin your day with breakfast at **The Grounds of the City**, a charming café in the heart of the CBD, inspired by the 1920s. Located at 500 George Street, it offers a perfect mix of rich coffee and delectable breakfast dishes. Choose from their menu, which features classics like avocado toast, poached eggs, and freshly baked pastries. The ambiance here is a delightful mix of old-world charm and contemporary style, providing an energizing start to your day.

9:00 AM - Sydney Opera House Tour

After breakfast, take a short walk to Circular Quay and make your way to the world-renowned **Sydney Opera House**. A guided tour (available hourly) offers a deep dive into its history, architecture, and the stories behind this UNESCO World Heritage site. The tour lasts about an hour, giving you insights into the engineering marvel that makes this building one of the most iconic structures globally.

10:30 AM - Royal Botanic Garden & Mrs. Macquarie's Chair

Exit the Opera House and stroll into the adjacent **Royal Botanic Garden**, an oasis of greenery in the heart of the city. Wander through themed gardens, see native Australian plants, and enjoy the peaceful atmosphere. Make your way to **Mrs. Macquarie's Chair**, a historic sandstone bench offering panoramic views of Sydney Harbor, the Opera House, and the Harbor Bridge. This is an ideal spot for photos and to take in the beauty of the harbor.

12:00 PM - Lunch at The Dining Room, Park Hyatt

For lunch, head to **The Dining Room** at the Park Hyatt Sydney, located at 7 Hickson Road, The Rocks. This elegant restaurant offers floor-to-ceiling windows with uninterrupted views of the Opera House.

The menu focuses on modern Australian cuisine, featuring fresh seafood, premium meats, and locally sourced produce. Dishes like grilled barramundi or lamb shoulder are popular choices, paired with a fine selection of Australian wines.

1:30 PM - Sydney Harbor Bridge Climb

After lunch, embark on the thrilling **Sydney Harbor Bridge Climb**. The climb takes about 3.5 hours, including preparation and the climb itself. During this adventure, you'll ascend to the summit of the bridge, 134 meters above sea level, where you'll be rewarded with 360-degree views of the city, the harbor, and beyond. This is a once-in-a-lifetime experience that provides a unique perspective of Sydney.

5:00 PM - Explore The Rocks

Post-climb, take some time to explore **The Rocks**, Sydney's historic district. Wander through the narrow, cobblestone streets lined with heritage buildings, boutique shops, and galleries. Visit **The Rocks Discovery Museum** to learn about the area's history, from its indigenous roots to its colonial past. If it's a weekend, explore **The Rocks Markets**, where you can find unique souvenirs, handmade crafts, and local art.

7:00 PM - Dinner at Quay

For a truly special dining experience, make a reservation at **Quay**, one of Australia's most-awarded restaurants. Located at Overseas Passenger Terminal, The Rocks, Quay offers a fine dining experience with breathtaking views of the Opera House and Sydney Harbor. Chef Peter Gilmore's menu is a celebration of Australian ingredients, with dishes that are as visually stunning as they are delicious. The tasting menu is highly recommended, offering a journey through the best of contemporary Australian cuisine.

9:30 PM - Drinks at Opera Bar

After dinner, head to **Opera Bar**, located at the base of the Sydney Opera House. This iconic open-air bar is a favorite among locals and visitors alike, offering an unbeatable view of the Harbor Bridge and the city skyline. Enjoy a cocktail, a glass of Australian wine, or a craft beer as you soak in the vibrant atmosphere. Live music often plays in the evenings, adding to the ambiance.

11:00 PM - Nightcap at The Doss House

If you're in the mood to continue the evening, wander back to **The Rocks** and visit **The Doss House**, a hidden speakeasy-style bar located at 77/79 George Street. Set in a heritage sandstone building, this cozy bar offers a range of whiskies, craft cocktails, and fine spirits. The intimate setting, with its exposed brick walls and vintage décor, makes it the perfect spot for a nightcap.

12:00 AM - Return to Your Accommodation

After a full day of exploring Sydney's most iconic sites, retire to your accommodation for a well-deserved rest. Whether you're staying in a luxury hotel like the Park Hyatt Sydney or a boutique option in The Rocks, you'll appreciate the comfort after a day packed with sightseeing, fine dining, and vibrant nightlife.

Day 2: Bondi Beach and Coastal Walks

On your second day in Sydney, immerse yourself in the laid-back beach culture that defines the city's coastal charm. From the iconic Bondi Beach to the breathtaking coastal walks that reveal stunning ocean vistas, this day is all about relaxation, natural beauty, and experiencing the best of Sydney's beachside lifestyle.

7:30 AM - Breakfast at Porch and Parlor

Start your day with breakfast at **Porch and Parlor**, a beloved Bondi café located at 17-18/110 Ramsgate Avenue. This spot is popular for its healthy, delicious breakfast options and relaxed beachy vibe. opt for their famous "Green Breaky Bowl" or avocado toast paired with a flat white or freshly pressed juice. The café's bright, airy atmosphere and proximity to the beach make it an ideal place to fuel up before a day of exploration.

9:00 AM - Bondi Beach

After breakfast, it's time to head to **Bondi Beach**, one of the world's most famous beaches. Whether you're here to swim, surf, or simply relax on the golden sands, Bondi offers something for everyone. If you're keen to hit the waves, consider taking a surf lesson from one of the local surf schools like **Let's Go Surfing**. For those who prefer a more relaxed morning, lay out your towel and enjoy the sun, or take a dip in the ocean. Lifeguards patrol the beach year-round, making it a safe spot to enjoy the water.

11:00 AM - Bondi Icebergs Club

Before embarking on your coastal walk, make a stop at the **Bondi Icebergs Club**, located at 1 Notts Avenue. This iconic establishment has been an integral part of Bondi's culture for over a century. The club's ocean pool is a must-visit, offering a unique swimming experience with waves crashing over the pool's edge. If you prefer not to swim, simply enjoy the stunning views of the ocean from the club's terrace.

12:30 PM - Lunch at North Bondi Fish

For lunch, head to **North Bondi Fish**, a trendy seafood restaurant located at 120 Ramsgate Avenue, right at the northern end of Bondi Beach. The menu features fresh, sustainable seafood with a focus on local ingredients. Enjoy dishes like kingfish ceviche, fish tacos, or their signature fish and chips. The relaxed beachside vibe, paired with views of the ocean, makes it the perfect spot for a leisurely lunch.

2:00 PM - Bondi to Coo gee Coastal Walk

After lunch, embark on the Bondi to **Coo gee Coastal Walk**, a 6-kilometer trail that offers some of the most spectacular coastal views in Sydney. The walk is well-marked and takes about 2-3 hours to complete at a leisurely pace, with plenty of time for stops along the way.

Tamayama Beach: Your first stop is Tamayama Beach, also known as "Glamorama" due to its popularity with Sydney's beautiful people. This small, picturesque beach is great for a quick dip or a rest in the sun.

Bronte Beach: Continue along the path to Bronte Beach, another popular spot for swimming and picnicking. Bronte Park, adjacent to the beach, is a lovely spot to relax or grab a coffee from one of the nearby cafés.

Clovelly Beach: Further along the walk, you'll reach Clovelly Beach, a narrow bay perfect for snorkeling due to its calm waters and abundant marine life. It's a great spot for a quick swim or a rest before continuing on your walk.

Gordons Bay: Just before reaching Coo gee, you'll pass by Gordons Bay, a hidden gem known for its crystal-clear waters and rocky shoreline. This secluded bay is a favorite spot for snorkeling and diving.

Coo gee Beach: Your final destination is Coo gee Beach, a lively beach with a laid-back vibe. Coo gee offers plenty of grassy areas for picnics, as well as several cafés and ice cream shops if you need a refreshment after your walk.

5:00 PM - Sunset at Coo gee Pavilion

After reaching Coo gee, relax and enjoy the sunset at **Coo gee Pavilion**, located at 169 Dolphin Street. This stylish venue offers a rooftop bar with panoramic views of the coastline. Order a cocktail or a cold beer, and soak in the breathtaking sunset over the Pacific Ocean. The Pavilion's rooftop is also a great spot to unwind with some snacks or a light meal.

7:00 PM - Dinner at Three Blue Ducks

For dinner, consider making a reservation at **Three Blue Ducks** in Bronte, located at 141-143 Macpherson Street. This farm-to-table restaurant focuses on sustainable and ethically sourced produce, with a menu that celebrates fresh, seasonal ingredients. Dishes like wood-fired lamb or grilled fish, paired with local wines, make for a memorable dining experience. The relaxed atmosphere and focus on quality food embody the essence of Sydney's beachside dining culture.

9:00 PM - Nightcap at Bondi Hardware

End your evening with a nightcap at **Bondi Hardware**, a trendy bar located at 39 Hall Street in Bondi.

The bar is named after the hardware store that once occupied the space and has a rustic, industrial vibe. The cocktail menu is creative, featuring unique concoctions like the "Hardware Margarita" or the "Eastern Suburbs Mule." If you're in the mood for something lighter, they also offer a range of craft beers and wines.

11:00 PM - Return to Your Accommodation

After a day of sun, sea, and scenic walks, return to your accommodation to rest up for the next day's adventures. Whether you're staying in Bondi or venturing back to the city, the relaxed pace of this beach day will leave you feeling refreshed and connected to Sydney's natural beauty.

Day 3: Discover Sydney's Culture and History

On your third day in Sydney, delve into the city's rich cultural heritage and vibrant history. From exploring world-class museums to walking through historic neighborhoods, this itinerary offers a deep dive into what makes Sydney a cultural and historical gem.

8:00 AM - Breakfast at Bills

Start your day with breakfast at Bills in **Surry Hills**, located at 359 Crown Street. Famous for its relaxed vibe and delicious breakfast options, Bills is an iconic Sydney café. The ricotta hotcakes with honeycomb butter are a must-try, along with their silky scrambled eggs. Pair your meal with a cup of their expertly brewed coffee or a refreshing juice. The café's airy, light-filled space offers a perfect beginning to your day of cultural exploration.

9:30 AM - Australian Museum

After breakfast, head to the **Australian Museum**, located at 1 William Street, just a short drive or walk from Surry Hills. The museum, established in 1827, is the oldest in Australia and offers a comprehensive insight into the natural history and indigenous cultures of Australia. Spend a couple of hours exploring the exhibits, which include everything from ancient fossils to Aboriginal artifacts. The museum's newly renovated spaces offer interactive displays that make history come alive, appealing to both adults and children alike.

12:00 PM - Walk Through Hyde Park

From the Australian Museum, take a stroll through **Hyde Park**, Sydney's oldest public park, located just across the street. The park is a green oasis in the heart of the city, with beautiful fountains, statues, and tree-lined avenues. Be sure to stop by the **Archibald Fountain**, a stunning centerpiece that commemorates the alliance between Australia and France during World War I. The park also houses the **ANZAC Memorial**, a poignant tribute to Australian soldiers.

12:30 PM - Lunch at The Grounds of the City

For lunch, make your way to **The Grounds of the City**, located at 500 George Street, a short walk from Hyde Park. This café offers a blend of vintage charm and modern sophistication, inspired by the bustling European cafés of the 1920s.

The menu features a range of dishes, from light salads to hearty sandwiches. Their grilled chicken sandwich or the fresh market fish are great options for a satisfying meal. The café's warm, welcoming ambiance provides a nice break in your day.

2:00 PM - Art Gallery of New South Wales

After lunch, head to the **Art Gallery of New South Wales**, located within The Domain, adjacent to the Royal Botanic Garden. This prestigious gallery houses an extensive collection of Australian, European, and Asian art. Spend a couple of hours exploring the various exhibitions, which range from traditional Aboriginal art to contemporary pieces. The gallery's stunning architecture and serene location make it a beautiful place to absorb Sydney's artistic heritage.

4:00 PM - The Rocks Historical Walking Tour

Next, make your way to **The Rocks**, one of Sydney's most historic neighborhoods. Join **The Rocks Walking Tour**, which departs from outside the **Rocks Discovery Museum** at 110 Argyle Street. The guided tour lasts about 90 minutes and takes you through the narrow, cobblestone streets of this old quarter. You'll learn about Sydney's colonial history, the area's transformation from a rough dockland to a bustling cultural precinct, and the stories of the convicts who first settled here. The tour also includes visits to heritage buildings and hidden laneways that showcase the unique character of The Rocks.

5:30 PM - Sydney Observatory

After your walking tour, visit the nearby **Sydney Observatory**, located at 1003 Upper Fort Street, Millers Point. The observatory, built in 1858, offers a fascinating look into the history of astronomy in Australia. Explore the exhibits that cover everything from ancient star maps to modern-day space exploration. If the skies are clear, take advantage of the daytime telescope viewings, where you can observe the sun, moon, and planets through the observatory's powerful telescopes.

7:00 PM - Dinner at The Glenmore

For dinner, head to **The Glenmore**, located at 96 Cumberland Street, The Rocks. This historic pub, established in 1921, offers stunning rooftop views of Sydney Harbor and the Opera House. The Glenmore's menu features classic Australian pub fare with a modern twist. Try their famous Glenmore burger, grilled barramundi, or a hearty steak. The rooftop bar is an excellent place to relax with a drink and enjoy the evening atmosphere, with the city lights creating a magical backdrop.

8:30 PM - Explore Circular Quay

After dinner, take a short walk to **Circular Quay**. This vibrant area is the gateway to Sydney's harbor and is bustling with activity, especially in the evening.

Stroll along the waterfront, take in the illuminated Opera House and Harbor Bridge, and perhaps indulge in gelato from one of the nearby vendors. Circular Quay is also home to several street performers and artists, adding to the lively atmosphere.

9:30 PM - Drinks at The Argyle

End your day with a visit to **The Argyle**, located at 18 Argyle Street, The Rocks. Housed in a historic sandstone building, The Argyle is a popular nightlife spot that offers multiple bars, each with its unique vibe. Whether you're in the mood for a quiet drink in the cozy lounge or a more upbeat atmosphere in the courtyard, The Argyle caters to all tastes. Try one of their signature cocktails, like the "Argyle Martini" or a classic mojito, as you unwind after a day of cultural immersion.

11:00 PM - Return to Your Accommodation

After exploring Sydney's rich culture and history, return to your accommodation for a restful night. Whether you're staying in a historic hotel in The Rocks or a modern apartment in the CBD, you'll appreciate the day's mix of history, art, and vibrant city life.

Day 4: Day Trip to the Blue Mountains

Escape the hustle and bustle of Sydney with a day trip to the majestic Blue Mountains, a UNESCO World Heritage-listed region known for its stunning landscapes, dramatic cliffs, dense eucalyptus forests, and quaint mountain towns. This day will be filled with breathtaking natural beauty, exhilarating walks, and memorable experiences that showcase the best of Australia's wilderness.

6:30 AM - Early Breakfast at The Grounds of Alexandria

Start your day early with breakfast at **The Grounds of Alexandria**, located at 7a/2 Huntley Street, Alexandria. This popular café and garden are known for its fresh, farm-to-table cuisine and vibrant atmosphere. Choose from a variety of hearty breakfast options, such as their signature eggs benedict or avocado toast, and enjoy a freshly brewed coffee. The Grounds is a bit of a detour but well worth the experience before your journey to the Blue Mountains.

7:30 AM - Depart for the Blue Mountains

After breakfast, begin your journey to the **Blue Mountains**. The drive from Sydney takes about 90 minutes, but if you prefer not to drive, you can take the train from Central Station to Kizomba, which takes approximately 2 hours. The train journey offers scenic views and is a relaxing way to start your day.

9:30 AM - Arrive in Kizomba

Upon arriving in **Kizomba**, the main town in the Blue Mountains, head straight to Echo Point Lookout, located at 23 Echo Point Road. This is one of the most iconic viewpoints in the Blue Mountains, offering panoramic views of the Jamison Valley and the famous Three Sisters rock formation.

The Three Sisters are a trio of sandstone peaks that have become one of Australia's most recognizable landmarks. Take your time to capture photos and soak in the stunning scenery.

10:30 AM - Scenic World

Next, make your way to **Scenic World**, located at the corner of Violet Street and Cliff Drive, Kizomba. Scenic World offers several unique ways to experience the Blue Mountains' natural beauty:

Scenic Skyway: Start with the Scenic Skyway, a glass-floored cable car that glides 270 meters above the Jamison Valley, offering incredible views of Kizomba Falls, the Three Sisters, and the vast expanse of the forested valley below.

Scenic Railway: After the Skyway, take a ride on the Scenic Railway, the world's steepest passenger railway. The thrilling descent takes you down into the lush rainforest on the valley floor.

Scenic Walkway: Once at the bottom, explore the Scenic Walkway, a 2.4-kilometer boardwalk through the ancient rainforest. This walk provides an up-close look at the diverse plant life and unique rock formations of the Blue Mountains.

Scenic Cableway: To return to the top, ride the Scenic Cableway, which offers more stunning views as you ascend back to the cliff top.

12:30 PM - Lunch at The Lookout Echo Point

For lunch, head back to Echo Point and dine at **The Lookout Echo Point**, located at 33 Echo Point Road. This café and restaurant offer a selection of casual dining options with a view. Enjoy dishes like a classic Aussie burger, fish and chips, or a fresh salad while gazing out over the Jamison Valley. The Lookout also has a range of vegetarian and gluten-free options.

1:30 PM - Wentworth Falls

After lunch, drive or take a short bus ride to **Wentworth Falls**, another highlight of the Blue Mountains, located along Falls Road. The Wentworth Falls track is a moderate walk that takes about 1-2 hours, depending on how far you want to go. The main lookout offers breathtaking views of the waterfall cascading down the cliffs into the valley below. For those feeling adventurous, continue along the track to the base of the falls, where you can experience the full force of the water and enjoy the tranquil surroundings.

3:00 PM - Laura Village

Next, visit the charming town of **Laura**, just a 10-minute drive from Wentworth Falls. Laura is known for its beautiful gardens, quaint shops, and cozy cafés. Take a stroll down Laura Mall, the town's main street, where you'll find unique boutiques, antique stores, and specialty food shops. Don't miss **Josepha's Fine Chocolates**, where you can sample and purchase artisanal chocolates made on-site.

If you're a fan of gardens, consider visiting the **Everglades House & Gardens**, a stunning 1930s home surrounded by 5.2 hectares of heritage-listed gardens. The gardens offer a peaceful retreat with beautiful flowers, fountains, and sweeping views of the Jamison Valley.

4:30 PM - Sunset at Godets Leap Lookout

For your final stop in the Blue Mountains, drive to **Godets Leap Lookout**, located in Blackheath, about a 20-minute drive from Laura. Godets Leap is known for its dramatic views of the Grose Valley and the towering Bridal Veil Falls. Arrive in time for sunset, when the setting sun casts a golden glow over the cliffs and valleys, creating a truly magical scene. This is one of the most photographed spots in the Blue Mountains and a perfect way to end your day.

6:00 PM - Return to Sydney

After a full day of exploring, it's time to head back to Sydney. The drive or train ride back will take about 90 minutes to 2 hours, giving you time to relax and reflect on the day's adventures.

8:00 PM - Dinner at The Apollo

For dinner back in Sydney, consider dining at **The Apollo** in Potts Point, located at 44 Macleay Street. This modern Greek restaurant offers a chic setting and a menu of traditional Greek dishes with a contemporary twist.

Start with their famous saganaki cheese, followed by a selection of shared plates like slow-roasted lamb shoulder or grilled octopus. The warm, inviting atmosphere and delicious food make The Apollo a perfect spot to end your day.

10:00 PM - Drinks at The Butler

After dinner, unwind with a drink at **The Butler**, located at 123 Victoria Street in Potts Point. This stylish cocktail bar offers panoramic views of the city skyline and a lush, tropical-themed interior. Enjoy a craft cocktail like the "Butler's Margarita" or a glass of Australian wine as you relax in the cozy ambiance.

11:00 PM - Return to Your Accommodation

After a day filled with natural wonders and mountain air, return to your accommodation for a well-deserved rest. The Blue Mountains Day trip is a perfect blend of adventure, relaxation, and breathtaking scenery, offering a memorable escape from the city.

Day 5: Sydney's Hidden Gems and Final Farewell

Your last day in Sydney is all about discovering the city's hidden gems—those lesser-known spots that capture the local charm and vibrant culture of this incredible city. From secret beaches to quirky neighborhoods, this day will offer you a more intimate experience of Sydney, ending with a memorable farewell to this amazing city.

8:00 AM - Breakfast at Room 10

Start your day with a cozy breakfast at **Room 10**, a beloved hole-in-the-wall café located at 10 Llanelli Place, Potts Point. This tiny café is a favorite among locals for its excellent coffee and delicious, simple breakfast options. Try their avocado toast with a twist, or enjoy their signature breakfast bowl packed with greens, grains, and poached eggs. The café's warm, laid-back atmosphere is the perfect way to begin your final day in Sydney.

9:30 AM - Explore the Paddington Reservoir Gardens

After breakfast, head to **Paddington Reservoir Gardens** at 251-255 Oxford Street, Paddington. This hidden oasis is one of Sydney's best-kept secrets. Once a vital part of the city's water supply, the reservoir has been transformed into a stunning sunken garden with Romanesque arches, tranquil water features, and lush greenery. Stroll through the gardens and take in the serene beauty of this unique urban space.

10:30 AM - Discover the Art Galleries of Chippendale

Next, make your way to the trendy **Chippendale neighborhood**, a hub for Sydney's contemporary art scene. Start at **White Rabbit Gallery**, located at 30 Balfour Street, which houses one of the world's largest and most significant collections of contemporary Chinese art.

The gallery spans four floors, with regularly changing exhibitions that are both thought-provoking and visually stunning.

After exploring White Rabbit, walk over to **Kensington Street**, a charming laneway filled with art galleries, street art, and creative spaces. **The Old Clare Hotel**, at 1 Kensington Street, often hosts art installations and is a great place to stop for a coffee or a drink.

12:30 PM - Lunch at Spice Alley

For lunch, head to **Spice Alley**, located behind Kensington Street. This vibrant and bustling food precinct offers a variety of Asian street food, with options ranging from Malaysian laksa to Vietnamese pho. Grab a table under the lanterns and indulge in a feast of flavors from different Asian cuisines. Spice Alley is a popular spot for locals, offering a casual yet authentic dining experience.

2:00 PM - Relax at Wendy's Secret Garden

After lunch, escape the city's hustle and bustle at **Wendy's Secret Garden**, located at 37 Lavender Street, Lavender Bay. This enchanting garden was created by Wendy Whiteley, the widow of the famous Australian artist Brett Whiteley, and is a labor of love filled with winding pathways, towering trees, and hidden sculptures. The garden offers stunning views of Sydney Harbor and is a perfect spot to relax and reflect on your trip.

3:30 PM - Stroll Through Balmain

Next, take a short ferry ride to the historic suburb of **Balmain**. Balmain is known for its charming streets lined with Victorian terraces, boutique shops, and cozy cafés. Explore **Darling Street**, the main thoroughfare, where you'll find a mix of designer boutiques, antique stores, and local markets. Stop by **The Cottage**, located at 342 Darling Street, for an afternoon tea or a refreshing drink. This quaint, rustic café is set in a beautifully restored heritage building, offering a peaceful retreat in the heart of Balmain.

5:00 PM - Visit the White Bay Cruise Terminal for a Sunset View

For a unique perspective of Sydney's skyline, head to the **White Bay Cruise Terminal**. While this might not be a typical tourist spot, it offers an incredible view of the sunset over the city. The terminal is located at 2041 James Craig Road, Rozelle, and from here, you can see the sun dip behind the Harbor Bridge, casting a golden glow over the water. It's a serene and often overlooked spot that provides a perfect backdrop for your final evening in Sydney.

7:00 PM - Dinner at The Boathouse on Blackwattle Bay

For your final dinner in Sydney, treat yourself to a meal at **The Boathouse** on Blackwattle Bay, located at 123 Ferry Road, Glebe. This waterfront restaurant is known for its fresh seafood and elegant dining experience. Enjoy dishes like their signature snapper pie or freshly shucked oysters as you take in the panoramic views of Blackwattle Bay and the city skyline. The Boathouse's intimate setting and exceptional cuisine make it an ideal spot for a memorable farewell dinner.

9:30 PM - Drinks at Shady Pines Saloon

After dinner, head back to the city for one last drink at **Shady Pines Saloon**, located at Shop 4, 256 Crown Street, Darlinghurst. This hidden bar, known for its quirky, wild west theme, is a local favorite. The laid-back vibe, excellent whiskey selection, and classic country tunes create a fun and relaxed atmosphere. It's a great place to wind down, enjoy a nightcap, and toast to the unforgettable experiences you've had in Sydney.

11:00 PM - Final Stroll and Goodbye

As your night comes to an end, take a final stroll through the city's streets. Walk along the harbor, past the illuminated Opera House and the Harbor Bridge, and soak in the beauty of Sydney at night. This peaceful moment is the perfect way to say goodbye to this incredible city.

12:00 AM - Return to Your Accommodation

Return to your accommodation for your final night in Sydney, reflecting on the diverse experiences, stunning landscapes, and vibrant culture you've encountered over the past five days.

Top-Rated Guided Tours

Sydney offers an array of guided tours that provide in-depth insights into its rich history, vibrant culture, and stunning natural beauty. Here are some top-rated guided tours in Sydney:

1. Sydney Opera House Tour

The Sydney Opera House Tour takes you behind the scenes of one of the world's most iconic buildings. This guided tour explores the Opera House's stunning architecture, including its famous shells, theaters, and backstage areas. You'll learn about the history of its construction, the design challenges faced by architect Jørn Utzon, and the Opera House's role in Sydney's cultural life. The tour includes fascinating stories about the performances and artists that have graced its stages.

Meeting Point: Sydney Opera House Welcome Centre, Bennelong Point, Sydney

Highlights: Iconic architecture, backstage access, history of the Opera House

Tour Provider: Sydney Opera House Tours

Duration: 1 hour

Contact: +61 2 9250 7250

2. The Rocks Walking Tour

The Rocks Walking Tour takes you through Sydney's oldest neighborhood, offering a glimpse into the city's colonial past. The tour covers cobblestone lanes, historic buildings, and hidden alleyways, all while sharing stories of convicts, settlers, and the area's transformation over the centuries. You'll explore key sites such as Cadman's Cottage, the Argyle Cut, and the charming pubs that have stood the test of time. The guide provides a mix of history, local lore, and cultural insights.

Meeting Point: Clocktower, Argyle Street, The Rocks, Sydney

Highlights: Cadman's Cottage, Argyle Cut, historic pubs, local lore

Tour Provider: The Rocks Walking Tours

Duration: 1.5 hours

Contact: +61 2 9247 6678

3. Sydney Harbor Bridge Climb

The Sydney Harbor Bridge Climb is an exhilarating experience that offers panoramic views of the city and beyond. This guided climb takes you to the summit of the Sydney Harbor Bridge, where you'll enjoy breathtaking views of the Opera House, the harbor, and the city skyline. The guide provides safety instructions, a brief history of the bridge, and commentary on the landmarks visible from the top. This tour is suitable for those looking for an adventure with a unique perspective of Sydney.

Meeting Point: 3 Cumberland Street, The Rocks, Sydney

Highlights: Summit of the Sydney Harbor Bridge, panoramic city views, unique adventure

Tour Provider: Bridge Climb Sydney

Duration: 3.5 hours

Contact: +61 2 8274 7777

4. Bondi Beach and Coastal Walk Tour

This guided tour combines Sydney's famous Bondi Beach with the scenic coastal walk that stretches from Bondi to Coo gee. You'll start with a stroll along Bondi Beach, learning about its surfing culture and local history. The tour then follows the coastal path, passing stunning cliffs, secluded beaches, and rock pools. Along the way, the guide shares stories about the area's natural history, Aboriginal heritage, and local wildlife. It's a fantastic way to experience Sydney's coastal beauty.

Meeting Point: Bondi Pavilion, Queen Elizabeth Drive, Bondi Beach

Highlights: Bondi Beach, coastal walk, cliffs, Aboriginal heritage

Tour Provider: Walks 101 Sydney

Duration: 2.5 hours

Contact: +61 2 8354 1000

5. Sydney City Highlights Bus Tour

The Sydney City Highlights Bus Tour provides a comprehensive overview of the city's top attractions in comfort. This guided tour covers major landmarks such as the Sydney Opera House, Sydney Harbor Bridge, Darling Harbor, and the Royal Botanic Garden. The tour also includes stops at Mrs. Macquarie's Chair for a perfect photo opportunity and a visit to the historic district of The Rocks. The guide offers commentary on Sydney's history, architecture, and culture, making it an ideal introduction to the city.

Meeting Point: Circular Quay, Sydney

Highlights: Sydney Opera House, Sydney Harbor Bridge, Darling Harbor, Royal Botanic Garden

Tour Provider: AAT Kings Sydney Day Tours

Duration: 3.5 hours

Contact: +61 2 9028 5182

6. Sydney Ghost Tour

The Sydney Ghost Tour delves into the eerie and haunted history of the city. Taking place after dark, this walking tour explores Sydney's most haunted locations, including the old military barracks, historic pubs, and hidden alleyways. The guide shares chilling tales of ghost sightings, mysteries, and the darker side of Sydney's past. It's a thrilling experience for those interested in the paranormal or Sydney's more sinister history.

Meeting Point: Sydney Town Hall, George Street, Sydney

Highlights: Haunted sites, ghost stories, historical mysteries

Tour Provider: Lantern Ghost Tours Sydney

Duration: 2 hours

Contact: +61 1300 390 119

7. Sydney Whale Watching Tour

The Sydney Whale Watching Tour offers a chance to see majestic humpback whales as they migrate along the coast. This guided boat tour takes you out into the open waters off Sydney's coast, where you'll have the opportunity to see whales breaching, tail-slapping, and playing in their natural habitat. The guide provides information about whale behavior, migration patterns, and the marine environment. This tour is a must for nature lovers and those looking for a unique Sydney experience.

Meeting Point: Circular Quay, Wharf 6, Sydney

Highlights: Humpback whales, marine life, coastal views

Tour Provider: Captain Cook Cruises Sydney

Duration: 3 hours

Contact: +61 2 9206 1111

8. Sydney Harbor Sunset Cruise

The Sydney Harbor Sunset Cruise offers a picturesque way to end your day in Sydney. This guided cruise takes you around the harbor as the sun sets, providing stunning views of the city's landmarks illuminated by the golden light. You'll sail past the Sydney Opera House, Sydney Harbor Bridge, and the city skyline, with a guide offering commentary on the history and significance of these sites. The cruise often includes drinks and canapés, making it a relaxing and scenic experience.

Meeting Point: King Street Wharf, Sydney

Highlights: Sunset over Sydney Harbor, Opera House, Harbor Bridge, city skyline

Tour Provider: Sydney Harbor Cruises

Duration: 2 hours

Contact: +61 2 8274 7777

9. The Blue Mountains and Wildlife Tour

This full-day tour takes you out of the city to explore the stunning Blue Mountains, a UNESCO World Heritage site. The tour includes visits to scenic viewpoints like Echo Point, where you can see the famous Three Sisters rock formation and a walk through the ancient rainforest. You'll also stop at a wildlife park to see native Australian animals such as kangaroos, koalas, and wombats. The guide provides insights into the geology, flora, and fauna of the Blue Mountains, as well as Aboriginal culture.

Meeting Point: Central Station, Sydney

Highlights: Blue Mountains, Three Sisters, Echo Point, Australian wildlife

Tour Provider: Blue Mountains Day Tours

Duration: 10 hours

Contact: +61 2 9660 9999

10. Aboriginal Heritage Tour

The Aboriginal Heritage Tour offers a unique insight into the culture and traditions of Sydney's First Nations people. This guided tour takes place in the Royal Botanic Garden, where you'll learn about Aboriginal uses of native plants for food, medicine, and tools. The guide, an Aboriginal elder, shares stories passed down through generations, providing a deep understanding of the land and its significance to the Gadigal people. The tour is an enriching experience that connects you to Sydney's ancient heritage.

Meeting Point: Royal Botanic Garden, Mrs. Macquarie's Road, Sydney

Highlights: Aboriginal culture, native plants, traditional stories

Tour Provider: Royal Botanic Garden Sydney

Duration: 1.5 hours

Contact: +61 2 9231 8111

11. Sydney Harbor Kayak Tour

The Sydney Harbor Kayak Tour offers an active and unique way to explore the iconic harbor. This guided tour takes you paddling past famous landmarks such as the Sydney Opera House, Harbor Bridge, and Fort Denison. As you glide through the water, your guide provides insights into the history of the harbor, stories of early settlers, and the significance of the sites you pass. The tour is suitable for both beginners and experienced kayakers, providing a close-up experience of Sydney's stunning waterfront.

Meeting Point: Rose Bay Wharf, Rose Bay, Sydney

Highlights: Sydney Opera House, Harbor Bridge, Fort Denison, paddling experience

Tour Provider: Sydney Harbor Kayaks

Duration: 2.5 hours

Contact: +61 2 9960 4389

12. Sydney Street Art Tour

The Sydney Street Art Tour takes you through the vibrant streets of Newtown, an inner-city suburb known for its eclectic art scene. This guided walking tour explores the colorful murals, graffiti, and street installations that adorn the walls of Newtown's laneways. Your guide, often a local artist, will explain the stories behind the artworks, the techniques used, and the impact of street art on Sydney's cultural landscape. It's an engaging way to experience the city's creative pulse and discover hidden artistic gems.

Meeting Point: Newtown Station, King Street, Newtown, Sydney

Highlights: Street murals, graffiti, local art scene, artist-led insights

Tour Provider: Culture Scouts Sydney

Duration: 2 hours

Contact: +61 422 066 110

Chapter 15: Practical Information

Money and Currency

Currency Basics

Local Currency: The official currency of Sydney, Australia, is the Australian Dollar (AUD), symbolized as "$" or "A$" to differentiate it from other dollar-denominated currencies. It is abbreviated as AUD.

Denominations:

- **Coins:** 5 cents, 10 cents, 20 cents, 50 cents, $1, and $2.
- **Banknotes:** $5, $10, $20, $50, and $100.

Exchanging Currency

Before Departure: It is often advisable to exchange a small amount of your home currency into Australian dollars before arriving in Sydney for initial expenses such as transportation, snacks, or tips.

At the Airport: Sydney Airport has several currency exchange kiosks and ATMs. However, be aware that exchange rates at airports are typically less favorable, and fees may be higher.

Currency Exchange Offices: Located throughout Sydney, especially in central business districts and tourist areas. Major companies include Travelex, Currency Exchange International, and Forex. These offer competitive rates and lower fees.

Banks: Major banks such as Commonwealth Bank, Westpac, ANZ, and NAB provide currency exchange services. Banks generally offer good rates but may charge a service fee.

Hotels: Many hotels offer currency exchange services, though often at a less competitive rate than banks or dedicated exchange offices.

Online Services: Some travelers use online services to order currency for pickup or delivery. These services often offer competitive rates and can be convenient.

Using ATMs

Availability: ATMs are widely available throughout Sydney, including at airports, shopping centers, convenience stores, and bank branches.

Fees: Using ATMs for cash withdrawals can be convenient, but be mindful of potential fees. Your home bank may charge a foreign transaction fee, and the ATM operator may also charge a fee.

Exchange Rates: ATMs typically offer competitive exchange rates, often better than those at exchange offices.

Safety: Use ATMs in well-lit, busy areas and avoid withdrawing large amounts of cash at once.

Credit and Debit Cards

Acceptance: Credit and debit cards are widely accepted throughout Sydney, including in hotels, restaurants, shops, and attractions. Visa, MasterCard, and American Express are the most commonly accepted cards.

Contactless Payments: Tap-and-go (contactless) payments are popular and widely accepted in Sydney. Cards with this feature can be used for quick and easy transactions.

Foreign Transaction Fees: Check with your card issuer about any foreign transaction fees. Some cards are designed for travelers and do not charge these fees.

Dynamic Currency Conversion: Some merchants may offer the option to charge your card in your home currency instead of AUD. This is known as Dynamic Currency Conversion (DCC) and often comes with less favorable exchange rates. It's generally better to choose to pay in AUD.

Traveler's Cheques

Usage: Traveler's cheques are largely obsolete in Sydney due to the widespread use of ATMs and credit cards. If you do use them, they can be cashed at some banks and exchange offices.

Fees: Be prepared for potential fees and lower exchange rates when cashing traveler's cheques.

Budgeting and Cost of Living

Accommodation: Sydney offers a range of accommodation options from budget hostels to luxury hotels. Expect to pay around $30-50 per night for hostels, $100-200 for mid-range hotels, and $250+ for luxury stays.

Food and Drink: Budget travelers can find meals for around $10-15 at casual eateries or food courts. Mid-range restaurant meals typically cost $20-40 per person, while fine dining can exceed $100 per person.

Transportation: A single bus or train ticket in the city center costs around $4-6. Daily public transport passes and Opal cards offer more economical options for frequent travelers.

Attractions: Many of Sydney's top attractions, such as the Sydney Opera House and Taranga Zoo, charge entrance fees ranging from $30-50. However, there are also numerous free attractions like beaches and parks.

Tipping and Service Charges

Tipping Culture: Tipping is not as common in Sydney as it is in some other countries. However, it is appreciated for excellent service. A 10% tip is generous for restaurant service. Rounding up the fare for taxi drivers and leaving small tips for hotel staff is also common.

Service Charges: Some restaurants may add a service charge for large groups or on public holidays. Always check your bill to see if a service charge has been included.

Financial Safety Tips

Monitor Your Accounts: Regularly check your bank and credit card statements for any unauthorized transactions.

Secure Your Cards: Keep your cards in a safe place and avoid carrying large amounts of cash.

Lost or Stolen Cards: Report lost or stolen cards immediately to your bank. Most banks have 24-hour hotlines for emergencies.

Language and Communication

English: The Primary Language

English is the primary language spoken in Sydney, making it easy for most international travelers to communicate. While Australian English is generally similar to British and American English, it has its unique slang and colloquialisms that can be both charming and confusing for newcomers.

Understanding Australian Slang

Australian slang, often referred to as "Aussie slang," is prevalent in Sydney. Here are some common terms and phrases you might encounter:

- Arvo - Afternoon
- Brekkie - Breakfast
- Gudya - Hello
- Mate - Friend
- No worries - No problem / You're welcome
- Servo - Gas station
- Sunnis - Sunglasses
- Thongs - Flip-flops
- Tucker - Food
- Macca's - McDonald's

Familiarizing yourself with these terms can enhance your interactions with locals and make your experience more enjoyable.

Multiculturalism and Other Languages

Sydney is a multicultural city with a diverse population. As a result, many languages are spoken throughout the city. Commonly spoken languages other than English include:

- Mandarin
- Cantonese
- Arabic
- Vietnamese
- Greek
- Italian

Many public signs, restaurant menus, and informational brochures are available in multiple languages to accommodate non-English speaking residents and tourists.

Indigenous Languages

Sydney is part of the traditional lands of the Eora Nation, and Aboriginal languages were the original tongues spoken in the area. Although these languages are not commonly spoken today, there is a growing movement to revive and preserve them. You may encounter some Indigenous words and phrases, especially at cultural sites and events.

Learning Basic Phrases

Here are some basic English phrases that might be helpful during your stay in Sydney:

- Hello - Hi
- How are you? - How's it going?
- Please - Please
- Thank you - Thanks
- Excuse me - Pardon me
- Sorry - Sorry
- Yes - Yeah
- No - Nah

Communication Tips

Politeness: Australians are generally friendly and informal, but polite manners are always appreciated. Use "please" and "thank you" regularly.

Directness: Australians value straightforwardness. Don't be surprised if people are direct in their communication; it's not considered rude.

Humor: Australians have a unique sense of humor, often involving sarcasm and irony. Joining in the light-hearted banter can be a good way to connect with locals.

Body Language: Maintain eye contact during conversations to show attentiveness. A firm handshake is a common greeting gesture.

Safety Tips

Ensuring your safety while traveling in Sydney involves understanding the city's dynamics, being aware of potential risks, and taking practical precautions. Here are comprehensive safety tips for travelers visiting Sydney:

General Safety Tips:

Stay Informed: Before your trip, research about Sydney's neighborhoods, current events, and any travel advisories. Stay updated on local news and weather conditions.

Emergency Contacts: Save emergency numbers such as police (000), ambulance (000), and fire services (000) on your phone. For non-emergency assistance, you can dial 131 444.

Travel Insurance: Ensure you have comprehensive travel insurance that covers medical emergencies, theft, and trip cancellations. Keep a copy of your insurance policy and contact details handy.

Public Behavior: Respect local laws and customs. Avoid public intoxication, excessive drinking, and disorderly conduct, which can attract unwanted attention or lead to legal consequences.

Stay Connected: Keep your phone charged and have a backup power source. Share your itinerary and accommodation details with family or friends.

Personal Safety:

Pickpocketing and Theft: Keep valuables like passports, cash, and electronics secure. Use a money belt or a secure bag with anti-theft features. Avoid displaying expensive items openly.

ATMs and Card Safety: Use ATMs in well-lit, populated areas. Shield your PIN when withdrawing cash. Notify your bank of your travel plans to prevent card issues.

Night Safety: Stick to well-lit and populated areas at night. Use licensed taxis or ride-sharing services for transport after dark. Avoid walking alone in unfamiliar or isolated areas.

Beach Safety: Swim only at patrolled beaches between the red and yellow flags. Follow lifeguards' instructions and be cautious of rip currents. Supervise children closely.

Traffic Safety: Look right first when crossing the road in Sydney, as vehicles drive on the left side. Use designated pedestrian crossings and obey traffic signals.

Health and Medical Tips:

Medical Care: Australia has high-quality medical services, but healthcare can be expensive for visitors. Carry essential medications and a first aid kit.

Sun Protection: Protect yourself from the sun's UV rays, which can be intense in Australia. Use sunscreen, wear hats, sunglasses, and lightweight clothing to avoid sunburn.

Food and Water: Tap water in Sydney is safe to drink. Practice good hygiene and opt for bottled water if unsure. Be cautious of food hygiene, especially at street stalls.

Cultural and Social Etiquette:

Respect Indigenous Culture: Learn about and respect Aboriginal culture and heritage. Seek permission before photographing sacred sites or individuals.

Local Etiquette: Australians are generally friendly and casual. Use polite language and observe social norms, such as queuing and tipping in restaurants.

Environmental Awareness: Respect Sydney's natural environment. Dispose of waste responsibly and follow guidelines for protected areas and national parks.

Transportation Safety:

Public Transport: Sydney's public transport system (trains, buses, ferries) is generally safe and reliable. Use reputable taxi services or ride-sharing apps like Uber.

Driving: If renting a car, familiarize yourself with Australian road rules. Carry your driver's license, and avoid driving under the influence of alcohol or drugs.

Health and Medical Services

Sydney, Australia's largest city and a global metropolis, boasts a comprehensive network of health and medical services that cater to residents, visitors, and tourists alike. Here's an overview of the health and medical services available in Sydney:

Hospitals and Medical Centers

Public Hospitals:

Royal Prince Alfred Hospital (RPAH): Located in Camperdown, RPAH is a major teaching hospital affiliated with the University of Sydney. It offers a wide range of medical and surgical services, including emergency care, intensive care, and specialty clinics.

Sydney Hospital and Sydney Eye Hospital: Situated in the central business district (CBD), Sydney Hospital provides general medical services, while Sydney Eye Hospital specializes in eye care and ophthalmology.

Westhead Hospital: Located in Western Sydney, Westhead Hospital is a major tertiary referral hospital with comprehensive medical, surgical, and specialized services.

Private Hospitals:

St. Vincent's Private Hospital: Part of the St. Vincent's Health Australia network, this hospital in Darlinghurst offers a range of specialized medical and surgical services, including cardiac care, oncology, and maternity services.

North Shore Private Hospital: Situated in St Leonard's, North Shore Private Hospital provides advanced medical, surgical, and maternity services in a private setting.

Prince of Wales Private Hospital: Located in Randwick, this hospital offers a wide range of medical and surgical specialties, including orthopedics, maternity, and oncology.

Emergency and After-Hours Care

Emergency Departments (ED): Major public hospitals such as RPAH, Westhead Hospital, and Royal North Shore Hospital have 24/7 emergency departments equipped to handle medical emergencies.

After-Hours GP Services: Several medical centers and clinics across Sydney offer after-hours GP services for non-emergency medical issues. Patients can access these services through the National Home Doctor Service or local medical centers with extended hours.

General Practitioners (GPs) and Medical Clinics

General Practices: Sydney has numerous general practices located throughout the city and suburbs, offering primary healthcare services, preventive care, and chronic disease management.

Bulk-Billing Clinics: Many GPs offer bulk-billing services, where patients with a Medicare card can receive consultations at no cost or with minimal out-of-pocket expenses.

Specialist Care and Allied Health Services

Specialist Clinics: Sydney hosts a wide range of specialist medical clinics, including cardiology, neurology, dermatology, and more, often affiliated with major hospitals and medical centers.

Allied Health Services: These include physiotherapy, psychology, occupational therapy, and dietetics, available both through hospitals and private practices.

Mental Health Services

Public Mental Health Services: Sydney offers public mental health services through hospitals like RPAH and community mental health centers providing counseling, crisis intervention, and psychiatric care.

Private Mental Health Clinics: Private psychiatrists and psychologists operate across Sydney, offering outpatient therapy, counseling, and specialized treatment programs.

Dental Care

Dental Clinics: Dental services are available through public hospitals, private dental clinics, and community health centers across Sydney. Emergency dental services are also accessible through certain hospitals.

Pharmacy Services

Pharmacies: Pharmacies (chemists) are abundant throughout Sydney, providing prescription medications, over-the-counter medications, and health-related products. Some pharmacies offer after-hours services and home delivery.

Health and Wellness Programs

Community Health Centers: Local health centers run programs promoting health education, immunizations, maternal and child health, and chronic disease management.

Fitness and Wellness Facilities: Sydney boasts numerous fitness centers, yoga studios, and wellness centers offering exercise programs, nutritional counseling, and alternative therapies.

Telehealth Services

Telehealth Options: Increasingly, healthcare providers in Sydney offer telehealth services, enabling patients to consult with doctors remotely via phone or video calls for non-urgent medical issues.

Travel Health Services

Travel Clinics: Located in major hospitals and medical centers, travel clinics provide vaccinations, travel health advice, and medications tailored to international travelers visiting regions with specific health risks.

Accessibility and Support Services

Accessibility Services: Hospitals and medical centers in Sydney are equipped with facilities for people with disabilities, including accessible parking, ramps, and specialized equipment.

Multilingual Services: Many healthcare providers offer interpreter services and multilingual healthcare professionals to accommodate Sydney's diverse population.

Electricity and Adapters

When traveling to Sydney, it's essential to understand the electricity standards and the type of adapters you may need. Here's a comprehensive guide:

Electricity Standards in Sydney

Sydney, like the rest of Australia, operates on a standard voltage of 230V and uses Type I electrical plugs and sockets. Here are the key details:

Voltage: The standard voltage in Sydney is 230V, with a frequency of 50Hz.

Plug Type: Australia uses Type I plugs, which have two flat pins in a V-shape, plus a grounding pin (a total of three pins). The pins are angled in such a way that devices are grounded for safety.

Adapters and Converters

To use your electronic devices from other countries in Sydney, you may need:

Adapter Plug: If your devices have plugs that are different from Type I (e.g., Type A, Type B, Type C plugs), you'll need an adapter to fit into Australian sockets. Adapters simply change the shape of the plug so it can fit into the outlet.

Voltage Converter (if applicable): Many modern electronic devices, such as laptops and smartphones, are designed to be compatible with a range of voltages (typically 100V-240V). These devices only require a plug adapter and can handle the higher voltage in Australia without a voltage converter. However, always check the voltage rating on your device's power adapter or charger to ensure compatibility.

Where to Buy Adapters

You can purchase adapters and converters from various places:

Airports: Most international airports have stores selling travel essentials, including adapters.

Electronics Stores: Places like JB Hi-Fi, Harvey Norman, and Officeworks stock adapters and converters.

Department Stores: Stores like Target, Kmart, and Big W often have a travel section where you can find adapters.

Using Electrical Appliances Safely

Power Surges: Australia occasionally experiences power surges or fluctuations. Consider using surge protectors for sensitive electronics like laptops and cameras.

Water and Electricity: Be cautious around water and electrical appliances. Bathrooms in Australia typically have separate switches for lights and power outlets for added safety.

Tips for Travelers

Check Your Device Compatibility: Before traveling, check if your devices support 230V. Most modern electronics are dual voltage (100V-240V) but always verify.

Buy Before You Go: It's advisable to purchase adapters in your home country before traveling to ensure you have the correct ones ready upon arrival.

Multi-Plug Adapters: If you have multiple devices to charge, consider a multi-plug adapter or a power strip with a Type I plug.

Time Zone and Climate

Sydney operates within the Australian Eastern Standard Time (AEST) zone for most of the year, which is UTC+10:00. However, during daylight saving time (DST), the time zone shifts to Australian Eastern Daylight Time (AEDT), which is UTC+11:00.

Standard Time (AEST):

Offset: UTC+10:00

Observance: From the first Sunday in April until the first Sunday in October.

Daylight Hours: During AEST, Sydney typically experiences longer daylight hours in the summer and shorter daylight hours in the winter.

Daylight Saving Time (AEDT):

Offset: UTC+11:00

Observance: From the first Sunday in October until the first Sunday in April of the following year.

Purpose: Daylight saving time in Sydney is implemented to make better use of daylight during the longer days of summer, thereby reducing energy consumption and promoting outdoor activities.

Key Points:

Transition Dates: The transition between AEST and AEDT occurs on the specified Sundays at 2:00 AM local time when clocks are adjusted forward or backward by one hour.

Impact on Business and Daily Life: The time zone changes impact various aspects of life, including business hours, transportation schedules, and outdoor activities. Many businesses adjust their opening and closing hours to align with daylight hours and to accommodate customer preferences during different seasons.

Coordination: The time zone is coordinated across the state of New South Wales and other regions of eastern Australia to ensure consistency in scheduling and communication.

Time Zone Boundaries: Sydney's time zone is part of the broader Australian Eastern Standard Time zone, which extends across the eastern states of Australia, including New South Wales, Victoria, Queensland, Tasmania, and the Australian Capital Territory.

International Communication: Understanding Sydney's time zone is crucial for international travelers and businesses conducting operations across different time zones worldwide. It helps in scheduling meetings, flights, and logistics effectively.

Public Awareness: Public announcements and reminders are typically made in the media and online platforms ahead of time zone changes to ensure that residents and visitors are aware of the upcoming adjustments and can plan accordingly.

Tipping Guidelines

Tipping etiquette in Sydney, and Australia more broadly, differs somewhat from countries like the United States where tipping is customary in many situations. Here's a comprehensive guide to tipping in Sydney:

Restaurants and Cafés:

General Practice: Tipping is not obligatory or expected in most restaurants, cafés, or bars in Sydney. Australia has a minimum wage system that does not rely on tips to supplement income.

Optional Service Charge: Some higher-end restaurants may include a service charge (often 10%) on the bill, especially for larger groups. In such cases, tipping additional amounts is not necessary.

Discretionary Tipping: If you receive exceptional service and wish to leave a tip, rounding up the bill or leaving 5-10% is considered generous and appreciated but not expected.

Hotels:

Porters and Baggage Handlers: It is customary to tip porters or baggage handlers who assist with luggage, especially in hotels with no additional charge for the service. A tip of AUD 1-2 per bag is appropriate.

Housekeeping: Tipping housekeeping staff is not expected but leaving a small amount (AUD 2-5 per night) for extended stays as a gesture of appreciation is appreciated.

Taxis and Transportation:

Taxis: Tipping taxi drivers is not mandatory, but rounding up the fare or adding a small amount as a gratuity for good service is common practice.

Ride-sharing: Similarly, tipping ride-sharing drivers (e.g., Uber) is optional. Some passengers round up to the nearest dollar or add a small amount as a token of appreciation for good service.

Other Services:

Tour Guides: Tipping tour guides is discretionary. For exceptional service, consider a tip of AUD 5-10 per person for a half-day tour and more for longer tours.

Spas and Salons: Tipping in spas and salons is not customary in Australia, as service charges are typically included in the pricing.

Cultural Considerations:

No Pressure: Australians generally do not expect tips as part of their income. Service staff are paid at least minimum wage, and tipping is seen as a bonus rather than a requirement.

Acknowledgment of Good Service: Tipping is often seen as a gesture of appreciation for exceptional service rather than a social obligation.

Payment Methods:

Cash Tips: While cash tips are appreciated, many places now accept tips via card payment methods, making it convenient for patrons who may not carry cash.

Internet and Wi-Fi Access

Internet Connectivity:

1. Broadband Services:

Sydney has widespread availability of broadband services, including ADSL, Cable, and increasingly, Fiber-to-the-Premises (FTTP) connections.

Major internet service providers (ISPs) such as Telstra, Optus, TPG Telecom, and Aussie Broadband offer various broadband plans with competitive speeds ranging from ADSL2+ (up to 24 Mbps) to high-speed NBN (National Broadband Network) and FTTP connections (up to 1 Gbps).

2. National Broadband Network (NBN):

The NBN rollout in Sydney has significantly enhanced internet speeds and reliability across many suburbs. NBN offers different technologies like Fiber to the Node (FTTN), Fiber to the Curb (FTTC), and FTTP, providing faster and more stable internet connections compared to traditional ADSL.

3. Mobile Internet:

Sydney boasts extensive 4G and 5G mobile network coverage provided by major carriers such as Telstra, Optus, Vodafone, and TPG Telecom (including brands like Vodafone and iiNet). Mobile internet speeds are generally reliable and fast, especially in urban areas and along major transport routes.

4. Public Wi-Fi:

Many public spaces, including cafes, libraries, parks, and transport hubs (like train stations and airports), offer free or paid public Wi-Fi services. Sydney City Council and businesses in tourist areas often provide free Wi-Fi zones, enhancing connectivity for residents and visitors.

Mobile Connectivity:

1. 4G and 5G Coverage:

Major mobile carriers in Sydney offer comprehensive 4G coverage across the metropolitan area. The rollout of 5G networks is expanding, offering faster speeds and improved latency for mobile internet users, particularly in densely populated areas and business districts.

2. Carrier Networks:

Each major carrier has invested in expanding its network infrastructure to meet the growing demand for mobile data services. Coverage maps and network reliability vary, but generally, Sydney's urban areas have strong mobile reception with consistent data speeds.

3. Mobile Plans and Packages:

Sydney residents can choose from a variety of mobile plans tailored to different data needs, including prepaid and postpaid options. Carriers offer competitive pricing on data, calls, and international roaming packages, catering to both individual users and families.

Connectivity Tips:

Comparison Shopping: Compare internet and mobile plans from different providers to find the best deal for your needs, whether it's speed, data allowance, or customer service.

Public Wi-Fi Security: Exercise caution when using public Wi-Fi networks, especially for sensitive transactions. Use a VPN (Virtual Private Network) for added security.

NBN Availability: Check the NBN rollout map to see if your area is serviced by NBN or other high-speed broadband technologies for optimal internet performance.

Network Reception: Consider carrier coverage maps and reviews to ensure reliable mobile service in your home and work areas.

Local Customs and Etiquette

General Cultural Etiquette:

1. Greetings:

Handshakes: A firm handshake is common in formal settings. Men and women usually shake hands upon meeting.

Greetings: Australians often greet with a casual "Hello" or "Hi." Close friends and acquaintances may use first names.

Respect: Use titles like Mr., Mrs., or Ms. until invited to use first names.

2. Personal Space:

- Australians value personal space and tend to stand at arm's length during conversations.
- Respect privacy and avoid intrusive questions about personal matters.

3. Punctuality:

- Being on time is appreciated in professional and social settings.
- Inform hosts or colleagues if you anticipate being late.

4. Respect for Indigenous Culture:

- Acknowledge and respect the traditional custodians of the land, the Aboriginal and Torres Strait Islander peoples.
- Learn about local Indigenous cultures and histories with sensitivity.

Social Etiquette:

1. Dining Etiquette:

Tipping: Tipping is not mandatory but is appreciated for exceptional service.

Table Manners: Use utensils rather than hands for most foods. Wait until everyone is served before starting to eat.

2. Socializing:

- Australians enjoy casual conversations and a sense of humor.
- Avoid sensitive topics like politics and religion unless invited by your hosts.

3. Alcohol:

Drinking alcohol in moderation is common. Respect designated drinking areas and public intoxication laws.

Respectful Behavior:

1. Environmental Awareness:

- Australians value environmental conservation. Use recycling bins and minimize waste.
- Respect natural habitats and wildlife, especially in national parks and coastal areas.

2. Public Behavior:

- Maintain a calm demeanor in public spaces and on public transport.
- Follow local laws, including no-smoking areas and noise restrictions.

3. Dress Code:

- Sydney has a relaxed dress code, but smart casual attire is appropriate in formal settings.
- Beachwear is acceptable at beaches but cover up when leaving the beach.

Cultural Sensitivity:

1. Multicultural Society:

Sydney is culturally diverse, with communities from various ethnic backgrounds. Embrace diversity and show respect for different cultures.

2. Language:

- English is the primary language. Use simple and clear language if communicating with non-native speakers.
- Learn a few basic greetings and phrases in English for courtesy.

3. LGBTQ+ Community:

Sydney has a vibrant LGBTQ+ community. Show respect and support for LGBTQ+ rights and events.

Practical Tips:

Transportation: Follow transport rules and give up seats for elderly or disabled passengers.

Photography: Ask permission before taking photos of individuals, especially in cultural or religious settings.

Emergency Services: Dial 000 for emergencies and follow instructions from authorities.

Emergency Contacts and Numbers

Emergency Numbers

Emergency Services (Police, Fire, Ambulance):

- **Dial:** 000 (or 112 from mobile phones)
- **Description:** For immediate assistance in emergencies such as accidents, crimes, fires, or medical emergencies.

Police Assistance Line (Non-emergency):

- **Dial:** 131 444
- **Description:** For reporting non-urgent crimes, theft, property damage, or to contact local police stations.

Fire and Rescue NSW (Non-emergency):

- **Phone:** 02 9265 2999
- **Description:** For non-urgent inquiries or to report fire safety concerns.

Ambulance Service of NSW (Non-emergency):

- **Phone:** 1300 655 566
- **Description:** For medical advice or non-urgent medical transport needs.

Health Services

Emergency Departments (Hospitals):

- **Royal Prince Alfred Hospital:** Missenden Road, Camperdown - 02 9515 6111
- **St. Vincent's Hospital:** 390 Victoria Street, Darlinghurst - 02 8382 1111
- **Royal North Shore Hospital:** Reserve Road, St Leonard's - 02 9926 7111

Health direct Australia:

- **Dial:** 1800 022 222
- **Description:** National health helpline providing 24/7 health advice and information.

Transport and Travel

Transport Info (Public Transport):

- **Phone:** 131 500
- **Description:** For information on trains, buses, ferries, and light rail services in Sydney and surrounding areas.

Sydney Airport (Kingsford Smith):

- **General Inquiries:** 02 9667 9111
- **Flight Information:** 02 9667 6055
- **Lost Property:** 02 9667 9111

Utilities and Services

Electricity and Gas Emergencies:

- **Ausgrid (Electricity):** 13 13 88
- **Jemena (Gas):** 13 19 09

Water Supply (Sydney Water):

- **Emergencies:** 13 20 90

Tourism and Visitor Information

Destination NSW (Visitor Information):

- **Phone:** 02 9931 1111
- **Website:** https://www.visitnsw.com/

City of Sydney Council (General Inquiries):

- **Phone:** 02 9265 9333
- **Website:** https://www.cityofsydney.nsw.gov.au/

Legal Aid and Support

Legal Aid NSW:

- **Phone:** 1300 888 529
- **Description:** Legal assistance and advice for individuals who cannot afford a lawyer.

Consulates and Embassies

United States Consulate General Sydney:

- **Phone:** +61 2 9373 9200

British Consulate-General Sydney:

- **Phone:** +61 2 9247 7521

Consulate General of Canada Sydney:

- **Phone:** +61 2 9364 3000

Embassy of New Zealand Sydney:

- **Phone:** +61 2 8256 2000

Additional Contacts

Crime Stoppers (Anonymous Reporting):

- **Phone:** 1800 333 000
- **Website:** https://www.crimestoppers.com.au/

NSW Fair Trading (Consumer Affairs):

- **Phone:** 13 32 20
- **Website:** https://www.fairtrading.nsw.gov.au/

Poisons Information Centre:

1. **Phone:** 13 11 26
2. **Description:** For advice on poisoning or suspected poisoning incidents.

Note:

- Ensure to dial 000 for emergencies requiring immediate police, fire, or medical assistance.
- For non-emergency situations, use the respective non-emergency contact numbers provided.
- Save these numbers in your contacts for quick access in case of emergencies or inquiries while in Sydney.

Useful Apps and Websites

Tourism and Local Information

1. Destination NSW

- **Website:** Destination NSW

Official tourism website for New South Wales (NSW), offering comprehensive information on Sydney's attractions, events, accommodations, and travel tips. It provides guides to regions, maps, and itineraries for visitors.

2. City of Sydney

- **Website:** City of Sydney

Official website for the local government authority, providing information on council services, community programs, events, and initiatives in Sydney. It also offers resources for residents, businesses, and visitors.

3. Sydney.com

- **Website:** Sydney.com

Official tourism website for Sydney, managed by Destination NSW, featuring things to do, attractions, dining options, accommodation listings, and upcoming events in and around Sydney.

4. Time Out Sydney

- **Website:** Time Out Sydney

Online guide to the best of Sydney's restaurants, bars, attractions, events, and entertainment. It includes reviews, recommendations, and articles on local culture and nightlife.

Transportation

1. Transport for NSW

- **Website:** Transport for NSW

Official transport information and services for NSW, including Sydney trains, buses, ferries, light rail, and road transport. Provides timetables, trip planning tools, service updates, and fare information.

2. Sydney Airport

- **Website:** Sydney Airport

The official website for Sydney Airport, offers flight information, terminal maps, parking details, transport options to and from the airport, and services available at the airport.

Events and Entertainment

1. What's On Sydney

- **Website:** What's On Sydney

City of Sydney's official guide to events, festivals, exhibitions, markets, and cultural activities happening in Sydney. It includes both free and ticketed events across various venues.

2. Sydney Opera House

- **Website:** Sydney Opera House

Official website for the Sydney Opera House, featuring information on performances, tours, dining options, and venue hire. It provides booking details and virtual tours of the iconic architectural landmark.

Local News and Information

1. ABC Sydney

- **Website:** ABC Sydney

Local news, weather updates, and feature stories from the Australian Broadcasting Corporation (ABC) covering Sydney and NSW. It includes radio programs and podcasts.

2. The Sydney Morning Herald

- **Website:** The Sydney Morning Herald

Leading newspaper website providing local news, sports, business, entertainment, and opinion pieces relevant to Sydney. It also covers national and international news.

Government Services

1. Service NSW

- **Website:** Service NSW

One-stop shop for NSW Government services and transactions, including driver's licenses, vehicle registrations, birth certificates, and more. It offers online services and information on service centers.

2. NSW Government

- **Website:** NSW Government

Official website of the NSW Government, providing information on policies, programs, initiatives, and resources for residents, businesses, and visitors in New South Wales.

Health and Emergency Services

1. NSW Health

- **Website:** NSW Health

Official website for health information, services, and resources in NSW, including hospitals, health alerts, public health campaigns, and COVID-19 updates.

Education and Schools

1. NSW Department of Education

- **Website:** NSW Department of Education

The official website for education services and information in NSW, including public schools, curriculum resources, enrolment information, and educational programs.

Weather and Climate

1. Bureau of Meteorology

- **Website:** Bureau of Meteorology

Australia's National Weather Agency provides up-to-date weather forecasts, warnings, radar maps, climate information, and historical weather data for Sydney and NSW.

Community and Support Services

1. Reach Out Australia

- **Website:** Reach Out Australia

Online mental health and well-being support for young people and their families, offering information, resources, and access to support services in Sydney and nationwide.

Business and Economy

1. Business NSW

- **Website:** Business NSW

Support and resources for businesses in NSW, including advice on starting a business, industry insights, economic updates, and information on grants and funding opportunities.

Basic Australian Slang

Learning basic Australian slang can add fun and authenticity to your interactions with Aussies. Here's a comprehensive guide to some commonly used Australian slang terms and expressions:

Greetings and Conversational Slang

- Gudya - Short for "Good day", a casual greeting meaning hello.
- Mate - A widely used term for friend or buddy.
- How yak going? - How are you? Used instead of "How are you doing?"
- Arvo - Afternoon (e.g., "See you this Arvo").
- Barbie - Barbecue, a popular social gathering involving cooking outdoors.
- Brekkie - Breakfast (e.g., "Let's grab brekkie").
- Coppa - Cup of tea or coffee (e.g., "Let's have a cupper").
- Heaps - A lot, plenty (e.g., "Thanks heaps!").

Everyday Australian Expressions

- No worries - No problem, it's okay.
- Strewth - Expression of surprise or disbelief.
- Bloke - A man.
- Sheila - A woman.
- Ripper - Excellent, great (e.g., "That's a ripper of a day!").
- Bogan - A term for someone considered uncultured or unsophisticated.
- Aussie - An Australian person or something quintessentially Australian.

Food and Drink Slang

- Sanger - Sandwich (e.g., "I'll have a sausage sanger").
- Snag - Sausage.
- Chook - Chicken (e.g., "Throw a chook on the barbie").

- Pav - Pavlova, a popular dessert.
- Beckie - Biscuit or cookie.

Australianisms for Places and Things

- Servo - Service station or gas station.
- Maccas - McDonald's.
- Uni - University.
- Footy - Football, often refers to Australian Rules Football or Rugby League.
- Outback - Remote and rural areas of Australia.
- Bush - The countryside or remote areas away from cities.

Regional and Indigenous Slang

- Yarn - A chat or conversation.
- Deadest - Genuine.
- Cobber - Friend or mate.
- Abby - A small freshwater crayfish found in Australian rivers and dams.

Tips for Using Australian Slang

Context Matters: Slang usage can vary by region and context, so pay attention to how and when others use it.

Listen and Learn: The best way to learn slang is to listen to locals and ask for explanations if you're unsure.

Use Sparingly: Don't overuse slang terms; moderation helps you sound natural.

Packing List: What to Bring for Every Season in Sydney

Summer (December - February)

Weather: Hot and humid, with occasional heatwaves and summer storms.

Clothing:

- Lightweight Clothing: T-shirts, shorts, dresses, and skirts made of breathable fabrics like cotton or linen.
- Swimwear: Essential for beach visits and water activities.
- Sun Protection: Wide-brimmed hats, sunglasses, and sunscreen (SPF 30+).
- Light Jacket or Sweater: Evenings can cool down, especially near the coast.
- Comfortable Walking Shoes: Sandals or sneakers for exploring.

Accessories:

- Beach Towel: For beach visits.
- Reusable Water Bottle: Stay hydrated.
- Daypack or Beach Bag: Carry essentials when out and about.
- Portable Fan or Misting Spray: Useful during heatwaves.

Miscellaneous:

- Travel Adapter: Australia uses Type I plugs (230V, 50Hz).
- Medications: Personal prescriptions and basic first-aid kit.
- Reusable Shopping Bag: Useful for groceries or souvenirs.

Autumn (March-May)

Weather: Mild to warm days, cooling down towards May.

Clothing:

- Light Layers: Long-sleeve shirts, light sweaters, and cardigans.
- Jeans or Pants: For cooler evenings.
- Light Scarf: Optional for cooler mornings or evenings.
- Light Jacket: Waterproof or windproof for occasional rain.

Accessories:

- Umbrella: Light, compact umbrella for unexpected showers.
- Comfortable Walking Shoes: Sneakers or flats.

Miscellaneous:

- Camera: Capture the changing colors of autumn foliage.
- Daypack or Tote Bag: Carry essentials during outings.

Winter (June - August)

Weather: Cool to mild temperatures, occasional rain and wind.

Clothing:

- Warm Layers: Long-sleeve tops, sweaters, and thermal underwear.
- Jeans or Pants: Comfortable for daily wear.
- Waterproof Jacket: Windproof and waterproof for rainy days.

- Scarf, Gloves, and Beanie: Keep warm during cooler days and evenings.

Footwear:

- Closed-toe Shoes: Comfortable boots or sneakers.

Accessories:

- Umbrella: Essential for rainy days.
- Daypack or Tote Bag: Carry essentials while exploring.

Miscellaneous:

- Reusable Shopping Bag: Useful for local markets or shopping.

Spring (September - November)

Weather: Mild temperatures, increasing sunshine.

Clothing:

- Light Layers: T-shirts, long-sleeve shirts, and light sweaters.
- Jeans, Pants, or Skirts: Comfortable for changing temperatures.
- Light Jacket or Cardigan: For cooler mornings or evenings.

Footwear:

- Comfortable Walking Shoes: Sneakers or flats.

Accessories:

- Hat and Sunglasses: Sun protection as days become sunnier.
- Daypack or Tote Bag: Carry essentials during outings.

Miscellaneous:

- Reusable Water Bottle: Stay hydrated during outdoor activities.
- Camera: Capture spring blooms and outdoor events.

Visitor Information Centers

1. Sydney Visitor Centre - Darling Harbor

Location: 33 Wheat Rd, Darling Harbor, Sydney NSW 2000

Services:

- **Information Desk:** Staffed by knowledgeable locals who provide personalized advice and recommendations on attractions, tours, and events in Sydney.
- **Maps and Brochures:** Free maps, guides, and brochures covering Sydney's attractions, public transport, and dining options.
- **Bookings:** Assistance with booking tours, activities, and accommodations in Sydney and nearby regions.
- **Souvenirs:** Retail section offering Sydney-themed souvenirs, gifts, and memorabilia.
- **Operating Hours:** Daily, typically from 9:30 AM to 5:30 PM (may vary seasonally)

2. Sydney Visitor Centre - The Rocks

Location: Argyle St, The Rocks, Sydney NSW 2000

Services:

- **Guided Walks:** Offers guided walking tours of The Rocks, highlighting its historical significance, architecture, and cultural heritage.
- **Local Expertise:** Staff provide insights into The Rocks' attractions, markets, and dining scene.
- **Ticket Sales:** Sells tickets for local attractions and events, including ferry rides and harbor cruises.
- **Visitor Information:** Detailed information on nearby landmarks like the Sydney Harbor Bridge and the Museum of Contemporary Art.
- **Operating Hours:** Daily, typically from 9:30 AM to 5:30 PM (may vary seasonally)

3. Sydney Airport Visitor Information Centre

Location: Arrivals Hall, Terminal 1 (International), Sydney Airport, Mascot NSW 2020

Services:

- **Airport Information:** Provides information on transportation options, airport facilities, and nearby accommodations.
- **City Guides:** Offers maps, guides, and brochures to help visitors navigate Sydney and plan their stay.
- **Transport Assistance:** Assists with booking shuttle services, taxis, and public transport to and from the airport.
- **Tourist Information:** Advice on attractions, tours, and activities in Sydney and beyond.
- **Operating Hours:** Daily, typically from early morning to late evening, aligned with flight schedules.

Travel Insurance

When planning a trip to Sydney, travel insurance is an essential component to ensure peace of mind during your travels. While Australia is a safe and modern country with excellent healthcare facilities, having travel insurance protects you from unexpected expenses, accidents, and emergencies that could arise. Whether it's medical emergencies, trip cancellations, or lost belongings, the right insurance can save you significant time, stress, and money.

1. Why You Need Travel Insurance for Sydney

Travel insurance is crucial because it covers various aspects that could potentially disrupt your trip:

Medical Emergencies: Australia has a high-quality healthcare system, but as a traveler, you may not be covered under Medicare (Australia's public healthcare). Hospital stays, emergency treatment or doctor visits can be expensive for international visitors.

Trip Cancellations or Interruptions: Travel plans may change due to unforeseen reasons like family emergencies, natural disasters, or airline strikes. Travel insurance can help you recover some or all of your non-refundable trip costs.

Lost or Stolen Belongings: Whether your luggage gets lost at the airport or you lose your items during your trip, insurance can help you recover the cost of lost items such as passports, electronics, or luggage.

Travel Delays: If your flights are delayed, your insurance may cover accommodation, meals, and other expenses incurred due to the delay.

Adventure Sports Coverage: Sydney is famous for its outdoor activities like surfing, diving, and hiking. If you're planning on participating in adventure sports, ensure your travel insurance covers accidents or injuries related to these activities.

2. Types of Travel Insurance Coverage

There are various types of travel insurance policies to choose from depending on your needs. Here are the most common types of coverage:

Medical Coverage: This covers emergency medical expenses, hospital stays, and medical evacuations. Some policies may also cover pre-existing medical conditions, but these typically require higher premiums.

Trip Cancellation/Interruption: If you need to cancel or cut short your trip due to unforeseen circumstances (illness, injury, family emergencies), this coverage helps recover the non-refundable expenses you've already paid for flights, accommodations, or tours.

Baggage and Personal Belongings Coverage: This covers lost, stolen, or damaged luggage and personal items during your trip. It may also include compensation for delayed luggage.

Accidental Death or Dismemberment: Provides financial benefits to you or your beneficiaries in the event of a serious accident resulting in permanent disability or death during your trip.

Adventure and Sports Coverage: If you're planning on engaging in activities such as surfing, scuba diving, or skydiving, ensure that your insurance plan covers these activities. Many standard travel insurance plans exclude extreme or high-risk sports.

Travel Delay Coverage: This reimburses expenses like accommodation, meals, and transportation if your trip is delayed for reasons like weather conditions or airline issues.

Rental Car Insurance: If you plan to rent a car in Sydney, make sure your travel insurance covers car rentals in case of accidents, theft, or damage.

3. What to Look for When Choosing Travel Insurance

When selecting travel insurance for your trip to Sydney, there are a few key factors to consider:

Comprehensive Medical Coverage: Ensure that your policy includes comprehensive medical coverage, particularly if you're from a country without a reciprocal healthcare agreement with Australia.

Emergency Evacuation and Repatriation: This is crucial in case of serious injuries that may require you to be transported back to your home country for treatment.

Coverage for Lost or Stolen Items: Given that Sydney is a busy city and the potential for lost or stolen belongings exists, make sure you have sufficient coverage for your valuables.

Policy Exclusions: Read the fine print to understand what isn't covered. Many policies exclude pre-existing conditions, high-risk activities, or travel to certain areas deemed unsafe due to political instability or natural disasters.

Adventure Sports Coverage: If you plan to participate in surfing, scuba diving, or hiking in national parks, check that these activities are covered, or add adventure sports coverage if necessary.

Policy Limits: Ensure the coverage limits are sufficient for your needs. For example, check that medical coverage is high enough to handle worst-case scenarios, such as a medical evacuation.

Duration of Coverage: Make sure the policy covers the entire duration of your stay in Sydney. If you plan to visit other countries, ensure your policy covers multiple destinations.

24/7 Emergency Assistance: Choose a provider that offers 24/7 emergency assistance, which can be crucial in case you need help during an emergency abroad.

4. Recommended Travel Insurance Providers for Sydney

Here are some well-known travel insurance providers that offer comprehensive policies for international travelers heading to Sydney:

World Nomads: This is a popular choice for adventurous travelers, offering coverage for a wide range of activities like surfing, diving, and hiking. Their plans include medical coverage, trip interruption, and emergency evacuation.

Allianz Travel Insurance: Allianz offers several plans for different budgets, including trip cancellation, emergency medical coverage, and coverage for delayed or lost baggage.

InsureandGo: Known for its budget-friendly plans, InsureandGo offers affordable yet comprehensive coverage for medical emergencies, trip cancellations, and lost belongings. They also offer coverage for pre-existing conditions.

Cover-More: An Australian-based provider that offers solid plans for visitors to Australia. Their policies cover medical expenses, cancellations, and adventure activities, making it a good choice for those planning outdoor activities in Sydney.

AXA Travel Insurance: AXA offers a range of plans, from basic to comprehensive. Their more inclusive plans cover medical emergencies, repatriation, and personal belongings.

5. Costs of Travel Insurance

The cost of travel insurance can vary widely based on several factors, including:

Length of Your Trip: Longer trips generally mean higher insurance premiums.

Age: Older travelers typically pay higher premiums.

Coverage Type: Basic plans are cheaper but offer limited coverage. More comprehensive plans with higher coverage limits will cost more.

Pre-existing Conditions: If you need coverage for pre-existing medical conditions, expect higher premiums.

On average, travel insurance costs between 4% and 10% of your total trip cost. For example, if your trip costs AUD 5,000, you can expect to pay between AUD 200 and AUD 500 for travel insurance, depending on the level of coverage.

6. Tips for Buying Travel Insurance for Sydney

Buy Early: Purchase your travel insurance as soon as you book your trip. This ensures that you're covered for any cancellations or changes leading up to your departure.

Compare Plans: Use comparison websites like Squaremouth or InsureMyTrip to compare different travel insurance policies and find the best coverage for your needs.

Check Your Credit Card: Some credit cards offer limited travel insurance if you book your trip using that card. However, this is usually insufficient for comprehensive coverage, so read the fine print and consider additional coverage if needed.

Read the Policy Details: Always read the policy document to fully understand what's covered and what's not. Pay particular attention to exclusions and any requirements for filing a claim.

Keep a Copy of Your Policy: Carry a copy of your travel insurance policy with you, including the emergency contact number and your policy number, in case you need to claim while traveling.

Chapter 16: Day Trips and Excursions

10 Amazing Day Trips from Sydney

1. Blue Mountains National Park

The Blue Mountains National Park is a must-visit destination for nature lovers. This UNESCO World Heritage site is renowned for its dramatic landscapes, deep valleys, towering sandstone cliffs, and dense eucalyptus forests. The park offers numerous hiking trails, with the iconic Three Sisters rock formation being a highlight. Visitors can take in breathtaking views from Echo Point Lookout or ride the Scenic Railway, the world's steepest passenger railway. For those interested in Aboriginal culture, guided tours are available to explore the ancient rock art and learn about the indigenous heritage of the area. The park also boasts diverse wildlife, including kangaroos, koalas, and vibrant bird species. Whether you're interested in bushwalking, birdwatching, or simply soaking in the serene environment, the Blue Mountains offer a perfect escape from the city.

Distance: 80 kilometers

Travel Time: 1.5 hours by car

2. Hunter Valley

Hunter Valley is Australia's oldest wine region, making it a perfect day trip for wine enthusiasts. This picturesque region is home to over 150 wineries, offering a variety of wine-tasting experiences. Visitors can tour vineyards, enjoy gourmet meals at one of the many fine dining restaurants, or explore boutique cheese and chocolate shops. Beyond wine, Hunter Valley offers hot air ballooning experiences, providing a bird's-eye view of the lush vineyards and rolling hills. Art galleries, spa retreats, and local markets also add to the charm of this region. Whether you're a wine connoisseur or simply looking to relax in a beautiful setting, Hunter Valley promises a day of indulgence and relaxation.

Distance: 160 kilometers

Travel Time: 2 hours by car

3. Royal National Park

The Royal National Park is the second oldest national park in the world, offering a mix of coastal scenery, bushland, and waterfalls. Visitors can hike the Coast Track, which spans 26 kilometers along rugged cliffs, offering stunning ocean views. The park is also home to Attomole Beach, a secluded spot perfect for swimming and picnicking. Other attractions include the Figure Eight Pools, natural rock pools shaped like the number eight, and the Audley Boatshed, where you can rent kayaks and paddle along the Hacking River. The park's diverse ecosystems make it a haven for wildlife, with opportunities to spot native birds, wallabies, and echidnas.

Distance: 36 kilometers

Travel Time: 45 minutes by car

4. Palm Beach

Palm Beach is a stunning coastal suburb known for its golden sands, crystal-clear waters, and luxury homes. It's also the filming location for the popular Australian TV show Home and Away. Visitors can hike up to Barrenjoey Lighthouse for panoramic views of the coastline and explore the historic lighthouse keeper's cottage. The beach itself is perfect for swimming, surfing, or simply relaxing. For a unique experience, take a ferry to nearby Etta long or explore the Pittwater region by boat. Palm Beach also offers a range of dining options, from casual beachside cafes to upscale restaurants, making it a perfect destination for a laid-back day by the sea.

Distance: 41 kilometers

Travel Time: 1.5 hours by car

5. Kiama

Kiama is a charming coastal town famous for its natural blowholes, where seawater is forced through a narrow opening in the rocks, creating spectacular spouts of water. The larger of the two blowholes, known simply as "The Blowhole," can shoot water up to 25 meters in the air. Visitors can explore the scenic Kiama Coastal Walk, which offers breathtaking views of the coastline and leads to other attractions like Cathedral Rocks and the Little Blowhole. The town itself is quaint, with boutique shops, cafes, and historic buildings. Kiama also has beautiful beaches, ideal for swimming, surfing, and picnicking.

Distance: 120 kilometers

Travel Time: 1.5 hours by car or 2 hours by train

6. Port Stephens

Port Stephens is a water lover's paradise, offering a wide range of activities such as dolphin watching, snorkeling, and sandboarding on the towering Stockton Sand Dunes. The area is home to over 150 bottlenose dolphins, and cruises are available year-round for close-up encounters. For those looking for adventure, Tomori Head Summit Walk provides panoramic views of the coastline, and the nearby Wormy Conservation Lands are perfect for 4WD tours. The beaches in Port Stephens are pristine, making them ideal for swimming, kayaking, and stand-up paddleboarding. The region is also known for its fresh seafood, particularly oysters, which can be enjoyed at local restaurants.

Distance: 200 kilometers

Travel Time: 2.5 hours by car

7. Jervis Bay

Jervis Bay is famous for having some of the whitest sands in the world, particularly at Hyams Beach. This coastal gem is ideal for swimming, snorkeling, and exploring marine life. The calm, clear waters are home to dolphins, and between May and November, you can also spot migrating whales. The Broderie National Park, located within the bay, offers bushwalking trails, botanical gardens, and Aboriginal cultural experiences. The park's Murrays Beach is another highlight, offering tranquil waters and excellent snorkeling opportunities. The combination of stunning beaches, rich wildlife, and cultural heritage makes Jervis Bay a perfect day trip destination.

Distance: 200 kilometers

Travel Time: 2.5 hours by car

8. Wollongong

Wollongong is a vibrant coastal city offering a mix of natural beauty and cultural attractions. The Sea Cliff Bridge is a must-see, offering breathtaking views as it winds along the coastline. Visitors can explore the Nan Tien Temple, the largest Buddhist temple in the Southern Hemisphere, or relax on the city's pristine beaches, such as North Wollongong Beach and Austinmer Beach. The city also has a lively arts scene, with galleries, museums, and street art.

For outdoor enthusiasts, the Illawarra Escarpment offers excellent hiking and mountain biking trails, with lookouts providing panoramic views of the coast.

Distance: 85 kilometers

Travel Time: 1.5 hours by car or train

9. Southern Highlands

The Southern Highlands region is a perfect blend of quaint villages, lush gardens, and stunning waterfalls. Bowral, the largest town in the area, is known for its beautiful gardens, antique shops, and the Bradman Museum, dedicated to the legendary cricketer Sir Donald Bradman. The region is also famous for its cool-climate wines, with several vineyards offering wine tasting and tours. Fitzroy Falls is a highlight, with walking trails offering views of the 81-meter waterfall plunging into the valley below. The Southern Highlands also boasts several historic sites, charming cafes, and boutique shops, making it a delightful day trip from Sydney.

Distance: 110 kilometers

Travel Time: 1.5 hours by car

10. Kangaroo Valley

Kangaroo Valley is a tranquil retreat, known for its lush landscapes, rolling hills, and charming countryside. Visitors can explore the historic Hampden Bridge, Australia's last surviving wooden suspension bridge, or paddle down the Kangaroo River in a canoe. The valley is also home to Morton National Park, where you can find the stunning Fitzroy Falls and enjoy various bushwalking trails. Kangaroo Valley's quaint village offers a range of local produce, including honey, olives, and wine. With its serene environment and abundance of outdoor activities, Kangaroo Valley provides a peaceful escape from the hustle and bustle of city life.

Distance: 160 kilometers

Travel Time: 2 hours by car

Conclusion

Sydney is a vibrant, world-class city that offers a dynamic blend of iconic landmarks, cultural experiences, natural beauty, and exciting activities. From the architectural marvels of the Sydney Opera House and Harbour Bridge to the pristine beaches like Bondi and Manly, Sydney offers something for every traveler. Its rich history, bustling markets, eclectic neighborhoods, and hidden gems provide endless opportunities for exploration.

Whether you're indulging in the thriving food scene, discovering lesser-known attractions, enjoying outdoor adventures, or immersing yourself in local culture, Sydney caters to all kinds of travelers. Budget-conscious visitors will find a range of affordable options, from public transport and free activities to diverse dining spots and affordable accommodation. Meanwhile, travel insurance ensures that unforeseen circumstances won't hinder your enjoyment of this incredible destination.

Ultimately, Sydney is a city that captivates visitors with its energy, diverse experiences, and stunning landscapes, making it an unforgettable destination for travelers seeking both adventure and relaxation. Whether it's your first visit or a return trip, Sydney is bound to leave you with lasting memories and a desire to explore even more of what Australia has to offer.

Safe travels, and enjoy your Sydney adventure!

Printed in Great Britain
by Amazon

55986076R00188